MIDDLE AMERICAN INDIANS

GARLAND REFERENCE LIBRARY
OF SOCIAL SCIENCE
Vol. 332

VOCABULARIO

DE

LENGUA KICHE

COMPUESTO

POR EL APOSTOLICO ZELO DE LOS M.R.P. FRANCISCANOS de esta Santa Provincia del Dulcissimo Nombre de JESUS del Arzobispado de Guatemala.

AÑADIDO

Por el mismo Autor otro Diccionario corto de varios vocab? que faltaron: y distintos nombres de diversas aves.

COPIADO

Por D. Fermin Joseph Tirado, sujeto instruido en dicho Idioma. A costa del P. Joseph Joachin Henriquez Clerigo Presbytero domisiliario de dicho Arzobispado, y Teniente de Cura de la Parroquia de Sto Domº. Zacapula. Se añadieron à esta Copia los arboles de contang? y afinidad.

Año   1787.

Se comenzò esta Copia el dia dies de Agosto: y se terminò el dia trece de Octubre del mismo año. Consta de 216. fojas.
Ne scribam vanum, duc pia Virgo manum.

Eighteenth-century Dominican Quiché vocabulary (no. 590)

MIDDLE AMERICAN INDIANS
A Guide to the Manuscript Collection at Tozzer Library Harvard University

John M. Weeks

GARLAND PUBLISHING, INC. • NEW YORK & LONDON
1985

Library of Congress Cataloging-in-Publication Data

Tozzer Library.
  Middle American Indians.

  (Garland reference library of social science ;
v. 332)
  Includes index.
  1. Indians of Mexico—Manuscripts—Catalogs.
2. Indians of Central America—Manuscripts—Catalogs.
3. Tozzer Library—Catalogs. I. Weeks, John M.
II. Title. III. Series.
Z1209.2.M4T69 1985 [F1219] 016.972′00497 85-15929
ISBN 0-8240-8592-2

Printed on acid-free, 250-year-life paper
Manufactured in the United States of America

CONTENTS

INTRODUCTION

Tozzer Library at Harvard University is the repository for an important collection of manuscript facsimiles, transcripts, and extracts relating to the Spanish conquest of southern Mexico and northern Central America, and the development of early Hispano-Indian society in the colonial provinces of New Spain, Yucatán, and Guatemala. A portion of this collection, primarily administrative documents assembled by the Carnegie Institution of Washington History of the Yucatán Project has recently been inventoried (Weeks 1984). A more diverse and probably more significant part of the collection is presented here. These manuscripts are largely the legacy of Charles Pickering Bowditch, an early trustee and patron of the Peabody Museum of Archaeology and Ethnology at Harvard University.

Charles Pickering Bowditch

Researchers may require some introduction to the man who assembled the majority of manuscripts relating to Middle American Indians at Tozzer Library. Charles Pickering Bowditch was born in Boston, September 30, 1842, and was educated at Harvard College, class of 1863. He served in the Civil War as a lieutenant and captain in the 35th Massachusetts Volunteer Infantry, and later a captain in the 5th Massachusetts Volunteer Cavalry. After a trip to Yucatán in 1888, his primary avocation became

-1-

Charles Pickering Bowditch

(1842-1921)

the investigation of Middle American antiquities, with a defined

emphasis on the Maya system of writing. His *The Numeration, Calendar

Systems, and Astronomical Knowledge of the Mayas*, published in 1910,

was an important work, and established Bowditch as the most prominent

figure in the field of Maya writing at that time.

Bowditch was a generous benefactor of the Peabody Museum of

Archaeology and Ethnology at Harvard University from 1888 until his

death in 1921. He financed and planned a number of research expeditions

to the Maya region of southern Mexico and northern Central America.

These trips initiated a number of men who would later become important

figures in the field of Maya archaeology. A listing would include the

work of George Byron Gordon, Marshall Saville, and John G. Owens at

the ruins of Copán and in the Uloa Valley region of Honduras, Teobert

Maler in the Usumacinta River valley of Mexico and Guatemala, Edward

H. Thompson at the site of Chichén Itzá and elsewhere in northern

Yucatán, Alfred M. Tozzer, Raymond E. Merwin, and Clarence Hay in

Belize (British Honduras) and the Petén region of northern Guatemala,

Samuel K. Lothrop in Honduras, Herbert J. Spinden in southern Yucatán,

and Sylvanus G. Morley throughout most of the Maya lowlands.

The results of these expeditions are impressive and were published,

largely at Bowditch's expense, in six folio volumes of Memoirs and a

number of Papers of the Peabody Museum. Bowditch also subsidized the

publication efforts of other scholars, including George M. Allen, Ernst

Förstemann, William E. Gates, Carl E. Guthe, Philip A. Means, Zelia

Nuttall, Paul Schellhas, and George C. Vaillant.

In addition to these scholarly pursuits, Bowditch supported

the early growth and development of the Peabody Museum. The collections
of artifacts and other remains assembled as a result of Bowditch
financed expeditions today fill several exhibition halls at the
Museum. Specimens include sculpture from Copán, molds and plaster
casts of the principal stela and monuments from Copán and Quiriguá,
lintels and stela from Yaxchilán and Piedras Negras, as well as
sculptured stones from Chichén Itzá. Pottery collections were
retrieved from Copán and the Uloa Valley in Honduras, Holmul in
northern Guatemala, amd much of Yucatán, in addition to a diverse
collection of artifacts recovered from the famous *cenote* at Chichén
Itzá.

Furthermore, Bowditch was largely responsible for the establishment
of the teaching of anthropology at Harvard College, and provided for
several fellowships to promote continued research in Middle American
studies; these were a fellowship in American archaeology through the
Archaeological Institute of America, the Central American Fellowship at
the Peabody Museum, and the Bowditch Professorship of Mexican and
Central American Archaeology and Ethnology at Harvard University.

From the biased perspective of an ethnohistorian, the greatest
contribution made by Bowditch to Middle American anthropology was his
extremely successful attempt to bring together in one place a large
collection of books and manuscripts relating to the Indians of Mexico
and Central America. After consultation with Alfred M. Tozzer
regarding the direction of the Peabody Museum, Bowditch entered into an
agreement with William E. Gates through which the Museum would obtain
some 50,000 leaves of photographic reproductions of important manuscripts

of linguistic and historical value. In a letter dated October 17, 1912,

Bowditch outlines this arrangement with Gates:

> We [CPB and Tozzer] talked over the
> situation and we are both of the opinion
> that through your kindness the Peabody
> Museum will be in a position to offer
> students a greater opportunity to make
> advances in Central American studies,
> especially linguistics, than would have
> been possible a short time ago. You
> have asked me to tell you what the Peabody
> Museum would like, and so I would say
> that we should rather prefer, if we had
> our choice, that the reproduction of
> manuscripts and books should begin with
> the Yucatan Maya (*Motul dictionary,
> Chilam Balam,* etc.), and proceeding
> in order with dialects similar to the
> Maya until the Nahuatl is reached. But
> this preference is of slight moment and
> is not to be balanced at all with the
> needs of your studies. Therefore, I
> am ready to begin receiving at any time,
> the photographic reproduction of
> Central American manuscripts and books
> up to 50,000 pages (including Mexico under
> the name of Central America), as you may
> find it convenient to have duplicated for
> me.

Manuscripts were received by Bowditch from 1912 through 1920, and

by 1921, Tozzer (1921:356) was able to claim:

> ... this [collection at the Peabody
> Museum] comprises practically everything
> in manuscript form now extant on the
> languages of Central America and much of
> the material on Mexican linguistics.

In addition to the collection of manuscript photoreproductions

referred to by Tozzer, Bowditch had commissioned the English artist

Annie Hunter to prepare hand-colored facsimiles of several pictorial

manuscripts, including the *Codex Laud* (no. 376), *Codex Kingsborough*

(no. 374), and *Codex Dresden* (no. 371). At the time of his death

Bowditch was having prepared a copy of Fray Bernardino de Sahagún's magnificent sixteenth century *Historia general de las cosas de Nueva España* (nos. 518 and 519). He also supervised the English translation of several important Spanish texts relating to the early colonial lowland Maya; these works include Andrés de Avendaño y Loyola's 1697 *Relación* (no. 320) and Agustín Cano's 1695 *Informe* (no. 350) regarding early *entradas* into the Petén jungle of northern Guatemala, and the 1566 *Relación de las cosas de Yucatán* by the Franciscan bishop Diego de Landa (no. 431). To complete another aspect of the collection, Bowditch secured English translations of practically the entire works of Eduard Seler, Ernst Förstemann, and a number of other German scholars working in Middle America at the turn of the century.

Lastly, through the generosity of Bowditch, the library acquired several original manuscripts of early date. These are the *Cahabón Manuscript* in Kekchí (no. 348), *Compendio en la lengua quiché* (no. 383), Manuel Maldonado de Matos' 1770 *Arte de la lengua szinca* (no. 450), a nineteenth century catechism from Yucatán (no. 459), a Yucatec Maya herbal acquired in Mérida (no. 478), a volume of Quiché and Cakchiquel religious chants (no. 497), *Sermones en lengua pokonchí* from the late sixteenth century (no. 530), a Mexican catechism in Testerian hieroglyphs (no. 546), *Tratado en la lengua otomí* (no. 583), the 1787 *Vocabulario de lengua quiché* (no. 590), and the magnificent *Xiu Chronicles* (no. 600). These manuscripts collectively attest to the vision of Charles Pickering Bowditch.

Organization of the Guide

This guide is an introduction to a unique collection of manuscripts at Tozzer Library relating to Middle American Indians. In selecting items for inclusion, no attempt has been made to discriminate on the basis of quality. Because there is no universally accepted or standard definition of Middle America, it is applied here loosely to include Mexico and the Central American countries of Guatemala, Belize (British Honduras), Honduras, El Salvador, Nicaragua, Costa Rica, and Panama (see following map).

Three principal bibliographic sections are presented in the guide. These are the Bowditch-Gates Collection of photographic reproductions, Miscellaneous Manuscripts, including original documents as well as numerous typescripts, and the Bowditch German Translation Series.

Bowditch-Gates Collection

The Bowditch-Gates Collection includes predominately linguistic items photoreproduced by William E. Gates from European and American archives and later sold or given to Charles P. Bowditch. Tozzer Library holdings of Gates' reproductions represent only a segment of the total Gates Collection. No original manuscripts acquired by Gates are presently at Tozzer Library. In general, original manuscripts and rare imprint items are at the Latin American Library at Tulane University, or in the Robert Garrett Collection at Princeton University. A few such items are presumably in unknown hands or repositories. Photoreproductions made by Gates are not unique. He sold or presented copies of the same material to such institutions as the John Carter Brown Library at Brown University, Brigham Young University, and to

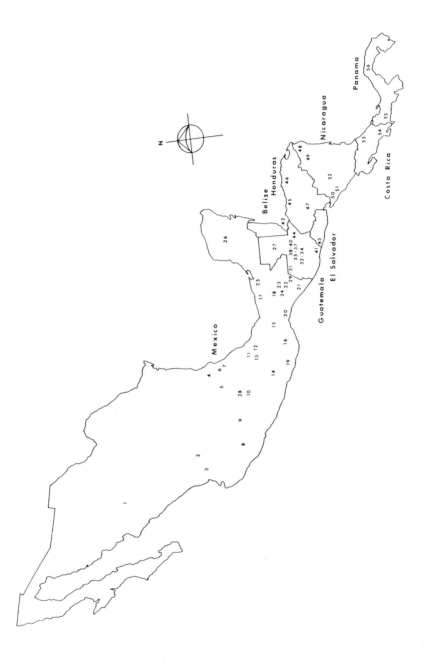

Map of Middle American Indian Language Groups

Achí (37)
Boruca (54)
Cakchiquel (32)
Carib (42)
Chiapanec (24)
Chicomuceltec (21)
Chinantec (12)
Chiriquí (55)
Chol (27)
Chontal (25)
Chortí (44)
Cora (3)
Cuicatec (13)
Cuna (56)

Huastec (4)
Huave (20)
Huichol (2)
Ixil (35)
Jacalteca (29)
Jicaque (45)
Kekchí (38)
Lenca (47)
Mam (30)
Mangue (51)
Matagalpa (52)
Matlaltzinga (28)
Mazahua (9)
Mazatec (11)

Miskito (48)
Mixe (15)
Mixtec (14)
Nahua(tl) (10)
Otomí (5)
Paya (46)
Pipil (43)
Pokomán (39)
Pokonchí (40)
Popoluca (17)
Quiché (33)
Subtiaba (50)
Sumo (49)
Talamanca (53)

Tarahumara (1)
Tarascan (8)
Tepehua (6)
Tlapanec (19)
Tojolabal (31)
Totonac (7)
Tzeltal (23)
Tzotzil (22)
Tzutuhil (34)
Uspantec (36)
Xinca (41)
Yucatec Maya (26)
Zapotec (16)
Zoque (18)

the Library of Congress Indian Languages Collection, and Manuscript
Division, Latin American Collection (Miscellaneous).

William E. Gates

William E. Gates was a shadowy and enigmatic personality. He
was born in Atlanta in 1863, and graduated from The Johns Hopkins
University in Baltimore in 1886. He pursued a career in law for a while
but eventually abandoned it for a successful printing enterprise in Cleveland, which published legal papers. By 1905 he was able to retire and
concentrate his energies on various other interests.

One of these interests was collecting books and manuscripts relating
to Middle American Indians. It appears that he acquired a reproduction of
the prehispanic Maya screenfold, *Codex Paris*, in 1898 and this intrigued
him and began a life-long curiosity about the Maya and their system of
writing. He soon realized that any knowledge of the Maya contained in
their writing must be based ultimately upon an intimate knowledge of their
language. He surveyed the literature of the field at that time using
published works and various auction and other sale catalogues and estimated
that over 100,000 pages existed on prehispanic and colonial Middle America.
Of this total, only 1% was in published or accessible form.

For much of the period between 1910 and 1920 Gates attempted to
recover every item on Middle American Indians, either by purchase, transcription, or photoreproduction. For the year 1914-1915 he hired a
professional collector who traveled through Mexico and Guatemala to find
materials in local parish and municipal archives. Still uncertain that
everything was found, he traveled the area on horseback in 1917 and 1918.

William Edmund Gates
(1863–1940)

Gates invested an extraordinary amount of money in this project and estimated that in 1915 alone, he spent in excess of $25,000 for books and manuscripts. By 1920 he was able to claim that he had obtained 95% of all relevant material in existence. Because all funds used were from his personal estate, there can be little doubt that by this time his finances were near exhaustion. In order to raise capital all material in the collection from north of the Maya region was turned over to the American Art Association in New York to be sold at auction. However, before the collection went on sale it was purchased by the Middle American Research Institute at Tulane University in New Orleans. Evidently as part of the conditions of sale, Gates was given a position there but stayed only for one year. In 1929 he sold another portion of his collection to Robert Garrett of Baltimore. These materials would eventually pass to Princeton University. Between 1930 and 1938 Gates was at The Johns Hopkins University where he undertook an impressive publication program of manuscript facsimiles using hand-made paper and hand-colored illustrations. He died in Baltimore in 1940, and the remainder of his collection was sold soon thereafter to Brigham Young University in Utah.

During his life, Gates provided two incomplete inventories of his extensive collection. In 1924 he offered a number of books, pamphlets, manuscripts, and photoreproductions of manuscripts and rare imprints at public sale. The sale catalogue, written by Gates and issued by the American Art Association of New York, listed 1580 items, each often containing several pieces. In the catalogue Gates devotes several pages to describing the way he assembled the linguistic part of his collection, followed by descriptions of these items, both printed and manuscript, arranged according to language.

The majority of these items became the property of the Middle American Research Institute library (presently Latin American Library) at Tulane University in New Orleans. A partial listing of Tulane holdings was made by Arthur E. Gropp in 1934. It is clear that not all items listed in the 1924 sale catalogue are at Tulane. In some instances the original manuscripts from which Gates made photoreproductions to be sold to various institutions were still privately held by Gates; the photoreproduction being listed in the catalogue formed the Tulane item, the same as other photoreproductions in the Peabody Museum, Library of Congress, Newberry Library, and elsewhere. Some items, originals and copies, listed in the 1924 sale catalogue were never received by Tulane.

In 1937, Gates prepared a second listing. Following his resignation from Tulane University he moved his operations and collections to Baltimore, where in 1930 he incorporated the Maya Society, with himself as President. The Maya Society was loosely connected with The Johns Hopkins University, but the collection remained under Gates' private domain. No part of his collection was ever in that university library. Gates issued a series of important publications, among them a short piece entitled *The Maya Society and its Work* (1937). In it he described his plans and provided an incomplete bibliographical inventory of 521 items.

The 1937 listing contains many items not mentioned in the 1924 catalogue. These include both photoreproduced items and original manuscripts, as well as photoreproductions of rare and scarce imprints. Many of the items given in the 1924 catalogue, even copies, are omitted from the 1937 catalogue.

Before his death in 1940, Gates dispersed this 'second' collection. While details are lacking, it seems around 1936 a substantial body of original items, manuscripts and typed copies, was purchased by Robert Garrett. Most, if not all, of these items do not appear in the 1924 catalogue, but are found in the 1937 listing. Around 1940 Garrett presented his purchased Gates' materials to the Institute for Advanced Studies at Princeton University. Later the Institute transferred them to the Division of Manuscripts and Rare Books of the University Library, where they are currently housed.

At the time of his death, Gates' heirs, principally his sister, Edith McComas, still retained some materials. These were primarily books he had acquired and photoreproductions of materials, copies of which he had already sold or given to various institutions. Through an arrangement with M. Wells Jakeman, then chair of the archaeology department, the final assemblage of Gates' material was sold in 1946 to Brigham Young University in Provo, Utah. The collection is presently housed in the archives section of the J. Reuben Clark, Jr. Library at the university.

There is little question of the significance of Gates' collection and its use to scholars of Middle American anthropology. He gathered into a central collection practically the entire corpus of early primary source material for the region and made much of it available to other scholars through exchanges with several institutions. By collecting these items Gates saved a great deal of information from eventual loss or destruction. Documents which may have remained little known and unused in private hands in the Americas and Europe were made available to researchers through Gates' activities.

Gates own assessment of his collection and its importance to

scholarship is consistent with modern evaluations. In a letter to Charles

Bowditch, dated October 31, 1918, Gates describes his collection and its

potential benefit to the Peabody Museum at Harvard University:

> The work has become famous, everyone knows
> it, and speaks of it as a monument. [Marshall]
> Saville was telling [W.H.] Holmes the other
> day, that if I never did any more, this manu-
> script collection was my monument; and so
> everyone joins in saying. It has taken un-
> limited time and pains, and both the work in
> general, and your particular part; I mean my
> own time revising and checks. Many times I
> had thrown away hundreds of prints, and nega-
> tives at once on a difficult manuscript, and
> ordered the whole done de novo. There have
> been cases where copies for you have cost me
> three times the stipulated figure. I have
> not kept detailed costs on individual manu-
> scripts, as there have been underway a dozen
> or more at a time, and from the time a batch
> was started until the prints went to you, it
> was often six months or a year ... As practical
> results, the one institution to get the great
> working benefit is, and for many years to come,
> will be, the Peabody. No one else will have
> a set for I see no possibility of my repeating.
> I have not the time, and it takes my time as
> well as the workers. It will be years before
> my collection will have a body of students
> around it on the Pacific as yours on the Atlantic,
> and meanwhile, you have made the Peabody the
> one absolutely essential place for students of
> this subject to go. Peabody holds the cards.

A total of 310 individual items comprising 27,400 manuscript leaves are in

the Bowditch-Gates Collection at Tozzer Library. Several of these pieces

have been bound to form larger items, such as:

a. Berendt, Karl Hermann [1817-1878]

Colección de pláticas doctrinales y sermones en lengua
maya, por diferentes autores, 1868.
Manuscript: 1 vol., photoreproduction; 20 cm.

<u>Original</u>: Berendt-Brinton Collection, University
of Pennsylvania.
<u>Entry Numbers</u>: 59, 115, 185, 250.
"A collection of Maya pieces, copied by Berendt;
the first part of the volume is devoted to a
copy of part of Domínguez [y Argais], suspended
by the acquisition of the printed copy ... the
origins of the pieces were in Yucatán, and I do
not know whether they still exist; that is,
except the *Modo de confesar*, the original of
which, dated 1803, was gotten by Berendt in
Campeche, and is now part of the Berendt
Collection" (Gates note).

C.A. 6 P 69

b. Brasseur de Bourbourg, Charles Etienne [1814-1874]

Documentos originales sobre las entradas y misiones
de la provincia de Verapaz, del Lacandón y del
Petén Itzá; escritas por varios padres de la orden
de Santo Domingo de Guatemala, en los años 1636
a 1820.
<u>Manuscript</u>: 2 vols., photoreproduction; 32 cm.
<u>Original</u>: Bibliothèque Nationale, Paris.
<u>Entry Numbers</u>: 1, 3, 4, 9, 10, 32, 47, 63, 79,
97-99, 118, 155, 168, 196, 202, 203, 240, 268,
275
A collection of reports, decrees, and related
material dealing with Guatemala, Yucatán, and
the Dominican province of Chiapas, which stresses
the work of Dominican missionaries and the problems
created by unsubdued Maya Indians.

C.A. 6 D 660 G
C.A. 6 D 660 G Microfilm

c. Fischer, Augustin

Otomí language: five treatises copied from early
imprints or manuscripts, ca. 1866.
<u>Manuscript</u>: 1 vol., photoreproduction; 22 cm.
<u>Original</u>: Latin American Library, Tulane University.
<u>Entry Numbers</u>: 60, 61, 181, 183, 277

MEX 6 D 65

d. Palenque Papers

Documentos relativos a los descubrimientos hechos
en el pueblo de Palenque, provincia de Chiapas,
confinante con la Laguna de Términos, de las
ruinas de una gran ciudad, en tiempo de Felipé II
de España.
<u>Manuscript</u>: 1 vol., photoreproduction; 23 cm.
<u>Original</u>: British Museum, London.

Entry Numbers: 93, 94, 192, 214, 229, 241
A collection of manuscript copies of the
following: Spanish translation of the published
report of Del Río and Cabrera (London, 1822),
accounts by Calderón, Bernasconi, and Muñoz
(1795), and the 1813 Robles Domínguez and 1787
Del Río reports; also an incomplete copy of
Palacio's 1576 letter regarding the discovery
of Copán.
                              C.A. 3 P 19
                              C.A. 3 R 476d

e. Schuller-Berendt Miscellanea

    Manuscript: 1 vol., photoreproduction; 22 cm.
    Original: Berendt-Brinton Collection, University
    of Pennsylvania.
    Entry Numbers: 43, 45, 57, 128-130, 136, 149,
    169, 179, 182, 197, 230, 272, 303, 309
    "One volume defied every effort ... but because
    it was a lot of [Byron George] Gordon's manuscripts,
    some of them totally inaccessible save by the grace
    of Gordon ... Dr. Schuller got into his graces
    enough to make a number of copies ... most are in
    Spanish, and contain some of Berendt at his best,
    in original research into linguistic history,
    localities, etc. ... I got his collection loaned
    me, copied some things [by] typewriter, making you
    carbons, and the rest, which I had no time for, did
    the best I could. Made them into a volume, divided:
    General, Eastern, Guatemalan, Western, and Northern
    of Maya ... Much of Berendt's work in this line
    was straight "rescue" work; often the last speakers
    of the dialect died off while he was there at work"
    (Gates note).
                              C.A. 6 B 452m

f. Squier, Ephraim George [1821-1888]

    Collection of original documents relating to Guatemala,
    Honduras, Nicaragua, and Yucatán.
    Manuscript: 1 vol., photoreproduction; 33 cm.
    Original: Bancroft Library, University of California,
    Berkeley.
    Entry Numbers: 17, 62, 120, 186, 193, 278
    "A large part of these were obtained from the various
    Spanish archives and depositories by my friend,
    Buckingham Smith, Esq., late secretary of the legation
    of the United States in Spain ... others were procured
    during my residence in Central America, either in
    person or through the intervention of friends. And
    although all were collected with reference to individual

use in special studies, yet in view of their
wide interest and their importance in all
archaeological and historical investigations
concerning America, I conceive of no better
service could be done to general science
than to place them as rapidly as possible before
the public, and within the reach of students"
(Squier note).

C.A. 6 C 6

Miscellaneous Manuscripts

The Miscellaneous Manuscripts section of the guide comprises a

diverse group of manuscripts not subsumed under the Bowditch-Gates

Collection or the Bowditch German Translation Series categories. This

section includes a number of original early linguistic manuscripts

as well as a number of photoreproductions of important historical

value. In addition to these early items, Miscellaneous Manuscripts

includes more recent archaeological and ethnographic work in the Maya

region related to the Carnegie Institution of Washington. Also in

this section are a number of Bowditch manuscripts and the personal

notes of such scholars as Adela C. Breton, Charles E. Clark, Joseph

T. Goodman, Jackson S. Lincoln, Sylvanus G. Morley, Rudolf R. Schuller,

Edward H. Thompson, and Alfred M. Tozzer.

A total of 297 entries comprising 22,890 manuscript leaves are

in the Miscellaneous Manuscripts section. Several larger subcollections

are found within this group:

   g. Dieseldorff, Erwin P. [1868-1940]

   Ancient land titles of the Kekchí Indians, 1903.
   Manuscript: 1 vol., typewritten; 28 cm.
   Entry Numbers: 390, 391, 558, 559, 561
   Historical overview of the Cobán and San Pedro
   Carchá area of Alta Verapaz in Guatemala and
   transcripts of three seventeenth and eighteenth

century land titles in Kekchí and English.
C.A. 6 D 566 F

h. Four surveys made by the Carnegie Institution
of Washington in Guatemala during 1932.
Manuscript: 1 vol., typewritten; 28 cm.
Entry Numbers: 318, 319, 448, 606
"Besides the archaeological investigations
carried out at Uaxactun in the Department of
Petén, the seventh season of which concluded
during May of 1932, the Carnegie Institution
of Washington initiated four scientific
investigations in the highlands of Guatemala
whose preliminary reports are now ready for
publication" (anonymous pencil note). Includes
geographical research by Rollin and Wallace
Atwood, Felix W. McBryde, and Emmanuel G.
Ziess.
C.A. 1 C 215f

i. LaFarge, Oliver

Chol studies, by Oliver LaFarge and Ernest Noyes,
1932-1933.
Manuscript: 1 vol., typewritten; 28 cm.
Entry Numbers: 428, 429, 465
Includes material on Chol ethnohistory and linguistics,
and an English translation of Francisco Morán's
1685 *Confesionario en lengua cholti*.
C.A. 6 L 121c

j. McDougall, Elsie [1883-1961]

Dance texts from Alta Verapaz, Guatemala, 1931.
Manuscript: 1 vol., typewritten; 28 cm.
Entry Numbers: 323-326
Transcripts of four Kekchí dance dramas from the
nineteenth century.
C.A. 4 M 147d F

k. Tozzer, Alfred Marston [1877-1954]

Pamphlets.
Manuscript: 2 vols., typewritten; 28 cm.
Entry Numbers: 563-566, 569, 570, 572, 574, 575,
579-582
Transcripts of published works between 1902 and 1946.
C.A. 3 T 669p F

Bowditch German Translation Series

    The third section of the guide is a unique collection of English translations of articles originally published in German. This series developed out of Bowditch's interest in Maya calendrics and writing and his willingness to subsidize the translation efforts of Selma Wesselhöft and A. M. Parker. A few more recent items, translated by E. Wyllys Andrews IV and Mrs. Hans Fischel, have been included as well, but these pieces were not the result of the Bowditch program.

    A total of 8,178 manuscript leaves comprises 247 translated entries; these have been bound into the following volumes:

    1. Dieseldorff, Erwin P. [1868-1940]

        Miscellaneous pamphlets: texts and translations, 1893-1909.
        Manuscript: 1 vol., typewritten; 28 cm.
        Entry Numbers: 626-629
                    C.A. 3 D 56m E F

    m. Förstemann, Ernst Wilhelm [1822-1906]

        Miscellaneous pamphlets: texts and translations, 1887-1906.
        Manuscript: 1 vol., typewritten; 28 cm.
        Entry Numbers: 633, 636-650, 652-658
                    C.A. 1 F 77 E F

    n. Lehmann, Walter

        Miscellaneous pamphlets: texts and translations, 1905-1910.
        Manuscript: 1 vol., typewritten; 28 cm.
        Entry Numbers: 666-668, 670-675
                    MEX 1 L 53 E F
                    MEX 1 L 53 E Microfilm

    o. Ludendorff, Hans

        Researches in Maya astronomy: texts and translations, 1930-1936.
        Manuscript: 1 vol., typewritten; 28 cm.
        Entry Numbers: 681-690
                    C.A. 9 L 965u E F
                    C.A. 9 L 965u E Microfilm

p. Maler, Teobert [1842-1917]

    Miscellaneous pamphlets: texts and translations,
    1895-1902.
    Manuscript: 1 vol., typewritten; 28 cm.
    Entry Numbers: 692-694
                        C.A. 3 M 293m E F

q. Maler, Teobert [1842-1917]

    Yucatecan papers: texts and translations,
    1895-1928.
    Manuscript: 1 vol., typewritten; 28 cm.
    Entry Numbers: 692-695
                        C.A. 3 M 293yu E F

r. Miscellaneous Mexican and Central American
    pamphlets, 1882-1905.

    Manuscript: 3 vols., typewritten; 28 cm.
    Entry Numbers: 609-611, 613-615, 617, 619-621,
    623-625, 630-632, 651, 660, 661, 663, 676, 696,
    698, 701, 718-721, 746, 830, 848, 849, 852
                        MEX 1 M 68 E F
                        MEX 1 M 68 E Microfilm

s. Preuss, Konrad Theodor [1869-1938]

    Miscellaneous manuscripts: texts and translations,
    1900-1907.
    Manuscript: 1 vol., typewritten; 28 cm.
    Entry Numbers: 700, 702-704, 706-711, 713-717
                        MEX 1 P 92 E F
                        MEX 1 P 92 E Microfilm

t. Sapper, Karl [1866-1945]

    Miscellaneous pamphlets: texts and translations,
    1891-1906.
    Manuscript: 2 vols., typewritten; 28 cm.
    Entry Numbers: 722-733, 735-742
                        C.A. 1 Sa 69m E F
                        C.A. 1 Sa 69m E Microfilm

u. Seler, Eduard [1849-1922]

    Ancient Mexican studies: texts and translations,
    1899.
    Manuscript: 1 vol., typewritten; 28 cm.
    Entry Numbers: 774, 787, 803
                        MEX 3 Se 48am E F
                        MEX 3 Se 48am E Microfilm

v. Seler, Eduard [1849-1922]

    Collected works of Eduard Seler: texts and
    translations, 1902-1905.
    <u>Manuscript</u>: 8 vols., typewritten; 28 cm.
    <u>Entry Numbers</u>: 750-754, 756-759, 761-767, 770,
    771, 775, 776, 778, 779, 781-786, 788-792, 794,
    797-802, 804-806, 808-810, 812-814, 822, 823,
    825, 826, 828, 829, 831-836, 838-846
                               MEX 1 Se 48g E 2 F
                               MEX 1 Se 48g E 2 Microfilm

w. Seler, Eduard [1849-1922]

    Collected works of Eduard Seler. Cambridge, Mass. :
    Carnegie Institution of Washington, 1939.
    <u>Manuscript</u>: 4 vols., typewritten; 28 cm.
    <u>Entry Numbers</u>: 750-754, 756-759, 761-767, 770,
    771, 775, 776, 778, 779, 781-786, 788-792, 794,
    797-802, 804-806, 808-810, 812-814, 822, 823,
    825, 826, 828, 829, 831-836, 838-846
    Mimeograph edited, edited by J. Eric S. Thompson
    and F. B. Richardson, for limited distribution;
    slight emendations to volumes 4 and 5 by Thompson.
                               MEX 1 Se 48g E 3 F

x. Seler, Eduard [1849-1922]

    Miscellaneous pamphlets: texts and translations,
    1890-1911.
    <u>Manuscript</u>: 1 vol., typewritten; 28 cm.
    <u>Entry Numbers</u>: 747, 748, 752, 760, 764, 768, 772,
    773, 777, 780, 785, 793, 795, 811, 814-816, 818,
    819, 827
                               MEX 1 Se 48m E F
                               MEX 1 Se 48m E Microfilm

Entry Format

    Manuscript entries are arranged alphabetically by section and

follow a standardized format. Entries have been constructed with

the requirements of scholarly interest as a primary concern.

Some information therefore may have been omitted that would be of

interest primarily to bibliophiles.

    <u>Authorship</u>. Where known or imputed, authorship is indicated.

Uncertain authorship has been indicated with the use of brackets. If no author is given on the piece, entries are assumed to be anonymous and are listed under title. In those cases where it is possible to determine, dates of birth and death are provided.

Title. Preferred or variant titles, followed by date of composition, are given after authorship. An attempt has been made to modernize or at least standardize divergent and archaic orthographies, particularly in the case of Gates' photoreproductions. If no title is provided in the original, constructed title is indicated with the use of brackets. Place of publication, publisher, and publishing date are given for printed entries. Printed entries have been included if they possess marginal notations of some apparent scholarly value, or are photoreproductions of rare or early imprints.

Form. Form subdata indicates whether the item is printed or in manuscript format, and whether handwritten, typewritten, or photoreproduction. Pagination is usually given in leaves, and maximum physical dimension in centimeters.

Provenience. The present known location of original documents is given for items in the Bowditch-Gates Collection. This information has been determined from the piece itself or from various finding aids given in the references. Provenience data for Gates' photoreproductions are summarized in Table 1.

Annotations. An annotation field usually follows information on provenience or form. Most annotations for entries in the Bowditch-Gates Collection are taken from the piece itself or from sale catalogues. Annotations for items in the Miscellaneous Manuscripts section are of a

Table I. Concordance of Institutional Holdings for Gates Photoreproductions.

Entry Number	Brinton 1900	Butler 1937	Freeman 1966	Gates 1924	Gates 1937	Gates 1940	Omont 1925	Pilling 1885	Pinart 1883
1									
2	24			976	217	x		15	
3							52		738
4							52		738
5									
6	64	1655		1030	430	x		35b	
7	64?	1662		1029	429			35c	
8	62	1655			437				
9				635					
10				636					
11		1493			401	x	45	49	839
12	116	1518		954	117	x	38		11
13		1597		970	129	x			
14		1539		1004	357	x			
15					73	x		73	
16	150							73b	
17				627					
18		1494				x	40	118	23
19		1495				x	41	119	24
20	55	1540		991	322	x	9	121a	
21									
22		1688			448	x		139-143	
23		1689		1039	446	x		136	
24		1497			405	x			
25		1492		777	40				
26		1625		940	103	x			
27		1625		941		x			
28				992	323				
29		1541			391	x	58	169	51
30	13		484		391				
31									
32				603					
33	97			934	98	x		277	
34		1542			312?	x			
35				1043	453	x			
36		1519		953	116	x	39		76
37		1593			34	x		312	
38								312	
39		1593		757	32	x		312	
40		1593		757	32	x		312	

Table I. Concordance of Institutional Holdings for Gates Photoreproductions (continued).

Entry Number	Brinton 1900	Butler 1937	Freeman 1966	Gates 1924	Gates 1937	Gates 1940	Omont 1925	Pilling 1885	Pinart 1883
41		1543		1007	300	x	59	316	82
42	22				213			346	
43	121							363c	
44	96				462			363b	
45	152								
46	88				445	x			
47									
48		1676		746	30	x			
49				933	47	x			
50		1584				x	65		52
51	57	1498		1018	385	x		565b	
					395				
52	58	1546		1006	310	x		565a	
53				1024	410?	x			
					417?				
54		1674		748	29	x			
55		1675		747	28	x			
56		1549			331				
57									
58		1537		1021	408	x	54	596	198
59	46	1602			201			631a	
60		1642		724	9	x		660	
61		1644		724	9	x			
62									
63				637					
64		1600			131	x			
65	45	1614			148	x			
66	49				131	x			
67	49	1606		959	137	x			
68	42/13? 43/5? 49?				130	x			
69									
70		1611		958	134	x			
71		1619		956	133	x			
72		1621			135	x			
73	49								
74									
75	66			1033	432	x			

Table I. Concordance of Institutional Holdings for Gates Photoreproductions (continued).

Entry Number	Brinton 1900	Butler 1937	Freeman 1966	Gates 1924	Gates 1937	Gates 1940	Omont 1925	Pilling 1885	Pinart 1883
76		1471		808	47	x			
77		1561		998	227	x			
78		1567		999	226	x			
79			51	639					
80		1533			313	x			
81	67	1658		1034	434	x		853a	
82				935	92	x			
83				905	78	x			
84					82	x			
85				972	206?	x			
86					208	x		894	
87				973	207	x		892	
88		1500	86		375	x		907	
89	50	1601		960	128	x			
90									
91		1475		801	49	x			
92		1701		908	79	x	70	937	526
93									
94		1603		964	204	x			
95		1603		964	204	x			
96								1016	
97				620?					
98				621?					
99				620?					
100					452	x			
101	1	1610			119? 120?	x		1030	
102	3	1617			121	x		1030	
103		1647		733	8	x		1250	
104				924	85	x		1047	
105					202				
106		1677		745	26	x			
107	91	1531		1050	461	x		1056b	
108		1624		937	100	x			
109				1023	412	x			
110		1556		1001	228-264?	x			

Table I. Concordance of Institutional Holdings for Gates Photoreproductions (continued).

Entry Number	Brinton 1900	Butler 1937	Freeman 1966	Gates 1924	Gates 1937	Gates 1940	Omont 1925	Pilling 1885	Pinart 1883
111		1620		965	158-170?	x			
112									
113				995? 996?	247- 249?	x			
114		1604			158-170?				
115	23	1602		975	212	x		1064	
116		1545			318	x			
117		1590		1048	459	x			
118									
119									
120				602					
121		1647		733	8	x		1250	
122	102				83	x		1275	
123									
124						x		1308	
125				949	113	x			
126		1591		1047	460	x	382	1341	
127								1342	
128	122							1343	
129	122							1343	
130	107							1343a	
131	36			978	218	x		3976	
132									
133		1648			6	x		1401	
134				737	15	x		1401	
135					68	x		1400	
136									
137				610					
138									
139		1682		743	23	x			
140		1678? 1679?		743	19	x			
141					20	x			
142		1680		744	21				
143		1684			22	x			
144				919	75	x		1561	

Table I. Concordance of Institutional Holdings for Gates Photoreproductions (continued).

Entry Number	Brinton 1900	Butler 1937	Freeman 1966	Gates 1924	Gates 1937	Gates 1940	Omont 1925	Pilling 1885	Pinart 1883
145									
146					111	x	67	1564a	413
147	36			977	216	x		1613	
148	52	1501			387	x		1622	
149									
150					72	x		1280	
151		1558		944	327	x	61	1749	451
152		1583			317				
153		1469		803	51	x			
154					456	x			.
155				638					
156		1683		742	24	x			
157				809	48	x			
158									
159				905	78				
160	104			910	84	x		2281	
161									
162	118	1520						2284b	
163					139				
164		1599		966	126	x			
165		1609			138	x			
166				967	125				
167		1474		806	46	x			
168									
169	141								
170		1503	487	1012	400	x		2412	
171		1504			399			2414	
172		1502			399	x		2413	
173		1702		907	76	x			
174	103					x			
175		1560		993	325	x	62	2483	592
176					45				
177					31	x		2532	
178					141	x			
179									
180		1505	495		366?	x		2564	
181		1645		724	9	x			
182									
183		1649		723	9	x		2594	
184	93	1690			450	x		2599a	
185	26	1602			201			2599b	

Table I. Concordance of Institutional Holdings for Gates Photoreproductions (continued).

Entry Number	Brinton 1900	Butler 1937	Freeman 1966	Gates 1924	Gates 1937	Gates 1940	Omont 1925	Pilling 1885	Pinart 1883
186				632					
187	84	1527	749	1038	219	x		2629	
188		1660		1036	441	x	53	2631	641
189					442	x	51	2634	
190					439		50	2633	
191		1666		1037	440	x		2632	
192									
193				640					
194		1551			372				
195				740	253			2692	
196				600					
197	124								
198		1587		1002	320	x	12		
199	60	1612		971	152	x		2774b	
200		1521		951	114	x	37	2783	678
201		1522		952	115	x	36	2784	679
202									
203									
204				760	38	x			
205				945	88				
206		1616			200?				
207				629					
208				624					
209					3				
210					4	x	6		
211		1607			150	x			
212		1576			349				
213									
214									
215				961	203	x			
216		1562		997	330	x	13		
217				1025a	424	x	55	3035	745
218					305	x		4267	
219					305	x			
220		1563			307	x			

Table I. Concordance of Institutional Holdings for Gates Photoreproductions (continued).

Entry Number	Brinton 1900	Butler 1937	Freeman 1966	Gates 1924	Gates 1937	Gates 1940	Omont 1925	Pilling 1885	Pinart 1883
221		1704		947	109	x	66		
222		1705		948	110	x	68		752
223	109				108	x			
224		1624		938	101	x			
225									
226									
227				918	74	x		3239	
228				1026	415	x			
229									
230	140								
231		1667			443	x			
232								3425	
233	33					x		3415	
234	31					x		3424	
235									
236		1484		807	42	x			
237		1486		807	42	x			
238		1485			41	x		3445	
239		1478			44	x		3448	
240				633?					
241									
242		1645			7	x		3472	
243		1555		1003	368?	x	60		312
244		1569			356	x	11		
245		1508		1013	402	x			
246				1000	329	x			
247		1507		1014	388	x	44	3484	820
248									
249		1487			51				
250	47	1602			201	x		3561a	
251				962	199	x			
252		1663			436	x			
253		1596			35		22		
254		1664			435	x			
255		1685			25	x			
256		1618			205				
257									
258		1514			379–381?	x		4051	
259									
260		1530		1051	463	x		3820–3824	

-31-

Table I. Concordance of Institutional Holdings for Gates Photoreproductions (continued).

Entry Number	Brinton 1900	Butler 1937	Freeman 1966	Gates 1924	Gates 1937	Gates 1940	Omont 1925	Pilling 1885	Pinart 1883
261		1693			449	x			
262		1538		1020	413				
263		1572			347?	x			
					348?				
					351?				
264		1571			360?				
265					112	x			
266		1699			77				
267	54	1509		1016	392	x	15	3881	
268				611					
269		1573			316				
270				915	69	x			
271		1652		725	5	x	8	3955	
272									
273				905	78	x			
274	89				444	x		3963a	
275					634?				
276		1510	496		378	x		3980	
277		1653		724	9	x		3981	
278				601					
279		1665			426	x		4021	
280		1696			374	x	69	3562	
281		1581			350	x			
282		1511			396	x	5		
283									
284		1579			352	x			
285		1578			348	x	10		
286		1577			347	x	42		574
287		1697			374	x	3		
288		1575			353		4		
289		1512			353?	x		4022	
290		1511			376	x	46		932
291	51				386	x		4032b	
292	122							4045a	
293		1686			27				
294									
295		1496			384				
296		1506		1015	389	x	43		675
297		1626		939	102	x			
298					14	x			
299		1586			314	x			
300				925	86				

Table I. Concordance of Institutional Holdings for Gates Photoreproductions (concluded).

Entry Number	Brinton 1900	Butler 1937	Freeman 1966	Gates 1924	Gates 1937	Gates 1940	Omont 1925	Pilling 1885	Pinart 1883
301		1513			377?	x		4052	
302					123				
303	139							1486b	
304		1515			304	x		4265	
305		1516			303	x	57		50
306		1622			123	x			
307		1588			336?	x			
					342?				
308		1588			341	x			
309	56								
310					87	x		4279	

more general nature, and for the Bowditch German Translation Series

items, comments are restricted to original publication information.

Where titles contain sufficient content data, annotations have usually

been omitted.

Reproductions. Many of the items listed in the Bowditch-Gates

Collection may be found in other libraries. As a tentative finding

guide, this field provides information on the location of duplicates.

The following abbreviations are used:

AC/NL	Edward E. Ayer Collection Newberry Library Chicago, Illinois
BBC/UP	Berendt-Brinton Collection University Museum University of Pennsylvania Philadelphia, Pennsylvania
BL/UC	Bancroft Library University of California, Berkeley Berkeley, California
BYU	J. Rueben Clark Jr. Library Brigham Young University Provo, Utah
JCB/BU	John Carter Brown Library Brown University Providence, Rhode Island
LAL/TU	Latin American Library Tulane University New Orleans, Louisiana
LC	Latin American (Miscellaneous) Collection, Division of Manuscripts Library of Congress Washington, D.C.
RGC/PU	Robert Garrett Collection Princeton University Princeton, New Jersey

Call Number. As this guide is intended for the scholarly use of

a specific collection rather than general bibliographic purposes,

Tozzer Library call numbers have been included. All manuscripts in the collection are ordered and may only be retrieved by this number.

Indexes

A series of indexes have been provided in order to increase the usefulness of the collection for scholars in Middle American Indian ethnohistory and historical linguistics. These are arranged by personal and place names, and general subject areas. The headings used in constructing subject classifications are necessarily arbitrary and obviously cannot serve the needs of all users equally well. They relate more to personal research interests than to areas with which I am less familiar. Nevertheless, they should prove adequate for gaining access to most of the subject areas included in the collection.

Acknowledgments

The project of compiling this research guide to manuscripts relating to Middle American Indians was aided by several of my professional colleagues at Tozzer Library, especially Shari Grove, Marilyn Geller, and Joanne Soreno, as well as by members of the Department of Anthropology and the Peabody Museum of Archaeology and Ethnology at Harvard University.

Generous financial support was provided by Harvard University Library through the award of a Douglas W. Bryant Fellowship for 1984. Without this assistance, the completion of the project would have been delayed considerably. I wish to thank Hugh Amory, Chair, and members of the Selection Committee of the Bryant Fellowship, Russell O. Pollard, Lorna Daniels, and E. Louisa Worthington, for their interest and research and editorial assistance, and fostered many improvements. Her continued interest and ethusiasm for this project have greatly facilitated its completion. I thank her, and our daughter, Hillary Weeks, for their patience and understanding.

Most importantly, it must be recognized that this project would never have been possible without the vision of Charles P. Bowditch who recognized the potential of these materials for future generations of Middle Americanists.

The portrait of Charles Bowditch is taken from an oil painting made in 1910 by Ignace Gaugengigl, and was reproduced by Hillel Burger. It was provided through the courtesy of the Photographic Archives, Peabody Museum of Archaeology and Ethnology, Harvard University. The illustration of William Gates was copied from the frontispiece of the 1940 Gates Collection sale catalogue. All other illustrations are courtesy of the Tozzer Library, Harvard University.

All inquiries regarding restrictions on the use of this manuscript collection should be addressed to the Librarian, Tozzer Library, Harvard University, 21 Divinity Avenue, Cambridge, Massachusetts 02138.

Cambridge, Massachusetts
November 1984

ru mal xuyao xucipah kahaual chike la
huh upixah kihih mimaloßolah kehoh. uke
hohil vae usancioylah ticon, kachuch sancta
yglesia aregu rioh chikaßah vae uhih, que
he gu mim chika rapah mim chi kagaxgo bi
çah eulos sacerdotes, euça mahel dios eba
nal sermon, chiquiser monih uhih upixah
dios, egamol uçaßulil u ticon dios, rumalma
na chi koqueçah ugoheic dios, xauironohel
qui hih caqui sermonih pakaui varal chu
uach uleuh, aregu ri maih, chikarapah, maih
chi kagaxgobiçah, maih chika camiçah, ka
haual Jesuchristo. chikamac kalabal; que
hegu tachul ußalahih kahaual Jesu christo
pakaui ohgaßgoh. paquiuinaipu eami
nak, tachul naipu umilo, chul naipuuga
ma uçaßul ticon, ub̶ mana uhubamic

Compendio en la lengua quiché
acquired in Guatemala by Robert Burkitt (no. 383)

1. Abella, Francisco

   Informe hecho al Ilmo. señor arzobispo de Guatemala sobre el
   estado de las misiones de Verapaz, firmado por el R.P.Fr.
   Francisco Abella, de la orden de Santo Domingo, en 29 de
   diciembre de 1819.
   Manuscript: 5 leaves, photoreproduction; 32 cm.
   Original: Bibliothèque Nationale, Paris.
   Handwritten copy of the original by Brasseur de Bourbourg.
   Interesting for early geographic and ethnographic information
   on the Alta Verapaz region of Guatemala.
                                        BL/UC
                                        C.A. 6 D 660 G
                                        C.A. 6 D 660 G Microfilm

2. Acosta, José Antonio [1538-1600]

   Oraciones devotas que comprenden los actos de fe, esperanza,
   caridad y afectos para un cristiano, y una oración para pedir
   una buena muerte, en idioma yucateco, con inclusión del Santo
   Dios, a devoción del Pbro. José Antonio Acosta ... Mérida de
   Yucatán : Imprenta a cargo de Mariano Guzmán, 1851.

   Printed: 16 p., photoreproduction; 22 cm.
   Printed in two columns, Spanish and Yucatec Maya opposite.
   Acosta was born in Yucatán and was cura of Mocochá about 1812.
                                        BBC/UP, BYU, LC
                                        C.A. 6 Or 1

3. Aguilar, Francisco

   [Letter from fray Francisco Aguilar to fray Luis Escoto
   regarding Indian affairs in San Miguel Tucurú, Verapaz region,
   Guatemala, ca. 1815].
   Manuscript: 5 leaves, photoreproduction; 32 cm.
   Original: Bibliothèque Nationale, Paris.
   Handwritten copy of the original by Brasseur de Bourbourg.
                                        BL/UC
                                        C.A. 6 D 660 G
                                        C.A. 6 D 660 G Microfilm

4. [Letter from fray Francisco Aguilar regarding the retention
   of Indians from San Juan Chamelco in the parajes of Uacxac
   and Chamiquin, 1820].
   Manuscript: 2 leaves, photoreproduction; 32 cm.
   Original: Bibliothèque Nationale, Paris.
   Handwritten copy of the original by Brasseur de Bourbourg.
                                        BL/UC
                                        C.A. 6 D 660 G
                                        C.A. 6 D 660 G Microfilm

5. Aguilar, Francisco

Plática de los principales misterios de la religión en lengua
pocomchí, 1856.
Manuscript: 18 leaves, photoreproduction; 16 cm.
Original: Bibliothèque Nationale, Paris.
From an original manuscript obtained by Brasseur de Bourbourg
in Tactic, Verapaz region of Guatemala.
                                        BYU
                                        C.A. 6 Ag 9

6. Plática en lengua poconchí, [de] Fr. Francisco Aguilar,
cura de Tactic, 1822.
Manuscript: 12 leaves, photoreproduction; 16 cm.
Original: Berendt-Brinton Collection, University of Pennsylvania.
"Manuscript, copied from the original in the parochial archives
of Cahabón in Verapaz. The Pocomchí and Spanish are on opposite
pages. This is a copy of the first sermon in Pocomchí" (Brinton
1900:218).
                                        AC/NL, BYU, LAL/TU, LC
                                        C.A. 6 Ag 9

7. Sermón de Nuestra Señora del Rosario en lengua pocomchí, 1818.
Manuscript: 37 leaves, photoreproduction; 16 cm.
Original: Berendt-Brinton Collection, University of Pennsylvania.
In Gates' original (1924) list this item is attributed to Aguilar
but later lists (1937, 1940) give no author. Spanish and
Pokomchí are opposite.
                                        AC/NL, BYU, LC
                                        C.A. 6 Ag 9

8. Aguilera, Hipolito de

Doctrina cristiana en pocomchí, escrita por Fr.Hipolito
de Aguilera, predicador cura de este partido del pocomchí,
Santa María Tactic, 1741.
Manuscript: 7 leaves, photoreproduction; 16 cm.
Original: Berendt-Brinton Collection, University of Pennsylvania.
"Copied from a manuscript in the parochial archives of Cobán in
Verapaz" (Brinton 1900:218).
                                        AC/NL, BYU, LAL/TU, LC
                                        C.A. 6 Ag 9

9. Aguirre, Francisco Xavier de

Informe de don Francisco Xavier de Aguirre, alcalde mayor que fue
de la provincia de Verapaz a los señores de la junta del gobierno
del Real Consulado de Guatemala; escrito en la hacienda de Los
Llanos, a 3 de febrero de 1803.
Manuscript: 4 leaves, photoreproduction; 32 cm.
Original: Bibliothèque Nationale, Paris.
Handwritten copy of the original by Brasseur de Bourbourg.

A summary description of the Verapaz region, its topography, inhabitants, products, etc., with suggestions for development.
> BL/UC
> C.A. 6 D 660 G
> C.A. 6 D 660 G Microfilm

10. Aguirre, Rafael de

Representación verbal que hicieron a su P. cura los alcaldes presentes y pasados, con los demás indios principales de Cobán, fecha de Cobán, en 4 de septiembre de 1807.
Manuscript: 6 leaves, photoreproduction; 32 cm.
Original: Bibliothèque Nationale, Paris.
A reproduction of an oral petition presented by the leading Indians of Cobán to their parish priest, Rafael de Aguirre, requesting confirmation of their statements regarding the difficulty of paying taxes, with a confirmatory declaration by Aguirre.
> BL/UC
> C.A. 6 D 660 G
> C.A. 6 D 660 G Microfilm

11. [Alarcón, Baltasar de]

Sermones en lengua cakchiquel escritos por varios padres de la Orden de San Francisco, y recogidos por el M.R.M. padre Fr. Baltasar de Alarcón, procurador general de la misma orden, en la provincia del Dulce Nombre de Jesús de Guatemala, ca. 1575.
Manuscript: 170 leaves, photoreproduction; 22 cm.
Original: Bibliothèque Nationale, Paris.
Comprises 23 sermons in Cakchiquel, written by different authors at different times. "This is a volume by various writers, Franciscans, gathered together only by the Procurador General Alarcón" (Gates note). A pencil note on the manuscript states: "Title ought to be changed. Father Alarcón did not collect these 'sermones' at all ... as was supposed by Brasseur de Bourbourg and accepted by Gates."
> AC/NL, BYU, LC
> C.A. 6 Al 1

12. Albornoz, Juan de [d.1715]

Arte de la lengua chiapaneca, compuesto por el padre fray Juan de Albornoz, de la orden de Predicadores de la provincia de San Vicente de Chiapas y Guatemala, 1691.
Manuscript: 27 leaves, photoreproduction; 28 cm.
Original: Bibliothèque Nationale, Paris.
> AC/NL, BBC/UP, BYU, LAL/TU, LC
> C.A. 6 Al 1

13. Algunos apuntos sobre la historia antigua de Yucatán.

Manuscript: 14 leaves, photoreproduction; 17 cm.
Original: Bibliothèque Nationale, Paris.
"These notes on the gods and the Maya sounds are evidently
modern, but I know nothing of their author" (Gates 1924).
AC/NL, BYU, LAL/TU, LC
C.A. 6 Al 3

14. Algunos sermones en lengua quiché de Rabinal, ca. 1575.

Manuscript: 50 leaves, photoreproduction; 22 cm.
Original: Bibliothèque Nationale, Paris.
"A well written manuscript of the middle sixteenth century,
in a hand resembling closely that of Padre Vico, if not indeed
his autograph" (Gates 1924). This appears really to be a
collection of theologia material.
AC/NL, BYU, LAL/TU, LC
C.A. 6 R 11

15. Alvarado, Francisco de

Vocabulario en lengua mixteca, hecho por los padres de la orden
de Predicadores, que residen en ella y últimamente recopilado
y acabado por el padre fray Francisco de Alvarado, vicario de
Tamaculapa de la misma orden ... México : En Casa de Pedro Balli,
1593.

Printed: 204 leaves bound in 2 vols., photoreproduction; 22 cm.
"This must be ranked with the Cordova [Zapotec dictionary of 1571]
both in rarity and importance; and together they give comparative
Mixtec-Zapotec that must be the foundation of all that branch, as
is the Motul for Maya, Molina for Náhuatl, etc. With this is to
be put the excessively rare, almost unique, Hernández *Doctrina en
Mixteca*, 1568" (Gates note).
BYU, LC
MEX 6 Al 8

16. Alvarado, Lucas

Vocabularios de las lenguas vizeita y caché, 1873.
Manuscript: 2 leaves, photoreproduction; 22 cm.
Original: Berendt-Brinton Collection, University of Pennsylvania.
"Manuscript, original, 291 words in all, collected for Dr.
Berendt" (Brinton 1900:29).
BYU
C.A. 6 B 452m

17. Alvarado, Pedro de [c.1485-1541]

Cartas del adelantado don Pedro de Alvarado, escrita al rey y
de España y al capitán Hernando Cortés, sobre la conquista y
pacificación de los reinos de Guatemala, y la expedición que
hizo desde el puerto de Iztapa a Perú, 1524 hasta 1541.

Manuscript: 21 leaves, photoreproduction; 33 cm.
Original: Real Academia de la Historia, Madrid.
Handwritten copy of the original document in the Muñoz
Collection by Buckingham Smith, March 1857.
                                   BL/UC
                                   C.A. 6 C 6

18. [Angel, Fr.]

Arte de lengua cakchiquel, compuesto por el padre fray Angel,
ca. 1775.
Manuscript: 188 leaves, photoreproduction; 16 cm.
Original: Bibliothèque Nationale, Paris.
"The author's name is very doubtful, but the manuscript is
useful, and there is also a vocabulary which Brasseur de
Bourbourg had in the same hand" (Gates note).
                                   AC/NL, LAL/TU
                                   C.A. 6 An 4

19. Vocabulario de la lengua cakchiquel, compuesto por el padre
fray Angel, de la orden de Nuestro Padre de San Francisco,
ca. 1775.
Manuscript: 225 leaves bound in 2 vols., photoreproduction; 22 cm.
Original: Bibliothèque Nationale, Paris.
"The authorship is not a certainty; the manuscript was Brasseur's,
and he named it Angel, from the note: 'Padre Angel begs those who
use this book to be careful of their language, and not use
miswords to the natives'" (Gates note).
                                   AC/NL, BYU, LC
                                   C.A. 6 An 4

20. Anleo, Bartolomé de [d.1692]

Arte de la lengua quiché, compuesto por N.M.R.P. fray Bartolomé
Anleo, religioso menor de N.S.P. San Francisco, ca. 1660.
Manuscript: 67 leaves, photoreproduction; 17 cm.
Original: Bibliothèque Nationale, Paris.
"The present manuscript was acquired by the Bibliothèque Nationale
in Paris. It is a photograph of a 1744 transcription by Fray
Ramírez de Utrilla" (Gates note). On ff. 65v-66 is the following
note: "Este arte de lengua quiché fue compuesto por N.M.R.P.Fr.
Bartholomé de Anleo, cuyo original tuvo N.M.R.P.Fr. Antonio Meliân
de Betancur, y su P.M.R. me lo dona a mi Fr. Antonio Ramírez de
Utrilla; de cuyo original fue traslado este de mi mano, y le acabé
en veinte y seis de agosto, en el pueblo de N.S.P. San Francisco
Sanahachel [i.e., Panajachel], año de 1744."
                                   AC/NL, BBC/UP, BYU, LAL/TU, LC
                                   C.A. 6 An 6

21. Ara, Domingo de [d.1572]

Arte de la lengua tzendal, ca. 1575.
Manuscript: 32 leaves, photoreproduction; 22 cm.
BYU
C.A. 6 Ar 1

22. Egregium opus fratris dominici de Hara, de comparacionibus
et similitudinibus. In festo sanctissimi sacramenti, modus
administrandi sacramentum matrimonii [en lengua de tzeltal],
ca. 1575.
Manuscript: 167 leaves, photoreproduction; 22 cm.
Original: Bibliothèque Nationale, Paris.
Includes a number of religious treatises in Tzeltal.
AC/NL, BYU, LC
C.A. 6 Ar 1

23. Vocabulario en lengua tzeltal, según el orden de Copanabastla,
1571.
Manuscript: 165 leaves, photoreproduction; 29 cm.
Original: Bibliothèque Nationale, Paris.
"We have Ara's dictionary and two texts from his pen; another
early text is Temporal; a recast of Ara's dictionary by Guzmán
in 1620, some sermons in 1675, and then almost absolutely
nothing [in Tzeltal] until the Pineda grammar and vocabulary
printed in 1888" (Gates 1924).
AC/NL, BL/UC, BYU, LAL/TU, LC
C.A. 6 Ar 11b

24. Arana Xahila, Francisco Hernández

[Memorial de Tecpán Atitlán].
Manuscript: 54 leaves, photoreproduction; 33 cm.
Original: Robert Garrett Collection, Princeton University.
"This is an independent translation, differing from Brinton
in places, and giving the whole of the latter part of the
manuscript after Kicab, and down to 1583, Brinton stopping
at 1559. It gives only the latter half of the whole,
beginning at leaf 29, ending with 55. The first part I have
noted and take it is lost" (Gates note).
AC/NL, BYU, LC
C.A. 6 H 3a G

25. [Araoz, Francisco Xavier de]

Vocabulario mexicana, 1598.
Manuscript: 137 leaves, photoreproduction; 22 cm.
Original: Latin American Library, Tulane University.
"The Araoz vocabulary is of somewhat less importance; but it
nearly fills the list now, with Molina and Sahagún, of Aztec
dictionaries" (Gates note).
AC/NL, BYU
MEX 6 Ar 6

26. Arrona, Ignacio

Confesionario en idioma mazateco, perteneciente a Ignacio
Arrona quien lo nacía en diez y ocho de enero del año de 1797.
Manuscript: 17 leaves, photoreproduction; 33 cm.
AC/NL, BYU, LC
MEX 6 C 74

27. Cuaderno de idioma mazateco comenzado en el año de 1796.
Manuscript: 9 leaves, photoreproduction; 33 cm.
AC/NL, BYU, LC
MEX 6 C 74

28. Arte de la lengua quiché, 16 cent.

Manuscript: 40 leaves, photoreproduction; 31 cm.
Original: Robert Garrett Collection, Princeton University.
"This is one of the earliest artes I know, and though
anonymous, is, it seems to me, probably the prototype of
nearly all later ones" (Gates note).
BYU
C.A. 6 Ar 7
C.A. 6 C 280 Microfilm

29. Arte de lengua quiché [i.e., Cakchiquel], ilustrado con algunas
notas que están puestas al fin, para su perfecta inteligencia;
hechas por un aficionado a este idioma, 1793.

Manuscript: 109 leaves, photoreproduction; 22 cm.
Original: Bibliothèque Nationale, Paris.
AC/NL, BYU, LC
C.A. 6 Qu 4

30. Arte y doctrina en lengua cakchiquel, 1692.

Manuscript: 217 leaves, photoreproduction; 22 cm.
Original: American Philosophical Society, Philadephia.
"Contains a statement of doctrine, catechism, confessional,
brief religious discourses, as well as a grammar of the
Cakchiquel" (Freeman 1966:86).
BBC/UP, BYU, LC
C.A. 6 Ar 75

31. Avendaño y Loyola, Andrés de [fl.1695-1705]

Relación de los dos entradas que hice a la conversión de los
Ytzaes y Cehaches, 1696.
Manuscript: 66 leaves, photoreproduction; 32 cm.
Original: British Museum, London.
"The present manuscript is Avendaño's autograph report in full
of his entire journey [in 1696 from Yucatán with a letter from
Martín de Ursua to Canek at Petén Itzá], description of the

route, distances, happenings, etc. It contains a map of
the lake and island, with surrounding territory, and also
long descriptions of the situation of the districts and
parcialidades of the kingdom, a description of the buildings
and the customs, etc. The manuscript was one of those gathered
by Ramírez in Mexico, so that no copy of it probably got to
Spain, this being the original" (Gates note).

                 C.A. 2 Av 3

32. Azcona, Domingo de

    [Letter from fray Domingo de Azcona, a Dominican, regarding
Indian affairs in the Verapaz region of Guatemala, 1567].
Manuscript: 2 leaves, photoreproduction; 32 cm.
Original: Bibliothèque Nationale, Paris.
Handwritten copy of the original by Brasseur de Bourbourg.
Includes informes by the auditor Antonio Mejía and by
licenciado Valdés.

                 BL/UC
                 C.A. 6 D 660 G
                 C.A. 6 D 660 G Microfilm

33. Barreda, Nicolás de la

    Doctrina cristiana en lengua chinanteca añadida la explicación
de los principales misterios de la fe, modo de baptizar en
caso de necesidad, y de ayudar a bien morir, y método de
administración de sacramentos por el Br. D. Nicolás de la
Barreda, cura beneficiado y juez eclesiástico de beneficio de
S. Pedro de Yolos del obispo de Oaxaca ... México : Por los
Herederos de la Viuda de Francisco Rodriguez Lupercio, 1730.

    Printed: 95 p., photoreproduction; 22 cm.

                 BBC/UP, BYU
                 MEX 6 B 27

34. Barrera, Francisco

    Vocabulario en lengua quiché, 1745.
Manuscript: 100 leaves, photoreproduction; 22 cm.
"The title is very hard to read but the date 1745 is clear,
and a name Fr. Alberto Miguez. The Vocabulario runs from A to Z"
(Gates note).

                 AC/NL, LC
                 C.A. 6 B 27

35. Barrera, José de la

    Libro de lengua tzotzil con que se hallará la doctrina cristiana,
con preguntas y explicación administración de los sacramentos;
dos artes, varios sermones y otras cosas que el curioso puede
ver, para su aprovechamiento; compuesto de varios papeles por
el P.Pr.Fr. José de la Barrera quien pide a los que le sirviera

lo encomienden a dios, año de 1782.
Manuscript: 157 leaves, photoreproduction; 22 cm.
Original: Latin American (Miscellaneous) Collection, Library
of Congress, Washington, D.C.
"This volume by Barrera is the only real effort at a grammar
we have [for Tzotzil], so that any real work on the language
must rest on this and the folio dictionary" (Gates 1924).
BYU, LAL/TU
C.A. 6 B 27

36. Barrientos, Luis [d.1688]

Doctrina en lengua chiapaneca, escrita por el padre fray
Luis Barrientos de la orden de Predicadores, 1690.
Manuscript: 8 leaves, photoreproduction; 22 cm.
Original: Bibliothèque Nationale, Paris.
AC/NL, BYU, LAL/TU, LC
C.A. 6 Al 1

37. Basalenque, Diego [1577-1651]

Arte de la lengua matlaltzinga, compuesto por el padre
maestro fray Diego Basalenque de la orden de N.P.S. Agustín
de la provincia de Michoacán, anno domini 1640.
Manuscript: 125 leaves, photoreproduction; 15 cm.
"This monumental work is one of the finest things we have,
and substantially our sole reliance for the language" (Gates
note).
AC/NL, BYU
MEX 6 B 29

38. Arte de la lengua matlaltzinga muy copioso y así mismo una
suma y arte abreviado; compuesto todo por el padre maestro
fray Diego Basalenque de la orden de Nuestro Padre de San
Agustín de la provincia de Michoacán, año 1640.
Manuscript: 15 leaves, photoreproduction; 23 cm.
MEX 6 B 29

39. Vocabulario de la lengua castellana vuelto en la matlaltzinga,
por el padre maestro fray Diego Basalenque de la orden de
N.P.S. Agustín de la provincia de Michoacán, año 1642.
Manuscript: 206 leaves bound in 2 vols., photoreproduction; 14 cm.
AC/NL, BYU, LAL/TU, LC
MEX 6 B 29

40. Vocabulario de la lengua matlaltzinga vuelto en la castellana,
por el padre maestro fray Diego Basalenque de la orden de
N.P.S. Agustín de la provincia de Michoacán, año 1642.
Manuscript: 143 leaves, photoreproduction; 15 cm.
AC/NL, BYU, LAL/TU, LC
MEX 6 B 29

41. Basseta, Domingo [d.1699]

    Vocabulario español-quiché, 1698.
    Manuscript: 248 leaves bound in 3 vols., photoreproduction; 33 cm.
    Original: Bibliothèque Nationale, Paris.
    "A manuscript of the highest interest and value, being the
    volume constantly used by Brasseur [de Bourbourg] in his
    translation of the *Popol Vuh, Rabinal Achí*, etc., it is
    crowded to the margins with additions, minutely written,
    in Brasseur's hand" (Gates 1924). Entries are arranged Quiché-
    Spanish and Spanish-Quiché.
                    AC/NL, BYU. LAL/TU, LC
                     C.A. 6 B 294v

42. Beltrán de Santa Rosa María, Pedro

    Declaración de la doctrina cristiana en el idioma yucateco,
    por el R.P. fray Pedro de Beltrán Santa Rosa; añadiendole el
    acto de contrición en verso y en prosa ... Mérida de Yucatán :
    Imprenta del Gobierno por D.M. Isac Rodríguez, 1816.
    Printed: 12 leaves, photoreproduction; 22 cm.
    "It is the ordinary and approved text for instructing the
    Indians in their religious duties" (Brinton 1900:209-210).
                    BBC/UP, LC
                     C.A. 6 B 419d

43. Berendt, Karl Hermann [1817-1878]

    Apuntes y estudios sobre la lengua chiapaneca, Tuxtla Gutiérrez,
    1869-1870.
    Manuscript: 4 leaves, photoreproduction; 22 cm.
    Original: Berendt-Brinton Collection, University of Pennsylvania.
    "Manuscript, rough draft, contains notes on history, grammar,
    relationship, calendar, etc., of the Chiapanecs" (Brinton
    1900:25).
                    BYU
                     C.A. 6 B 452m

44.   Apuntes sobre la lengua chaneabal, con un vocabulario, 1870.
    Manuscript: 14 leaves, photoreproduction; 22 cm.
    Original: Berendt-Brinton Collection, University of Pennsylvania.
    Includes a vocabulary of 416 words and a preface on the litera-
    ture and distribution of Chaneabal.
                    BYU
                     C.A. 6 B 46

45.   Vocabulario de los indios de San José de Costa Rica, 1867.
    Manuscript: 4 leaves, photoreproduction; 22 cm.
    Original: Berendt-Brinton Collection, University of Pennsylvania.
    "Manuscript, original. Contains 128 words, It is a dialect or
    corruption of the Talamanca" (Brinton 1900:29).
                    BYU
                     C.A. 6 B 452m

46. Berendt, Karl Hermann [1817-1878]

    Vocabulario de la lengua pocomán, compilado de [Thomas] Gage
    y [Karl] Scherzer, por C.H.B., 1867.
    Manuscript: 7 leaves, photoreproduction; 22 cm.
    Original: Berendt-Brinton Collection, University of Pennsylvania.
    "You will see in this a number of Gordon pieces, Pocomám and
    Pokonchí. Some are pretty poor copies, but they were the best
    I could get" (Gates note).
                                BYU
                                C.A. 6 B 452vo

47. Blazquez, Agustín

    [Letter from fray Agustín Blazquez regarding the dispersion
    of Indians in the Alta Verapaz region of Guatemala, 1820].
    Manuscript: 3 leaves, photoreproduction; 32 cm.
    Original: Bibliothèque Nationale, Paris.
    Handwritten copy of the original by Brasseur de Bourbourg.
                                BL/UC
                                C.A. 6 D 660 G
                                C.A. 6 D 660 G Microfilm

48. Botello Movellan, Joseph Zepherino

    Catecismo breve en lengua tarasca y recopilación de algunos
    verbos los más comunes para el uso de la misma lengua dispuesto
    por el Br.Dn. Joseph Zepherino Botello Movellan, año de 1756.

    Printed: 108 p., photoreproduction; 15 cm.
    "The vocabulary takes the last 84 pages" (Gates 1924).
                                AC/NL, BYU, LAL/TU, LC
                                MEX 6 B 65

49. Boucara, A.

    Diccionario y diálogos, castellano y chinanteco, 1860.
    Manuscript: 22 leaves, photoreproduction; 22 cm.
    "Fourteen pages of phrases, and the rest a vocabulary; all
    have the Chinantec words with both their Spanish and French
    equivalents" (Gates note).
                                BYU
                                MEX 6 D 54

50. [Brasseur de Bourbourg, Charles Etienne (1814-1874)]

    Vocabulario de las lenguas quiché y cakchiquel, ca. 1850.
    Manuscript: 74 leaves, photoreproduction; 33 cm.
    Original: Bibliothèque Nationale, Paris.
    "This bears no name, but is Brasseur's writing. It is an
    effort at an ordered and compiled Quiché-Cakchiquel dictionary"
    (Gates note).
                                AC/NL, BYU, LC
                                C.A. 6 B 736v

51. Calendario de los indios de Guatemala, 1685.

Manuscript: 27 leaves, photoreproduction; 22 cm.
Original: Berendt-Brinton Collection, University of Pennsylvania.
Transcribed from the original in Guatemala City by Karl H.
Berendt, 1878.
AC/NL, BYU, LC
C.A. 6 C 128c

52. Calendario de los indios de Guatemala, 1722.

Manuscript: 31 leaves, photoreproduction; 22 cm.
Original: Berendt-Brinton Collection, University of Pennsylvania.
Transcribed from the original in Guatemala City by Karl H.
Berendt, 1877.
AC/NL, BYU, LC
C.A. 6 C 128k

53. Calendario en lengua kekchí, 1733.

Manuscript: 8 leaves, photoreproduction; 33 cm.
Original: Robert Garrett Collection, Princeton University.
"A remnant of the native divinatory ritual" (Gates note).
BYU, LC
C.A. 6 D 65
C.A. 6 D 659 G Microfilm

54. Calendario tarasco de Michoacán, 1756.

Manuscript: 6 leaves, photoreproduction; 22 cm.
Original: Bibliothèque Nationale, Paris.
"With a signed note by Veytia that he had copied it from a
manuscript in Boturini's hand, found in the possession of
Gorraez, one of those who had seized the Boturini manuscripts"
(Gates 1924).
AC/NL, BYU, LAL/TU, LC
MEX 6 M 58

55. Calendario tarasco y náhuatl, 16 cent.

Manuscript: 18 leaves, photoreproduction; 22 cm.
Original: Bibliothèque Nationale, Paris.
AC/NL
MEX 6 T 17

56. [Calvo, Tomás]

Vocabulario de la lengua quiché, 1726.
Manuscript: 72 leaves, photoreproduction; 22 cm.
Original: Robert Garrett Collection, Princeton University.
"Sections for conversational phrases, unusual at this early
date; also seven leaves of music and words" (Gates 1937).
AC/NL, LC
C.A. 6 C 12

57. Canciones en lengua maya.

Manuscript: 5 leaves, photoreproduction; 22 cm.
Original: Berendt-Brinton Collection, University of Pennsylvania.
Handwritten copy of the original by Rudolf Schuller, 1868.
BYU
C.A. 6 B 452m

58. [Cardenas, Tomás de (d.1577)]

Arte en lengua cacchí de Cobán en la Vera Paz, compuesto por
el Illmo. Sr. don fray Tomás de Cardenas de la orden de
Predicadores, cuarto obispo de Cobán, ca. 1570.
Manuscript: 75 leaves, photoreproduction; 22 cm.
Original: Bibliothèque Nationale, Paris.
"This manuscript was given to Brasseur de Bourbourg from the
episcopal archives of Cobán, by Ignacio Coloche, and is of
exceptional importance" (Gates note).
AC/NL, BYU, LAL/TU, LC
C.A. 6 C 18

59. Carvajal, Francisco León

Discurso para el descendimiento del Señor, por don Francisco
Carvajal, presbítero; copiado del original manuscrito en poder
del párroco del Santiago en Mérida, Pbro. D. Nic. Delgado,
noviembre 1868.
Manuscript: 20 leaves, photoreproduction; 20 cm.
Original: Berendt-Brinton Collection, University of Pennsylvania.
"Copied from the original in Mérida ... The language of the
Discurso is considered a model of elegant style and pure diction
in Maya" (Brinton 1900:12).
AC/NL, BYU, LC
C.A. 6 P 69

60. Castaño, Bartolomé [1601-1672]

Lo que precisamente debe saber el cristiano, por el padre
Bartolomé Castaño de la Compañia de Jesús.
Manuscript: 8 leaves, photoreproduction; 22 cm.
Original: Latin American Library, Tulane University.
Handwritten copy of the original by Augustin Fischer, ca. 1866.
AC/NL, BYU, LC
MEX 6 D 65

61. Catecismo y breve explicación de la doctrina cristiana en idioma
otomí.

Manuscript: 17 leaves, photoreproduction; 22 cm.
Original: Latin American Library, Tulane University.
Handwritten copy of the original by Augustin Fischer, ca. 1866.
AC/NL, BYU, LC
MEX 6 D 65

62. Chávez, Gabriel de

Relación de la provincia de Meztitlán, por Gabriel de Chávez, alcalde mayor, 1579.
Manuscript: 10 leaves, photoreproduction; 33 cm.
Original: Real Academia de la Historia, Madrid.
Handwritten copy of the original in the Muñoz Collection by Buckingham Smith, March 1857.
BL/UC
C.A. 6 C 6

63. Chica, Manuel María de la

Informe hecho al Illmo. señor arzobispo de Guatemala sobre el estado de las misiones de Verapaz, firmado por el R. padre Fr. Manuel de la Chica, Ord. Predicadores, fecho del convento de Santo Domingo de Guatemala a 23 de octubre de 1819.
Manuscript: 8 leaves, photoreproduction; 32 cm.
Original: Bibliothèque Nationale, Paris.
"Report on missionary work and Indian affairs at Chamelco; includes a great number of place names and locations on his visit to the Lacandón and to the Petén" (Gates 1924).
BL/UC
C.A. 6 D 660 G
C.A. 6 D 660 G Microfilm

64. Chilam Balam of Calkini

Manuscript: 15 leaves, photoreproduction; 32 cm.
Includes a history of the settlement of Calkini, the conquest by Montejo, and other sixteenth century events in Yucatán. Parts of the document date from 1579 through 1821. A Gates copy made from photographs by Teobert Maler.
AC/NL, BYU, LC
C.A. 7 C 436ca 2

65. Manuscript: 117 leaves, photoreproduction; 22 cm.
Original: Robert Garrett Collection, Princeton University.
Gates gives "Recetarios de indios" on wrapper. It is also known as "El libro de los médicos de Yucatán".
BBC/UP, BYU, LC
C.A. 6 B 64ca

66. Chilam Balam of Chumayel

Manuscript: 67 leaves, photoreproduction; 22 cm.
Original: Robert Garrett Collection, Princeton University.
The manuscript is an illustrated text compiled by Juan José Hoil in 1782 and includes rituals, prophesies, chronicles, and material related to astronomy, cosmology, and other subjects. "Probably the Berendt copy of the manuscript found by Morley in Yucatán and given to him by Gates" (Tozzer note).
BBC/UP, BYU, LC
C.A. 7 C 436ch G

67. Chilam Balam of Ixil

   Manuscript: 25 leaves, photoreproduction; 22 cm.
   Includes an eighteenth century *Lunario o calendario maya*
   and *Libro de medicina de Ixil.* "Copy made about 50 years ago
   [i.e., 1875] in Yucatán, from a manuscript formerly belonging
   to Pío Pérez, and now lost" (Gates 1924).
                                   AC/NL, BBC/UP, BYU, LC
                                   C.A. 7 C 436ti 2

68. Chilam Balam of Kaua

   Manuscript: 141 leaves, photoreproduction; 32 cm.
   Original: Robert Garrett Collection, Princeton University.
   The Kaua is the largest of the books of Chilam Balam and
   contains diverse texts written in Yucatec Maya including
   divinatory almanacs, prayers, medical recipes, calendrical
   tables, cosmological and astrological subjects, and katun
   prophecies (Gibson and Glass 1975:383). This is a photographic
   copy of the original made by Teobert Maler.
                                   BBC/UP, BYU, LAL/TU, LC
                                   C.A. 7 C 436ka 2

69. Manuscript: 89 leaves, photoreproduction; 22 cm.
   A partial copy of leaves 61-150 made by William E. Gates.
                                   LC
                                   C.A. 7 C 436ti 2

70. Chilam Balam of Nah

   Manuscript: 32 leaves, photoreproduction; 33 cm.
   Original: Robert Garrett Collection, Princeton University.
   Contains a calendar count, with ancient day names, and a
   section on astronomy. Also includes several herbal remedies.
                                   AC/NL, BYU, LAL/TU, LC
                                   C.A. 7 C 436na 2

71. Chilam Balam of Tekax

   Manuscript: 18 leaves, photoreproduction; 32 cm.
   "In character it comes nearer the Kaua than the other known
   ones. Of the three elements that make a 'Chilam Balam,' it
   has two, the medical knowledge, so much of which appears under
   the Libro judío title, and the current calendars of good and
   bad days" (Gates note).
                                   AC/NL, BYU, LAL/TU, LC
                                   C.A. 7 C 436te 2

72. Chilam Balam of Tizimín

   Manuscript: 35 leaves, photoreproduction; 22 cm.

A photographic reproduction of the original in the
collection of Carrillo Ancona in Mérida. The text is preceded
by explanatory notes by Manuel Luciano Pérez and Crescencio
Carrillo Ancona.

> AC/NL, BYU, LAL/TU, LC
> C.A. 7 C 436ti 2

73. Manuscript: 26 leaves, photoreproduction; 46 cm.
Original: Robert Garrett Collection, Princeton University.

> BBC/UP, LAL/TU, LC
> C.A. 7 C 436ti 3 F

74. Manuscript: 26 leaves, photoreproduction; 32 cm.
A photographic reproduction by Gates of Maler's photographs
of the original in Mérida.

> C.A. 7 436ti 4

75. [Co, Basilio]

Doctrina cristiana en lengua pokomchí, Tactic, 1810.
Manuscript: 22 leaves, photoreproduction; 16 cm.
Original: Robert Garrett Collection, Princeton University.
A note by Karl H. Berendt states: "La presente doctrina se ha
copiado de un cuaderno en 8° con 22 fajas útiles. Lleva la
inscripción 'Para el uso de Basilio Co, año de 1810.' El cura
del pueblo de Tactic me lo consiguio prestado de un indio en el
barrio de San Jacinto en el mismo pueblo. Va copiado aquí con
la ortografía de su original, Cobán, agosto de 1875."

> BBC/UP, BYU, LC
> C.A. 6 Ag 9

76. Codex Aubin of 1576

Manuscript: 79 leaves, photoreproduction; 22 cm.
Original: British Museum, London.
"This manuscript belonged to Aubin; in 1851 he had it drawn by
hand at the Sourds–Muets Institute with naturally great defects.
This edition has likewise become so unproducible that Boban
noted the only copy he could find in Goupil's time was one Aubin
had kept for himself" (Gates note). A picture chronicle covering
Aztec history from Aztlán to the year 1607.

> BYU, LC
> MEX 7 F 466g

77. Cofradía del Rosario, ordenanzas de 1689, en lengua quiché.

Manuscript: 11 leaves, photoreproduction; 36 cm.
Original: Robert Garrett Collection, Princeton University.

> AC/NL, BYU, LAL/TU, LC
> C.A. 6 L 61 F
> C.A. 6 L 61 Microfilm

78. Cofradía de Vera Cruz de Totonicapán, ordenanzas de 1777, en lengua quiché.

Manuscript: 26 leaves, photoreproduction; 36 cm.
Original: Robert Garrett Collection, Princeton University.
             AC/NL, BYU, LC
             C.A. 6 L 61 F
             C.A. 6 L 61 Microfilm

79. [Collection of] Costumbres, leyendas y tradiciones de Yucatán.

Manuscript: 21 leaves, photoreproduction; 32 cm.
Items included were originally published in the Registro yucateco, Mérida, Yucatán, ca. 1845. Selections describe the customs, legends, cities, and other features of Yucatán.
             BL/UC
             C.A. 6 D 660 G
             C.A. 6 D 660 G Microfilm

80. Compendio de sermones en la lengua quiché, 1711-1713.

Manuscript: 248 leaves, photoreproduction; 22 cm.
Original: Tozzer Library, Harvard University.
Consists of 62 sermons.
             AC/NL, BYU, LC
             C.A. 6 C 73
             C.A. 6 C 280 Microfilm

81. Confesionario en castellano y pokonchí, Tactic, 1814.

Manuscript: 20 leaves, photoreproduction; 22 cm.
Original: Berendt-Brinton Collection, University of Pennsylvania.
A note by Karl H. Berendt states: "El original del presente Confesionario es un manuscrito en 16mo de 42 fajas útiles en el archivo parrochial del pueblo de Tactic. Y me lo presto para sacar copia el cura de aquel pueblo, fray Silvestro Mijangos, Dominico expulsado de Chiapas, Cobán, agosto de 1875."
Arranged in two columns, Pocomchí and Spanish.
             AC/NL, BYU, LC
             C.A. 6 C 76

82. Confesionario en idioma cuicateca para los principiantes e ignorantes, como Ojeda.

Manuscript: 6 leaves, photoreproduction; 32 cm.
"Closely written in double columns, Cuicatec and Spanish" (Gates note).
             BYU
             C.A. 6 D 659 G Microfilm
             MEX 6 C 76

83. Córdova, Juan de

Adiciones al arte zapoteca [de Levanto], ca. 1575.
Manuscript: 72 leaves, photoreproduction; 22 cm.
Original: Latin American Library, Tulane University.
Includes the following: Cuenta en zapoteca, Bautismo, Viático,
Extrema-unción, Matrimonio, Interrogación a los testigos,
Amonestaciones, Confesionario, Comandamientos, y Pláticas y
conversaciones.
LC
MEX 6 L 575a

84. Vocabulario en lengua zapoteca hecho recopilado por el muy
reverendo padre fray Juan de Córdova, de la orden de Predicadores,
que reside en este Nueva España ... México : Pedro Ocharte, 1578.
Printed: 430 leaves bound in 3 vols., photoreproduction; 22 cm.
"This is the one supreme Zapotec monument. There is no perfect
copy in existence, though this photocopy is complete, being made
up from two" (Gates note).
BYU
MEX 6 C 81

85. Coronel, Juan [1569-1651]

Arte en lengua de maya; recopilado y enmendado por el P.F. Ioan
Coronel de la orden de S. Francisco, guardia del convento de
Tekax ... México : Imprenta de Diego Garrido por Adriano Cesar.
Printed: 55 leaves, photoreproduction; 16 cm, 1620.
"From the only known copy of the first printed Maya grammar"
(Gates 1924).
BYU, LC
C.A. 6 C 81a

86. Discursos predicables con otras diversas materiales espirituales,
con las doctrinas Xpas., y los artículos de la fe. Recopilados y
enmendados por el P.Fr. Joan Coronel de la orden del Seráfico
Padre S. Francisco, guardián del convento de Tekax, y lector de
la lengua; dirigido al ilustrisimo don Fr. Gonçalo de Salazar,
obispo de Yucatán y del consejo de Su Majestad ... México : Pedro
Gutiérrez, 1620.
Printed: 240 leaves bound in 2 vols., photoreproduction; 16 cm.
BYU, LC
C.A. 6 C 81

87. Doctrina cristiana en lengua maya; recopilado y enmendada por el
P.F. Ioan Coronel, de la orden de N.S.P.S. Francisco, guardián del
convento de Tekax, muy útil por los indios; dirigida al illustmo.
S. don fray Gonçalo de Salazar, del consejo de Su Majestad, obispo
de Yucatán ... México : Imprenta de Diego Garrido, 1620.
Printed: 26 leaves, photoreproduction; 16 cm.
"Only two copies of this imprint are known" (Gates 1924).
BYU, LC
C.A. 6 C 81

88. Coto, Tomás [b.1600]

Vocabulario de la lengua cakchiquel, o guatemalteca; nuevamente hecho y recopilado con sumo estudio trabajo y erudición por el P.F. Tomás Coto, Predicador y padre de esta provincia del S.S. Nombre de Jesús de Guatemala; en que se contienen todos los modos y frases elegantes con que los naturales la hablan y d. q. se pueden valer los ministros estudiosos para su mejor educación y enseño, 1651.
Manuscript: 476 leaves bound in 3 vols., photoreproduction; 33 cm.
Original: American Philosophical Society, Philadelphia.
The original of the Vocabulario was donated to the American Philosophical Society by Mariano Gálvez, governor of Guatemala. This work has entries in Spanish and Cakchiquel and contains a wealth of ethnographic information, largely drawn from earlier writers.
AC/NL, BYU, LC
C.A. 6 C 81

89. Crónica de Chicxulub, ca. 1562.

Manuscript: 20 leaves, photoreproduction; 36 cm.
Includes a history of the pueblo of Chicxulub, and of the conquest of that region of Yucatán; also includes a survey of town lands by several members of the Pech family, testified to February 7, 1542, a partial listing of Spanish conquerors, and a portion of an account by a member of the Pech family. Maya text with Spanish translation (Gibson and Glass 1975:389-390).
AC/NL, BBC/UP, BYU, LAL/TU, LC
C.A. 6 N 146t F

90. Manuscript: 13 leaves, photoreproduction; 33 cm.
"A copy made by Pío Pérez, from which the above was taken" (Gates note).
C.A. 6 N 146g

91. Crónica en lengua mexicana, with notes by J.M.A. Aubin.

Manuscript: 31 leaves, photoreproduction; 32 cm.
Original: Bibliothèque Nationale, Paris.
"One or more leaves at the beginning are gone, the text continuing with count year by year, with running text for 121 years and coming to Ce acatl, with the date 1519 in the margin ... last date 1589" (Gates 1924).
AC/NL, LAL/TU, LC
MEX 6 Az 7

92. Cueva, Pedro de la

Parábolas y ejemplos sacados de la naturaleza y de los costumbres del campo, aplicados a la moral cristiana, obra escrita en lengua zapoteca para el consuelo e instrucción de los naturales de la misma lengua por el R.P.M. fray Pedro de la Cueva, de la orden

Predicadores, 1701.
Manuscript: 136 leaves, photoreproduction; 17 cm.
Original: Bibliothèque Nationale, Paris.
AC/NL, BYU, LAL/TU, LC
MEX 6 C 91

93. Del Río, Antonio

Informe de Antonio del Río sobre el descubrimiento de Palenque,
fechado en junio 24 de 1787.
Manuscript: 11 leaves, photoreproduction; 33 cm.
Original: British Museum, London.
C.A. 3 P 19
C.A. 3 R 476d

94. Descripción de las ruinas de una ciudad antigua, descubierta en
el Palenque, en el reino de Guatemala, en la América española;
traducida de la relación original manuscrita del capitán don
Antonio del Río, seguida del Teatro Crítico Americana, o, investiga-
ción y explicación crítica respeto a la historia de los americanos,
por el doctor Pablo Félix Cabrera, de la ciudad de Nueva Guatemala.
Manuscript: 80 leaves, photoreproduction; 23 cm.
A Spanish translation of the 1822 London (Henry Berthoud) edition
of Del Rio's Relación.
C.A. 3 R 476d

95. Del ser de dios [en la lengua maya], ca. 1750.

Manuscript: 6 leaves, photoreproduction; 22 cm.
"Writing much better than ordinary, of about 1750, on the
nature of the Trinity" (Gates 1924).
AC/NL, BYU, LC
C.A. 6 V 85

96. Delgado, Damián

Compendio del arte quiché del P.Fr. Damián Delgado, ord.
Predicadores, siguiese la doctrina cristiana en lengua quiché
del mismo autor, con sermones del mismo padre y otros de la
orden de N.P. Santo Domingo.
Manuscript: 35 leaves, photoreproduction; 29 cm.
Original: Bibliothèque Nationale, Paris.
"A combination grammar, doctrina, and phrase book, formerly
belonged to Brasseur de Bourbourg; early enough to be valuable"
(Gates note). The arte occupies the first nine leaves and the
following 11 contain the doctrina; the remainder, various
subjects, including the salutation of Indian alcaldes in
transmitting the staff of office to each other.
BYU
C.A. 6 D 37

97. Delgado, Joseph

CLetter from the Dominican Joseph Delgado to the provincial of
the province of Santo Domingo, signed by Delgado and Juan Serrano,
of the proposal to be presented before the provincial. Relates to
the conduct of work among the Chol Indians, Rancho de San Lucas,
1682].
Manuscript: 5 leaves, photoreproduction; 32 cm.
Original: Bibliothèque Nationale, Paris.
Handwritten copy of the original by Brasseur de Bourbourg.
BL/UC
C.A. 6 D 660 G
C.A. 6 D 660 G Microfilm

98. CReport by the Dominican Joseph Delgado on the settlements,
inhabitants, and other features of the region between San Miguel
Manché and the territory of the Itzá Indians, based on his
journey begun on June 7, 1677, Bacalar, Yucatán, 1677].
Manuscript: 4 leaves, photoreproduction; 32 cm.
Original: Bibliothèque Nationale, Paris.
Handwritten copy of the original by Brasseur de Bourbourg.
BL/UC
C.A. 6 D 660 G
C.A. 6 D 660 G Microfilm

99. Viaje de Bacalar, y encuentro de los de Bacalar, los nombres
están en el derrotero que dí a V.P.M.R. etc.; carta fecha
octubre 28 del año de 1703.
Manuscript: 1 leaf, photoreproduction; 32 cm.
Original: Bibliothèque Nationale, Paris.
Handwritten copy of the original by Brasseur de Bourbourg.
BL/UC
C.A. 6 D 660 G
C.A. 6 D 660 G Microfilm

100. Diccionario grande castellano-tzotzil, ca. 1575.

Manuscript: 176 leaves, photoreproduction; 33 cm.
Original: Robert Garrett Collection, Princeton University.
"Sixteenth century Tzotzil dictionary, original destroyed after
this copy was known to have been made, and the only XVI [century]
Tzotzil in existence" (Gates note).
BYU, LC
C.A. 6 D 5

101. Diccionario de Motul en lengua [yucatec] maya, ca. 1575.

Manuscript: 668 leaves bound in 5 vols., photoreproduction; 23 cm.
Original: John Carter Brown Library, Brown University.
This is probably the most extensive colonial Yucatec Maya
dictionary known to date. In the 1850's Brasseur de Bourbourg
purchased a small two volume dictionary at a book stall in
Mexico City and later sold these to John Carter Brown. In 1865

Berendt obtained permission to make a copy and during the
following years added to and amended the vocabulary. Includes
entries in both Yucatec-Spanish and Spanish-Yucatec.
AC/NL, BBC/UP, BYU, LC
C.A. 6 C 498v G

102. Diccionario de San Francisco, 17 cent.

Manuscript: 204 leaves, photoreproduction; 32 cm.
"This work was found at the closing of the convent of
San Francisco in Mérida in 1820. It bears no date. The
original is lost but [Pío] Pérez made a copy and Berendt
made a copy from that of Pérez in 1870" (Brinton 1900:205-206).
Includes both Yucatec-Spanish and Spanish-Yucatec segments.
AC/NL, BBC/UP, BYU, LC
C.A. 6 D 54
C.A. 6 D 54 Microfilm

103. Discurso crítico de la doctrina otomí, 18 cent.

Manuscript: 16 leaves, photoreproduction; 22 cm.
"Anonymous author, apparently a native Otomí speaker, also
writer of Examen crítico de la gramática de Neve y Molina"
(Pilling 1885).
AC/NL, BYU,
MEX 6 N 41

104. Doctrina cristiana en el idioma totonaca, 1780.

Manuscript: 19 leaves, photoreproduction; 22 cm.
Original: Latin American Library, Tulane University.
Includes the Pater noster, Ave María, El Credo, and La Salve
regina in Totonac.
BYU
MEX 6 T 64

105. Doctrina cristiana en lengua maya, ca. 1775.

Manuscript: 17 leaves, photoreproduction; 22 cm.
"This little manuscript is very badly preserved, parts having
been water-soaked to complete illegibility. Its value will
only be in some linguistic forms possibly, its date being
apparently back of the XIX century corruptions of the language"
(Gates note).
BYU, LC
C.A. 6 D 65

106. Doctrina cristiana en lengua tarasca, 16 cent.

Manuscript: 40 leaves, photoreproduction; 22 cm.
The original was owned by Nicolás León.
AC/NL, BYU, LAL/TU, LC
MEX 6 D 65a

107. Doctrina cristiana y confesionario en lengua ixil, precedidos de un corto modo para aprender la lengua y ritual de matrimonio, [por] el cura párroco de Nebaj, 1824.

Manuscript: 24 leaves, photoreproduction; 17 cm.
Original: Berendt-Brinton Collection, University of Pennsylvania. "With a few grammatical notes, and the only known piece in the language" (Gates note).

> AC/NL, BYU, LAL/TU, LC
> C.A. 6 D 658g

108. Doctrina cristiana y vocabulario en la lengua matzahua [i.e., Mazatec], ca. 1775.

Manuscript: 24 leaves, photoreproduction; 22 cm.
"Manuscript, of later 18th century" (Gates note). Title page gives: "Confesionario en idioma mazateco, perteneciente a Ignacio Arrona quien lo hacía en diez y ocho de enero del año de 1797". On leaf 17 begins a vocabulary entitled: "Quaderno de idioma mazateco comencido en el año de 1796".

> AC/NL, LAL/TU, LC
> MEX 6 D 66

109. Documentos de Chamelco en lengua kekchí, 1540 et seq.

Manuscript: 16 leaves, photoreproduction; 33 cm.
Original: Robert Garrett Collection, Princeton University. "A manuscript of the earliest period, it containing copies or transcripts of wills, etc., of dates 1540, 1593, etc." (Gates note).

> BYU, LAL/TU, LC
> C.A. 6 D 65
> C.A. 6 D 659 G Microfilm

110. Documentos [de San Cristóbal Totonicapán y Santiago Momostenango] en la lengua quiché, 1689-1836.

Manuscript: 24 leaves, photoreproduction; 33 cm.
Original: Robert Garrett Collection, Princeton University. "Various wills and other similar matters" (Gates 1924).

> AC/NL, BYU, LC
> C.A. 6 V 85

111. Documentos de Ticul, en lengua [yucatec] maya, 1642-1761.

Manuscript: 36 leaves, photoreproduction; 36 cm.
"A short manuscript of early deeds and legal papers from that pueblo" (Gates note).

> AC/NL, BYU, LAL/TU, LC
> C.A. 6 D 65 F

112. Documentos en [lengua] kekchí, 1565 et seq.

Manuscript: 28 leaves, photoreproduction; 33 cm.
"These are quite interesting, especially in the scarcity of early
Kekchí; there is a deed written in 1565, original, and copies made
later. There is also a calendar, the only one of the kind I know
of, and a Doctrina" (Gates note).
BYU
C.A. 6 D 65
C.A. 6 D 659 G Microfilm

113. Documentos en la lengua quiché, 1762-1787.

Manuscript: 75 leaves, photoreproduction; 33 cm.
"A collection of wills and legal papers in Quiché for the years
1762-1787" (Gates note).
BYU
C.A. 6 D 659 G

114. Documentos y papeles en lengua [yucatec] maya, 1561 et seq.

Manuscript: 53 leaves, photoreproduction; 33 cm.
"These are a number of town documents, to which I have added
various odd Maya papers. Of special interest in these are the
personal letters written in Maya by Jacinto Pat and other Maya
leaders of the 1847 uprising; also a single leaf of a Maya
dictionary, by the writing, of the XVI century; as the leaf is 277,
and occurs in 'va', the whole volume must have been about 600
pages. Another fragment of the text is of the year 1571" (Gates
note). A carbon-copy of a typewritten translation from Yucatec
by Ralph L. Roys of a document relating to the founding of the
pueblo of Kochilá, dated April 21, 1561, is pasted in the back
of the volume.
AC/NL, LC
C.A. 6 D 659 G
C.A. 6 D 659 G Microfilm

115. Dominguez y Argaiz, Francisco Eugenio

Pláticas de los principales misterios de Nuestra Sta. Fe, con
una breve exhortación al fin del mundo con que deben excitarse al
dolor de las culpas; hechas en el idioma yucateco, por orden del
Illmo. y Rmo. Sr. Dr. y Mtro. D.F. Ignacio de Padilla, del
sagrado orden de San Agustín ... México : Imprenta del Real y Más
Antiguo Colegio de S. Yldefonso, 1758.
Printed: 24 p., photoreproduction; 20 cm.
"A very clean and perfect copy of this extremely scarce work"
(Gates note). Includes the following sections: La explicación de
N. Santa Fe, El misterio de la S.S. Trinidad, El de la encarnación
del verbo divino, El de la Eucaristía, La explicación del fin
último para que fue criado el hombre, que es solo Dios, y and
la explicación del modo con que deban excitarse al dolor de las
culpas.

AC/NL, BBC/UP, BYU, LC
C.A. 6 Or 1
C.A. 6 P 69

116. Elgueta, Manuel

Borrador para la formación del vocabulario de lengua quiché.
Manuscript: 24 leaves, photoreproduction; 33 cm.
AC/NL, BYU, LC
C.A. 6 T 83

117. Vocabulario mam y español, ca. 1909.
Manuscript: 9 leaves, photoreproduction; 33 cm.
Contains about 850 words.
AC/NL, BYU, LAL/TU, LC
C.A. 6 V 85

118. Escoto, Luis

[Letter from fray Luis Escoto regarding Indian affairs
in the Verapaz region of Guatemala, ca. 1820].
Manuscript: 2 leaves, photoreproduction; 32 cm.
Original: Bibliothèque Nationale, Paris.
Handwritten copy of the original by Brasseur de Bourbourg.
BL/UC
C.A. 6 D 660 G
C.A. 6 D 660 G Microfilm

119. Escuscimiento de los ahocoyes indios que están adelante de Cobán
junto a los lacandones, que hoy es el paraje de Los Dolores, y
muy cerca del río de Zacapulas [i.e., Río Chixoy], ca. 1690.

Manuscript: 43 leaves, photoreproduction; 32 cm.
Original: Bibliothèque Nationale, Paris.
Notes on the work of the friars among the Indians of Guatemala
and adjacent territory, including considerable material on
individual Dominicans and a few references to Franciscans, as
well as to royal decrees on the pacification of the Indians,
apparently based to a large extent on Remesal's *Historia general
de las indias occidentales*.
BL/UC
C.A. 6 D 660 G
C.A. 6 D 660 G Microfilm

120. Estrada de Salvago, Juan

Descripción de las provincias de Costa Rica, Guatemala, Honduras,
Nicaragua, y Tierra Firme y Cartegena, y toda la costa del norte,
de sus naturales, poblaciones, constelación de la tierra y su
cielo, su calidad, de su latitud, suelo y longitud, del temple que
en ella hay, etc.; escrita por el licenciado Juan Estrada de
Salvago, y dirigida a Madrid al muy y Magco. y M.R. Sr. el S. Fr.

Diego Guillen, comisario de la provincia de Cartago y Costa
Rica; con fecha de 6 de mayo de 1572.
Manuscript: 6 leaves, photoreproduction; 33 cm.
Original: Archivo General de Indias, Seville.
"From a copy in the Depósito Hidráfico of the Spanish government,
Madrid, 17 March 1857, Buckingham Smith."
BL/UC
C.A. 6 C 6

121. Examen crítico de la gramática otomí de Neve y Molina, 18 cent.

Manuscript: 58 leaves, photoreproduction; 22 cm.
"Anonymous writer, apparently a native speaker of Otomí;
severely critiques the Otomí grammar by Neve y Molina" (Pilling
1885).
AC/NL, BYU, LC
MEX 6 N 41

122. Feria, Pedro de [1524-1588]

Doctrina cristiana en lengua castellana y zapoteca por el
R.P. fray Pedro de Feria, prior provincial de la orden de los
frailes Predicadores de Santo Domingo en esta Nueva España ...
México : En Casa de Pedro Ocharte, 1567.
Printed: 232 p., photoreproduction; 23 cm.
"Copied from one of the two known copies. It has two leaves
supplied in manuscript in an early hand, but lacks the title,
and whatever preliminaries there may have been, as to which I
am not advised. There is a copy in the Bodleian, which I am
having checked up now, and if that copy can add anything to this,
I will have it done" (Gates note). This item was made from a
copy in the John Carter Brown Library in Providence.
BBC/UP, JCB/BU, LC
MEX 6 F 37

123. Filacapete, Martin

Cuaderno de idioma zapoteco del valle, que contiene algunas reglas
las más comunes del arte, un vocabulario algo copioso, un
confesionario, y otras cosas que verá el cristiano lector; se ha
escrito procurando todo lo posible imitar la pronunciación natural
de los indios; sacado lo más de los autores antiguos que
escribieron de este idioma, 1793.
Manuscript: 290 leaves bound in 2 vols., photoreproduction; 26 cm.
Original: John Carter Brown Library, Brown University.
"The vocabulary is much smaller than that of the Diccionario of
Cordova, but there is such a difference in the spelling of
words that it was thought wise to reproduce the manuscript"
(Gates note).
LC
MEX 6 G 93 1918
MEX 6 Q 2

124. Fletcher, Richard

Catecismo de los metódistas, no. I, Para los niños de tierna
edad; catecismo ti le letodistavol, no. II, Utial mehen
palaloob ... Londres : W.M. Watts, 1865.
Printed: 34 leaves, photoreproduction; 16 cm.
Fletcher was a Methodist missionary stationed in Corozal,
Belize, and wrote a catechism and a brief series of prayers
in Yucatec Maya.
BBC/UP, BYU, LC
C.A. 6 C 28

125. Fragmentos de idiomas; confesionarios en lengua zoque, chiapanec,
chaneabal, y zaaluta.
Manuscript: 19 leaves, photoreproduction; 33 cm.
Original: Robert Garrett Collection, Princeton University.
"Doctrinas, all short, but in various needed dialects, Chañabal,
Tzotzil, etc., and copied from a manuscript which I am afraid
has disappeared in the present revolution" (Gates note). Copied
from an original manuscript in the Icazbalceta Library by Vicente
de Andrade, for the use of Nicolás León, 1898.
BYU, LAL/TU, LC
C.A. 6 D 65 F

126. [Fuentes, Manuel]

Preguntas para administrar el santo sacramento del matrimonio
en mam, conformes al manual que usamos ... siguen las varias
partes de la Doctrina cristiana en mam y en castellano, etc., lo
todo hallado entre los papeles que defunto Sr. presbítero don
Manuel Fuentes, cura propio que fue de la parroquia de San Miguel
Ixtlahuacán, ca. 1750.
Manuscript: 8 leaves, photoreproduction; 22 cm.
Original: Bibliothèque Nationale, Paris.
One of the very few manuscripts in Mam.
AC/NL, BYU, LC
C.A. 6 F 95

127. Fuentes y Guzmán, Francisco Antonio de [c.1643-1700]

Extracto del tomo 2 de la obra titulada Recordación florida,
discurso historial, natural, militar y política del reino de
Guatemala; 2a parte, que escribe el capitán don Francisco
Antonio de Fuentes y Guzmán, vecino patrimonial y regidor de
la misma muy noble y muy leal ciudad de Guatemala, año de 1689.
Manuscript: 874 leaves bound in 4 vols., photoreproduction; 32 cm.
Original: Archivo General del Gobierno, Guatemala City.
"I have no words to exaggerate the importance of this document.
It is the lost second part, and though only in the form of a copy
by Mariano Padilla, still I do not know that the original is any
longer existent" (Gates note).

LC
C.A. 2 F 95

128. Fuertes, E.A.

Further notes on Huave, ca. 1870.
Manuscript: 3 leaves, photoreproduction; 22 cm.
Original: Berendt-Brinton Collection, University of Pennsylvania.
Includes comments by Karl H. Berendt.
BYU
C.A. 6 B 452m

129. Thirteen words in the Huave language, village of Dionisio, 1870.
Manuscript: 2 leaves, photoreproduction; 22 cm.
Original: Berendt-Brinton Collection, University of Pennsylvania.
Includes comments by Karl H. Berendt.
BYU
C.A. 6 B 452m

130. Vocabularios of the Zapoteco from Suchitán, Zoque from Chimalapa,
and Mixe from Guichiore, 1871.
Manuscript: 4 leaves, photoreproduction; 22 cm.
Original: Berendt-Brinton Collection, University of Pennsylvania.
"Manuscript. The collections of Mr. Fuertes were made for the
Smithsonian Institution. Dr. Berendt does not seem to have con-
sidered them very accurate" (Brinton 1900:23). Zoque and Mixe
place names in the title should probably read Suchitán and
Guichicore.
BYU
C.A. 6 B 452m

131. Gala, Leandro R. de la

U tz'ibhuun hach noh tzicbenil ahaucaan; ahmiatz Leandro R. de la
Gala, ti ú hach yamailoob, yanoob tú nachilcahtaliloob nohol y
chikín ti le luumcabil Yucatan laa ... Ho (Mérida) : U tz'alhuun
José D. Espinosa, 1870.
Printed: 8 p., photoreproduction; 22 cm.
A pastoral sermon by Bishop Gala, translated by José Pilar Vales;
printed in Spanish and Yucatec Maya.
BBC/UP, BYU, LC
C.A. 6 Or 1

132. Galindo, Juan [1802-1840]

Informe de la comisión científica formada para el reconocimiento
de las antigüedades de Copán por decreto de 15 de enero de 1834
del C. jefe supremo del estado de Guatemala, Dr. Mariano Gálvez.
Manuscript: 22 leaves, photoreproduction; 33 cm.
Original: Bibliothèque Nationale, Paris.
C.A. 2 G 13

133. Gaona, Juan de [1507-1560]

    Coloquios de la paz y tranquilidad cristiana; interlocutores un
    religioso y un colegial, en lengua otomí.
    Manuscript: 94 leaves, photoreproduction; 22 cm.
    "The Coloquios occupies a little less than half the volume,
    the rest being another text, in a hand that looks slightly
    different" (Gates note).
                                        AC/NL, BYU, LC
                                        MEX 6 G 15

134. Coloquios de la paz y tranquilidad cristiana; interlocutores un
    religioso y un colegial, en lengua matzahua, [por] Fr. Juan de
    Gaona.
    Manuscript: 146 leaves, photoreproduction; 22 cm.
    Original: Latin American Library, Tulane University.
    A handwritten copy by Fischer of Gaona's Coloquios from the
    Náhuatl to Mazahua.
                                        BYU, LC
                                        MEX 6 G 15

135. Coloquios de la paz y tranquilidad cristiana, en lengua mexicana ...
    México : En Casa de Pedro Ocharte, 1582.
    Printed: 122 leaves, photoreproduction; 22 cm.
                                        BYU, LC
                                        MEX 6 G 15

136. García y García, Apolonia

    Versos maya, 1863.
    Manuscript: 2 leaves, photoreproduction; 22 cm.
    "Estos versos fueron escritas en el año de 1863 por el Lic.
    Apolonia García y García, y dedicados a una señorita del pueblo
    de Tekantó, que no habla el idioma castellano como la generalidad
    del bello sexo de aquella localidad, sin embargo de entenderlo
    perfectamente." Handwritten copy of the original by Rudolf
    Schuller.
                                        BYU
                                        C.A. 6 B 452m

137. Gavarrete, Juan

    Colección de cartas escritas por diversos personajes al ayunta-
    miento de esta ciudad de Guatemala sacadas de su archivo secreto;
    las firmas son copiadas con exactitud, 1534-1691.
    Manuscript: 5 leaves, photoreproduction; 32 cm.
    Original: Bibliothèque Nationale, Paris.
    A collection of letters made by Gavarrete, written by various
    persons of the ayuntamiento of Guatemala. These ten letters are
    written by Pedro de Alvarado, Francisco Calderón, Alonso Maldonado,
    the Bishop of Guatemala, and two others.
                                        BL/UC
                                        C.A. 6 D 660 G
                                        C.A. 6 D 660 G Microfilm

138. Gavarrete, Juan

Lo siguente es tornado de un historiador anónimo de San Francisco
suyo manuscrito existe en el archivo del mismo convento; de las
grandes ciudades y poblaciones del reino de Guatemala, su sumento
y estención, su gobierno, y policía y majestad de sus leyes y
señores.
Manuscript: 3 leaves, photoreproduction; 32 cm.
Original: Bibliothèque Nationale, Paris.
The manuscript ends with the following: "solo axopal que hizo su
asiento en Utatlan."

BL/UC
C.A. 6 D 660 G
C.A. 6 D 660 G Microfilm

139. Gilberti, Maturino [d.1575]

Diccionario analítico en lengua tarasca, 1569.
Manuscript: 148 leaves, photoreproduction; 33 cm.
The dictionary begins with P and ends with Tz. "The loss
of the half of the dictionary is a great loss; it is not at all
the same as the printed work, 1559, but, as will be seen, an
analytical work, far more elaborate, classified with all the
various forms and derivatives under its root. In this respect
it is one of the most important works we have left in any dialect.
A very little reading shows it great value" (Gates note).

AC/NL, BYU
MEX 6 G 378dia F

140. Diccionario grande castellano-tarasco y tarasco-castellano,
16 cent.
Manuscript: 280 leaves, photoreproduction; 37 cm.
Original: Sociedad Mexicana de Geografía y Estadística, México.
"In a good clear writing, written after 1559" (Gates note).

AC/NL, BYU
MEX 6 G 378dit F

141. Discursos en la lengua tarasca, 16 cent.
Manuscript: 223 leaves, photoreproduction; 22 cm.
"About half the work is an interpretation in Tarascan of Latin
quotations from the Bible, and about half given to brief sermon"
(Gates 1940).

BYU
MEX 6 G 378ds

142. Siguiense unos breves sermones en la lengua de Michoacán,
ordenados por el P.F. Maturino Gilberti, fraile menor en la
dicha provincia, 16 cent.
Manuscript: 146 leaves, photoreproduction; 22 cm.

AC/NL, BYU
MEX 6 G 378s

143. Gilberti, Maturino [d.1575]

Tratado de la doctrina cristiana por fray Felipe Meneses al idioma [tarasca] de Michoacán, por fray Maturino Gilberti, dedicada al Sr. obispo doctor don Antonio Morales de Molina, 1568.
Manuscript: 211 leaves bound in 2 vols., photoreproduction; 22 cm.
                              AC/NL, BYU, LC
                              MEX 6 G 378de

144. González, Antonio

Traducción del catecismo castellano del P.M. Gerónimo de Ripalda de la compañia de Jesús en el idioma mixteco; por el R.P.Fr. Antonio Gonzáles, del orden de Predicadores, cura de la doctrina de Nochistlán y prior del convento de Cuilapa, con un resumen curioso de los principales misterios de nuestra catolica fe, y el modo de administrar el viático a los naturales en dicha idioma ... Puebla : Imprenta de la Viuda de Miguel de Ortega, 1719.
Printed: 114 p., photoreproduction; 16 cm.
"Only one copy known (or possibly two)" (Gates note).
                              BYU
                              MEX 6 G 59
                              MEX 6 R 481m

145. González, Juan de Dios

Reconocimiento que se manifesta por el adjunto plan de la provincia de Yucatán y parte de la costa de Honduras ... que de orden de D. Cristóbal de Sallar, governor de aquella provincia, ejecuto el año de 1766 [por] el ingeniero D. Juan de Dios González.
Manuscript: 31 leaves, photoreproduction; 29 cm.
Original: British Museum, London.
                              C.A. 6 R 27

146. González, Luis

Arte breve y vocabulario de la lengua tzoque, conforme se habla en el pueblo de Tecpatlán; dividido en dos partes, en la primera se trata de las cuatro partes de la oración, declinables, que son nombre, pronombre, verbo, y participio; la segunda se compone de un vocabulario, lo todo compuesto por el padre fray Luis González, de la orden de Predicadores, año de 1672.
Manuscript: 147 leaves, photoreproduction; 22 cm.
Original: Bibliothèque Nationale, Paris.
"Written in a very clear hand. The first part treats the parts of speech and the second is a vocabulary" (Gates 1940).
                              AC/NL, BYU, LC
                              MEX 6 G 59

147. Guerra, José María

Pastoral del ilustrísimo señor obispo dirigido a los indígenas
de esta diócesis ... Mérida de Yucatán : Impreso por Antonio
Petra, 1848.
Printed: 8 p., photoreproduction; 17 cm.
"The pastoral is given in both Spanish and Maya, the translation
into the latter tongue having been made, according to a note of
Dr. Berendt's, by don José Canuto Vela" (Brinton 1900:10).
BBC/UP, BYU, LAL/TU, LC
C.A. 6 Al 3

148. Guzmán, Pantaleón de

Compendio de nombres en lengua cakchiquel y significados de
verbos por imperativos y acusativos recíprocos, en doce tratados;
por el padre Predicador F. Pantaleón de Guzmán, cura doctrinero
por el Real Patronato de esta doctrina y curato de Santa María de
Jesús Paché; en veinte días del mes de octubre de mil setecientos
y cuatro años.
Manuscript: 175 leaves, photoreproduction; 23 cm.
Original: John Carter Brown Library, Brown University.
"A magnificent manuscript, very useful partly for its matter and
for its arrangement. One needs a dictionary in the ordinary order
for general reference with this, but the arrangement as well as the
magnificent writing of this makes it exceedingly useful" (Gates
note).
AC/NL, BBC/UP, BYU, LC
C.A. 6 G 99

149. Henderson, Alexander

A Short vocabulary of the Twaka Indians, together with a few
words of the San Blas Indians, both tribes of the Moskito Coast;
collected by Mr. Haly and communicated by the Rev. Alexander
Henderson, Baptist missionary in Belize, 1871.
Manuscript: 6 leaves, photoreproduction; 22 cm.
Original: Berendt-Brinton Collection, University of Pennsylvania.
"The English used to call the whole eastern coast from Belize
to Chiriqui Lagoon the Moskito Coast. The vocabularies were
collected by Mr. Haly, an English trader who lived for years
in Bluefields" (Gates note).
BYU
C.A. 6 B 452m

150. Hernández, Benito

Doctrina xpiana. en lengua mixteca, compuesta por el muy
reverendo padre fray Benito Herná[n]dez, vicario provincial
de la mixteca de la orden de Santo Domingo de la Nueva España ...
México : En Casa de Pedro Ocharte, 1568.
Printed: 382 p., photoreproduction; 22 cm.
BYU
MEX 6 H 43

151. Hernández Spina, Vicente

   Apuntamiento de la idioma quiché, 1854.
   Manuscript: 16 leaves, photoreproduction; 34 cm.
   Original: Bibliothèque Nationale, Paris.
   "Although modern, is well written and useful. Padre Spina was
   cura at [Santa Catarina] Ixtahuacán ... and took great interest
   in native matters" (Gates 1924).
                                    AC/NL, BYU, LAL/TU, LC
                                    C.A. 6 Sp 4

152. [Herrera, Francisco]

   Vocabulario en la lengua cakchiquel [i.e., Quiché], 1745.
   Manuscript: 100 leaves, photoreproduction; 22 cm.
   Original: Bibliothèque Nationale, Paris.
                                    AC/NL, LC
                                    C.A. 6 V 85

153. Homilies in Náhuatl, 1596.

   Manuscript: 157 leaves, photoreproduction; 22 cm.
   "This is valuable for its age, as must be an XVI manuscript,
   and for the exceeding beauty of the writing" (Gates note).
   "The first 16 pages have a church calendar, with the dates 1541,
   1542, probably the date of the manuscript, which is written
   throughout in an exquisitely regular formal hand" (Gates 1924).
   Contents include: Calendario, Epistolae et evangelia feria quarta
   cinerum, Incipiunt epistole et evangelia dominicalibus officiis
   congruentias que leguuntur traductanta in lingua mexicana, and
   Incipiuntur evangelia que per anni totius fractum leguntur in
   diebus festis.
                                    AC/NL, BYU, LC
                                    MEX 6 H 75

154. Infantado, El Duque de

   Proclama de 1803 en lengua tzotzil.
   Manuscript: 57 leaves, photoreproduction; 30 cm.
   Original: Robert Garrett Collection, Princeton University.
   "The present Proclama is one of my 'red mark' manuscripts,
   for all reasons, the scantiness of the material, its translation
   and notes, and also its wholly unique character as a Napoleonic
   document. I know nothing like it in any dialect. It is a translation apparently into that far-off native minor dialect of the
   appeal for aid against Napoleon issued from Cadiz by the junta,
   and throws a most interesting light on the situation at that
   time" (Gates note). A modern copy of the original and dated
   1906. Tzotzil and Spanish are on alternating pages.
                                    BYU, LC
                                    C.A. 6 P 94

155. Informe de los servicios hechos por la religión de Santo Domingo en
en la provincia de la Verapaz y tierras de Lacandones; relación
y memoria relativa a los asuntos de la provincia de Santo
Domingo de Guatemala, dirigido al muy ilustre señor don Antonio
Pedro de Echervers y Suvisa, año de 1724.
Manuscript: 38 leaves, photoreproduction; 32 cm.
Original: Bibliothèque Nationale, Paris.
Details of Spanish resettlement of the Lacandón Indians,and
Indian revolts in the Verapaz region at the end of the sixteenth
century. A handwritten copy of the original by Brasseur de
Bourbourg.

BL/UC
C.A. 6 D 660 G
C.A. 6 D 660 G Microfilm

156. Iriate, Joseph de

Sermones en la lengua tarasca, 1697.
Manuscript: 197 leaves, photoreproduction; 22 cm.
Original: Latin American Library, Tulane University.
"Thirteen sermons written in the Tarascan language in regular
even script" (Gropp 1935:285).

AC/NL, LC
MEX 6 Ir 4

157. León y Gama, Antonio de

[Studies of the Codex Aubin of 1576, by Antonio de León y Gama
and Joseph Marie Alexis Aubin].
Manuscript: 38 leaves, photoreproduction; 22 cm.
Original: Bibliothèque Nationale, Paris.
"These memoranda by Gama and Aubin are not only useful for the
study of the Codex [Aubin] of 1576, but are curious as showing
Aubin's habits, his notes on envelopes, printed notices, etc."
(Gates note). Includes a translation of the Náhuatl text into
French.

BYU
MEX 7 L 551s

158. [Letter from the Dominican provincial to the archbishop of
Guatemala regarding the work of Dominican missionaries,
particularly among the Chol-Lacandón Indians of Verapaz, late
17 cent.].
Manuscript: 2 leaves, photoreproduction; 32 cm.
Original: Bibliothèque Nationale, Paris.
Describes the treatment of the Lacandón and Itzá in missionary
settlements. Handwritten copy of the original by Brasseur de
Bourbourg.

BL/UC
C.A. 6 D 660 G
C.A. 6 D 660 G Microfilm

159. [Levanto, Leonardo]

Arte de lengua zapoteca, ca. 1725.
Manuscript: 50 leaves, photoreproduction; 22 cm.
Original: Latin American Library, Tulane University.
This *arte* is similar to Torralba's *Arte y confesionario zapoteca.*

LC
MEX 6 L 575a

160. Catecismo de la doctrina cristiana en lengua zapoteca, dispuesto por el M.R.P.Mtro. Fr. Leonardo Levanto, provincial que fue dos veces de la provincia de S. Hipolito Martír de Oaxaca, y una de la S. Miguel, y Santos Angeles de la Puebla, prior tres veces del convento grande, y otras tres del convento de recolección de N.P.Sto. Domingo Soriano, comisario del Smo. Rosario, asistente real, examinador synodal del obispado de Oaxaca, consultor del santo oficio y su corrector de libros ... Puebla : La Viuda de Miguel de Ortega, 1776.
Printed: 42 p., photoreproduction; 22 cm.
The approvals and licenses are dated 1732, probably the date of the first edition.

AC/NL, BBC/UP, BYU, LAL/TU
MEX 6 L 57

161. Libro de cofradía de Santa Cruz de Totonicapán, en lengua quiché, 1689 y 1777.

Manuscript: 37 leaves, photoreproduction; 36 cm.
Original: Robert Garrett Collection, Princeton University.
"Two manuscripts, in one cover, of rules for the cofradía, one of them with the text in both Quiché and Spanish; one of the seventeenth, the other early sixteenth century" (Gates note).

C.A. 6 L 61 F
C.A. 6 L 61 Microfilm

162. Libro de cuentas de la cofradía del Rosario en el pueblo de Suchiapa, desde 1796 hasta 1821, en lengua chiapaneca.

Manuscript: 121 leaves, photoreproduction; 15 cm.
Original: Berendt-Brinton Collection, University of Pennsylvania.
An account book, written largely in Chiapanec. A note by Karl H. Berendt gives: "contiene muchos apuntos en lengua chapaneca [sic], relativos a las contribuciones de los cofrades y a los gastos de la cofradía."

AC/NL, BYU, LC
C.A. 6 C 36

163. Libro de judío de Sotutá

Manuscript: 29 leaves, photoreproduction; 29 cm.
Original: Robert Garrett Collection, Princeton University.
"All in [Yucatec] Maya; these [herbal] recipes are simply
invaluable" (Gates note).
LAL/TU, LC
C.A. 6 L 61a

164. Libro de los Cocomes de Cacalchén, en lengua maya, 1647-1826.

Manuscript: 81 leaves, photoreproduction; 36 cm.
"Various documents from 1647 on, including a number of
ordenanzas promulgated from 1552 to 1583; also a number of
wills. A number of names of the Cocom family, the ancient
lords of Sotutá and the east of Yucatán, appear" (Gates 1924).
AC/NL, BYU, LAL/TU, LC
C.A. 6 L 61 F

165. [Libro de medicina maya]

Manuscript: 56 leaves, photoreproduction; 29 cm.
AC/NL, BYU, LC
C.A. 6 M 46

166. Libro de títulos de Ebtún en lengua maya, 1638 et seq.

Manuscript: 162 leaves bound in 2 vols., photoreproduction; 33 cm.
Collection of documents, primarily land titles and agreements,
relating to the pueblo of Ebtún, Cupul province, Yucatán.
BYU, LC
C.A. 6 T 54

167. Libro de tributos de San Pablo Teocaltitlán, 1574.

Manuscript: 29 leaves, photoreproduction; 21 cm.
Original: Bibliothèque Nationale, Paris.
A pictorial register of persons and tribute from San Pablo
Teocaltitlán, a part of Mexico City, "showing heads for the
Indians, each with his name written and in hieroglyph, and
tribute he had to pay to the encomendero; explanatory text in
Náhuatl, and signatures" (Gates 1924).
AC/NL, BYU, LAL/TU, LC
MEX 6 T 73

168. List of Indian families brought into Santa Catalina Chamiquin
from the Polochic mountains region, Verapaz, 1820.

Manuscript: 2 leaves, photoreproduction; 32 cm.
Original: Bibliothèque Nationale, Paris.
Handwritten copy of the original by Brasseur de Bourbourg.
BL/UC
C.A. 6 D 660 G
C.A. 6 D 660 G Microfilm

-73-

169. Loga del niño dios; representación escénica de los mangues en
     Namotivá, Santa Catarina, 1874.
     Manuscript: 4 leaves, photoreproduction; 22 cm.
     Original: Berendt-Brinton Collection, University of Pennsylvania.
     Text in corrupt Spanish with interspersed mangue words.
                                                    BYU, LC
                                                    C.A. 6 B 452m

170. Maldonado, Francisco
     Ramillete manual por los indios sobre la doctrina cristiana
     en la lengua cakchiquel, 1748.
     Manuscript: 79 leaves, photoreproduction; 22 cm.
     Original: American Philosophical Society, Philadelphia.
     "A copy made in 1748 of Maldonado's *Ramillete* or anthology
     of 12 dialogues, together with a copy of an unknown Doctrina
     cristiana of 1556" (Freeman 1966:86-87). On the first leaf is
     the following: "Arte pronunciación y ortografía de la lengua en
     el mismo idioma cakchiquel".
                                        AC/NL, BYU, LAL/TU, LC
                                        C.A. 6 M 29

171. Sermones super evangelia que in sanctorum festivitatibus leguntur;
     cum eorundem vitis et transitis idiomathe Guatemaltensi Cakchiquel,
     per fratrem Franciscum Maldonado, ordinis divi francisci predica-
     torem Olim que diffinitorem nominis Jesu Guatemaltensis provintiae
     alumun licet matriti natum, 1671.
     Manuscript: 153 leaves, photoreproduction; 33 cm.
     Original: Bibliothèque Nationale, Paris.
                                        AC/NL, BYU, LC
                                        C.A. 6 M 29

172. [Maldonado, Francisco]
     Theologia indorum en la lengua cakchiquel.
     Manuscript: 180 leaves, photoreproduction; 22 cm.
     Original: Bibliothèque Nationale, Paris.
     Pinart (1883:94) gives: "Ha nima vuh vae theologia indorum
     ru binaam".
                                        AC/NL, BYU, LC
                                        C.A. 6 M 29

173. [Martín, Juan]
     Vocabulario de la lengua castellana y zapoteca, 1696.
     Manuscript: 72 leaves, photoreproduction; 22 cm.
     A vocabulary from the pueblo of Nexitza in the Sierra Zapoteca.
                                        AC/NL, BYU, LAL/TU, LC
                                        MEX 6 V 85

174. Martínez, Alonso

Manual breve y compendioso para empezar a aprender la lengua
zapoteca y administrar en casa de necesidad; lo escribió fray
Alonso Martínez, de la orden de Sto. Domingo, y lo sujeta a la
santa madre iglesia católica romana y a su corrección y censura,
año de 1633.
Manuscript: 76 leaves, photoreproduction; 29 cm.
Original: John Carter Brown Library, Brown University.
"This volume is a photostatic reproduction of the Doctrina by
Alonzo Martínez, the original of which was formerly in the
possession of don José María Melgar of Vera Cruz. Dr. C.H. Berendt
undoubtedly made two copies of this work, one, the copy in the
John Carter Brown Library from which this reproduction is made,
and one in the Berendt Collection of the library of the museum
of the University of Pennsylvania" (Gates note).
BBC/UP, BYU, LC
MEX 6 M 36

175. Martínez, Marcos

Arte de la lengua utlateca ó kiché, vulgarmente llamado el arte
de Totonicapán, compuesto por el Rdo. padre fray Marcos Martínez
de la orden de Predicadores, ca. 1575.
Manuscript: 66 leaves, photoreproduction; 22 cm.
Original: Bibliothèque Nationale, Paris.
"Remesal read the Arte in the Franciscan convent in Totonicapán
and the priests there assured him it was the best grammar
written at that time" (Gates note).
AC/NL, LAL/TU, LC
C.A. 6 M 36

176. Matrícula de Huexotzingo, ca. 1559-1560.

Manuscript: 931 leaves bound in 3 vols., photoreproduction; 32 cm.
Original: Bibliothèque Nationale, Paris.
"A census ... of about 18 localities in the Huexotzingo region
and several localities farther south in Puebla" (Glass and Robert-
son 1975:134).
BYU, LC
MEX 7 H 87

177. Medina, Juan

Doctrinalis fidei in Mechuacanensium indorum lengua; aeditus ab
admodum reverendo patre fratre Joanne Metinensi, bethico,
Augustinii ordinis, & priore conventi cuisensis ... México :
Antonij Ricardi Typographie, 1577.
Printed: 280 p., photoreproduction; 32 cm.
"This is in every way the equal of a XVI manuscript; only two
copies of this work have survived, of which this, the Ramírez
copy, is apparently the best preserved" (Gates note).
BYU
MEX 6 M 47

178. [Mena, Francisco]

Libro grande de medicina en lengua maya, ca. 1725.
Manuscript: 88 leaves, photoreproduction; 21 cm.
Transcription of Maya medical texts owned by a resident of
Ticul, Yucatán, made by Mena for W.E. Gates.
BYU, LC
C.A. 6 L 61m

179. Mendoza, Jeremias

El Pueblo de Cacaopera, sus habitantes, sus costumbres, sus
industrias, su dialecto y otras varias apreciaciones
sobre el estado actual de su civilización, Yoloaiquín, 1895.
Manuscript: 15 leaves, photoreproduction; 22 cm.
BYU
C.A. 6 B 452m

180. [Mendoza, Juan de (1539-1619)]

Flor sanctorum, o vidas de santos en lengua cakchiquel, por
fray Juan de Mendoza, franciscano, ca. 1605.
Manuscript: 216 leaves bound in 2 vols., photoreproduction; 22 cm.
Original: American Philosophical Society, Philadelphia.
A collection of sermons in Cakchiquel. Freeman (1966:87) gives
the title as: "Uae rugotzlem Sant Andrés Apostol."
AC/NL
C.A. 6 V 67

181. Método breve para confesar a un indio en idioma otomí.

Manuscript: 17 leaves, photoreproduction; 22 cm.
Original: Latin American Library, Tulane University.
Handwritten copy of the original by Augustin Fischer, ca. 1866.
AC/NL, BYU, LC
MEX 6 D 65

182. [Mexican immigration to Yucatán].

Manuscript: 3 leaves, photoreproduction; 22 cm.
"A tradition preserved among the Indians of Yucatán concerning
this subject lead in the year 1618 in the villa of Valladolid
to an investigation for the sake of certain privileges and
distinctions of which a part has been preserved containing the
disposition and testimony copied hereafter" (Gates note).
BYU
C.A. 6 B 452m

183. Miranda, Francisco de [1720-1787]

Catecismo breve en lengua otomí; dispuesta por el P. Francisco
de Miranda de la compañía de Jesús ... México : Imprenta en la
Bibliotheca Mexicana, 1759.
Manuscript: 13 leaves, photoreproduction; 22 cm.

Original: Latin American Library, Tulane University.
Handwritten transcript of the original by Augustin Fischer, ca.
April 10, 1866.
AC/NL, BYU, LC
MEX 6 D 65

184. Modo de administrar los sacramentos en castellano y tzendal, 1707.
Manuscript: 24 leaves, photoreproduction; 21 cm.
Original: Berendt-Brinton Collection, University of Pennsylvania.
Transcript of the original document made in Tuxtla Gutiérrez by
K.H. Berendt, 1870.
AC/NL, BYU, LC
C.A. 6 M 42

185. Modo de confesar en lengua [yucatec] maya.
Manuscript: 20 leaves, photoreproduction; 20 cm.
Original: Berendt-Brinton Collection, University of Pennsylvania.
"Written in a clear, small hand, Spanish in one column, Maya
in the other. The name of the author is carefully blotted on the
first page and is illegible. The questions and answers extend
over a wide variety of topics, and form a valuable means of
studying the language. The manuscript was obtained in Campeche
by Dr. Berendt" (Brinton 1900:8).
BYU, LC
C.A. 6 P 69

186. Montero de Miranda, Francisco

Memoria sobre la provincia de Verapaz; al Illo. señor licenciado
Palacio del Consejo de S.M. y su oidor dignísimo en la Real
Audiencia de Guatemala, su muy servidor Francisco Montero de
Miranda, 1575.
Manuscript: 13 leaves, photoreproduction; 33 cm.
Original: Latin American Collection, University of Texas, Austin.
Handwritten copy of a version in the Muñoz Collection in the
Real Academia de la Historia, Madrid, by Buckingham Smith, March
1857.
BL/UC
C.A. 6 C 6

187. Morán, Francisco

Arte en la lengua choltí; doctrina en la lengua choltí;
vocabulario en la lengua choltí, 1689-1695.
Manuscript: 90 leaves, photoreproduction; 22 cm.
Original: American Philosophical Society, Philadelphia.
Morán was a Dominican who accompanied government forces in an
attempt to open a road from the Verapaz region to Laguna de
Términos. He wrote a vocabulary of Choltí which has disappeared,
but which had been copied with additions and notes of dialectic
differences. The present manuscript is a copy of this later work,
written between 1689 and 1695. The first three pages contain a

narrative in Spanish by Tómas Murillo, touching on the missions
in 1689-1692. Contents include the following: Arte en lengua
choltí que quiere decir lengua de milperos, Libro de lengua
choltí que quiere decir lengua de milperos, Confesionario en
lengua choltí, escrito en el pueblo de San Lucas Salac del
Chol, año de 1685, and Todo el vocabulario grande de M.R.P.
fray Francisco Morán, esta traducido en este libro, por el Abesedario
y algunos vocablos mas. The colophon of the manuscript gives:
"En este pueblo de Lacandones llamado de la Señora de Los Dolores
en 24 de junio, día San Juan, de 1695 años".

BBC/UP, BYU, LAL/TU, LC
C.A. 6 M 793a 2

188. Morán, Pedro

Arte breve y compendiosa de la lengua pocomchí, de la provincia
de la Verapaz, compuesto y ordenado por el padre fray Dionisio
de Çuñiga, y traducido en la lengua pocomán de Amatitlán, por
el fray Pedro Morán, en este convento de N.P. Santo Domingo
de Goathemala, 1720.
Manuscript: 9 leaves, photoreproduction; 33 cm.
Original: Bibliothèque Nationale, Paris.
"The only grammatical work for this language of so early a date
known. Well and closely written by an able linguist" (Gates note).

AC/NL, BYU, LC
C.A. 6 D 659 G Microfilm
C.A. 6 M 794v

189. Vidas de santos, en formas de homilias, en pokomán y castellano,
para los principiantes que comienzan a aprender la lengua
pokomán de Amatitlán, ordenados por el padre fray Pedro Morán,
en este convento de N.P. Santo Domingo de Goathemala, ca. 1720.
Manuscript: 87 leaves, photoreproduction; 33 cm.
Original: Bibliothèque Nationale, Paris.
"The Vidas de santos manuscript must be placed in the Theologia
indorum class; it has a special individual value in its method,
which for a large part translates phrase by phrase with a list of
special linguistic notes at the end of each Vida" (Gates note).
Homilies in Pokomán are interlined with Spanish translations.

BYU, LC
C.A. 6 D 659 G Microfilm
C.A. 6 M 794v

190. Vocabulario de nombres que comienzan en romance en la lengua
pokomán de Amatitlán, ordenado y compuesto por el padre fray
Pedro Morán, en este convento de N.P. Santo Domingo de Guatemala,
1720.
Manuscript: 91 leaves, photoreproduction; 34 cm.
Original: Bibliothèque Nationale, Paris.
"The present vocabulary started out to be one of nouns, but soon
broke, and gives a long and analytical analysis of adverbs
entitled Comparativos y superlativos en lengua pokomán" (Gates

note).
BYU, LC
C.A. 6 M 793bd

191. Vocabulario de sólo los nombres de la lengua pokomán, escrito
y ordenado por el padre fray Pedro Morán, en el convento
de N.P.Sto. Domingo de Goathemala, 1720.
Manuscript: 122 leaves, photoreproduction; 32 cm.
Original: Bibliothèque Nationale, Paris.
"The treatment of these works [by Morán] is delightful. The
words are all treated as honorable and prominent citizens of
a commonwealth; of one we will be told, 'this gentleman lives up
north, and does not drink our waters of Amatitlán'. The writing
is all very clear and regular, and the works are filled with
illustrations and careful analyses. There was no better work
done on any of these languages than that we have here" (Gates
1924). The vocabulary goes only as far as 'nach'.
AC/NL, BYU, LAL/TU, LC
C.A. 6 D 659 G Microfilm
C.A. 6 M 794bs

192. Muñoz, Juan Bautista

Carta en limpio de Juan Bautista Muñoz al marqués de Sonora, de
marzo de 1786, informando sobre el descubrimiento de Palenque.
[con los datos de Calderón y Bernasconi].
Manuscript: 5 leaves, photoreproduction; 33 cm.
Original: British Museum, London.
C.A. 3 B 456f P
C.A. 3 P 19
C.A. 3 R 476d

193. Extractos sueltos de varios libros de la colección de Muñoz
tocantes a la historia de las provincias centroamericanas.
Manuscript: 85 leaves, photoreproduction; 33 cm.
A collection of early documents gathered by the historian Muñoz
dating between 1545 and 1555. Coverage includes Guatemala,
Honduras, Nicaragua, Yucatán, and Zapotitlán.
BL/UC
C.A. 6 C 6

194. Nabe Tihonic; Doctrina en la lengua quiché.

Manuscript: 74 leaves, photoreproduction; 22 cm.
Original: Robert Garrett Collection, Princeton University.
AC/NL, LC
C.A. 6 Qu 4

195. Nagera Yanguas, Diego de [d.1637]

Doctrina y enseñan a en la lengua mazahua de cosas muy utiles, y
provechosas para los ministros de doctrina y para los naturales

que hablan la lengua mazahua; dirigido al ilustrísimo señor
don Francisco Manso y Zúñiga, arzobispo de México, del consejo
de Su Majestad y del Real de las Indias, por el licenciado
Diego de Nagera Yanguas, beneficado del partido de Xocotitlán;
comisario del Santo Oficio de la Inquisición y examinador en
la dicha lengua mazahua ... México : Juan Ruiz, 1637.
Printed: 179 leaves, photoreproduction; 22 cm.
                          BYU
                          MEX 6 Y 1

196. Navas y Quevedo, Andrés de la [1622-1702]

Informe del Rdo. padre prior del convento de Cobán al Ilmo. y
Rmo. Sr. don Fr. Andrés de las Navas y Quevedo, arzobispo de
Guatemala, sobre las misiones de Verapaz y ah-Izas [sic],
escrito en Cobán a 8 de febrero de 1685.
Manuscript: 14 leaves, photoreproduction; 32 cm.
Original: Bibliothèque Nationale, Paris.
"A closely written report by the prior of the Dominican convent at
Cobán defending the missionaries against complaints addressed to
the king of Spain by Olivera y Angulo, former alcalde mayor of
Cobán. Covers the period when the entrada was made, coincident
with the Ursúa expedition from Mérida" (Gates note). Handwritten
copy of the original made by Brasseur de Bourbourg, 1865.
                          BL/UC
                          C.A. 6 D 660 G
                          C.A. 6 D 660 G Microfilm

197. Noguera Victor [Jesús]

Vocabulario de la lengua popoluca de Matagalpa, 1855.
Manuscript: 5 leaves, photoreproduction; 22 cm.
Original: Berendt-Brinton Collection, University of Pennsylvania.
Handwritten copy of the original made by Karl H. Berendt, 1874.
                          BYU
                          C.A. 6 B 452m

198. Nombres de pájaros en lengua quiché y otras cosas, ca.1750.

Manuscript: 16 leaves, photoreproduction; 22 cm.
Original: Bibliothèque Nationale, Paris.
"A well-written manuscript" (Gates 1924).
                          AC/NL, BYU, LAL/TU, LC
                          C.A. 6 V 82

199. Noticias de varias plantas [de Yucatán] y sus virtudes.

Manuscript: 15 leaves, photoreproduction; 6 cm.
Original: Berendt-Brinton Collection, University of Pennsylvania.
"Copied from the original in Yucatán. It appears to have been
written about the beginning of the present century, and gives
the Maya names of many plants of supposed medicinal properties"
(Brinton 1900:15).
                          AC/NL, BYU
                          C.A. 6 B 452v

200. Nuñez, Juan

Algunas cosas curiosas en lengua chiapaneca; sacados de propósito
para doctrina de los indios y para que los padres que dependen
esta lengua se aprovechen de ellas por no aver in ella nada escrito;
los padres perdonen y resolvan el buen deseo que tuvo quien lo
trabajo por servirles y aprovechar los almas de los pobres, 1623.
Manuscript: 54 leaves, photoreproduction; 22 cm.
Original: Bibliothèque Nationale, Paris.
A series of homilies or sermons in Chiapanec.
AC/NL, BYU,
C.A. 6 N 92

201. Sermones de doctrina, en lengua chiapaneca; compuestos por el
R.P.Fr. Juan Nuñez, dominico, recogidos en la familia del Sr.
don Esteban Nucamendi, gobernador que fue de Acalá de Chiapas,
ca. 1625.
Manuscript: 83 leaves, photoreproduction; 22 cm.
Original: Bibliothèque Nationale, Paris.
AC/NL, BYU, LAL/TU, LC
C.A. 6 N 92

202. Nuñez de la Vega, Francisco

Copia de un carta relativa a la secta idolatra del nahualismo,
escrita por el Ilmo. Sr. don Francisco Nuñez del a Vega, obispo
de Chiapa, al Exmo. Sr. Capitán General a Guatemala, ca.1691.
Manuscript: 1 leaf, photoreproduction; 32 cm.
Original: Bibliothèque Nationale, Paris.
Extract copied from a letter by Francisco Nuñez de la Vega,
Dominican bishop of Chiapas, to the Captain General of Guatemala,
requesting the destruction of certain Indian writings on the
practice of nahualismo. This copy was made in 1859 from an
incomplete manuscript in the episcopal Archivo de San Cristóbal
at Ciudad Real de Chiapas by Brasseur de Bourbourg.
BL/UC
C.A. 6 D 660 G
C.A. 6 D 660 G Microfilm

203. Olivera y Angulo, Sebastián de

Carta de su majestad, escrita a Sebastián de Olivera y Angulo,
alcalde mayor de la Verapaz, 1676.
Manuscript: 1 leaf, photoreproduction; 32 cm.
Original: Bibliothèque Nationale, Paris.
Handwritten copy of the original by Brasseur de Bourbourg.
Regarding missions among the Chol, Itzá, Manché, and Lacandón
Indians.
BL/UC
C.A. 6 D 660 G
C.A. 6 D 660 G Microfilm

204. [Olmos, Andrés de (d.1571)]

Arte y vocabulario de la lengua mexicana, 1547.
Manuscript: 288 leaves bound in 2 vols., photoreproduction; 23 cm.
Original: Latin American Library, Tulane University.
"The XVI Arte and vocabulario, or better, verb-list, is a beautifully
written manuscript in red and black. It is very elaborate, and ...
seems probably in the first rank as early, first-hand grammatical
analysis" (Gates note).
BYU
MEX 6 Ar 7

205. Oraciones en la lengua chocho, ca.1650.

Manuscript: 10 leaves, photoreproduction; 23 cm.
"Well written and in perfect condition. A Doctrina etc. with
the Spanish version accompanying the Chocho phrases. Apart
from being the only known piece for the language, it is
especially valuable for its early date, as practically nothing
is extant for these minor Oaxaca dialects earlier than the
XVIII century" (Gates 1924).
BYU
C.A. 6 Or 1

206. Oraciones en la lengua maya de Teabo.

Manuscript: 15 leaves, photoreproduction; 22 cm.
Original: Robert Garrett Collection, Princeton University.
Miscellaneous short religious documents in Yucatec Maya.
AC/NL, LC
C.A. 6 Or 1t

207. Ordóñez de Villaquiran, Diego de Vera

Relación en el Consejo Real de las Indias hizo el licenciado
Antonio de León Pinelo, redactor de su Alteza, sobre la
pacificación y población de las provincias del Manché y
Lacandón, que pretende hacer don Diego de Vera Ordóñez de
Villaquiran, caballero de la orden de Calatrava, 1639.
Manuscript: 8 leaves, photoreproduction; 33 cm.
"The Villaquiran is probably unique, as such informes were not
public prints, and the present copy seems to be merely a proof-
sheet, with a number of corrections, most probably in the hand
of León Pinelo himself. It gives information which seems not
to have reached even so well informed a writer as Villaguitierre,
and in what it says of Fray Francisco Morán in his entrada to
the Lacandones in 1625, as well as various other data about
Chol territory, gives valuable historical links confirming the
localization of the Choltí tongue" (Gates note).
C.A. 2 L 11

208. Ordóñez y Aguiar, Ramón de

Notas de Chiapas y Palenque, recogida entre los borrones de don Ramón de Ordóñez y Aguiar.
Manuscript: 3 leaves, photoreproduction, 32 cm.
Original: Bibliothèque Nationale, Paris.
Handwritten copy by Brasseur de Bourbourg of notes by Ordóñez y Aguiar on various features of the ruins of Palenque and pueblos in Chiapas.

BL/UC
C.A. 6 D 660 G
C.A. 6 D 660 G Microfilm

209. [Oroz, Pedro (1521-1597)]

Evangeli a en las lenguas latina, otomí, náhuatl; incipiunt epistole et evangelia que in diebus dominicus et festibus per totius anni circulum leguntur; traducta in linguam mexicanam.
Manuscript: 251 leaves bound in 2 vols., photoreproduction; 22 cm.
"It is written in three columns, Latin in the central column, and Aztec and Otomí on each side, for easy comparison. The lettering is small but perfectly legible. No name and no date appear in the text. Gates assigns it to Oroz. Its value lies in the comparison of the native languages to the classical Latin" (Gates 1940).

LC
MEX 6 Or 6

210. Theologia indorum en la lengua otomí, 16 cent.
Manuscript: 76 leaves, photoreproduction; 22 cm.
Original: Bibliothèque Nationale, Paris.
No authorship appears on the manuscript although on the first page is given "del uso de fray F. Oroz". "The manuscript is of course XVI century, probably by Oroz's own hand. I know of no other surviving manuscript by him" (Gates note).

MEX 6 T 34

211. [Ossado, Ricardo]

Libro de judío [medicina] en lengua maya.
Manuscript: 78 leaves, photoreproduction; 16 cm.
Original: Tozzer Library, Harvard University.
On the first page is the following: "al Dr. LePlongeon, Mérida, abril 18 de 1883, Apolonia Tibaja".

AC/NL, BYU, LC
C.A. 6 Os 71

212. [Ossorio, Tomás]

Theologia indorum en lengua quiche de [San Sebastián] Lemoa.
Manuscript: 143 leaves, photoreproduction; 22 cm.
Original: Robert Garrett Collection, Princeton University.
"These versions were copied by a certain D. Tomás Ossorio,

escribano de San Sebastián Lemoa" (Tozzer note).

AC/NL, BYU, LC
C.A. 6 L 55

213. Padilla, Ignacio

Visita del obispado de Yucatán hecho por su obispo, su
ilustrísimo Sr. don fray Ignacio Padilla, y noticia del
estado de cada pueblo y de la capital, distancia de unos a otros,
y número de personas a quienes administró la confirmación, año de
1757.
Manuscript: 37 leaves, photoreproduction; 29 cm.
Original: British Museum, London.

C.A. 6 R 27

214. Palacio, Diego García de [d.1595]

Copia incompleta de una carta dirigida a Felipe II, el 8
de marzo de 1576, por el licenciado don Diego García de Palacio,
oidor de la Real Audiencia de Guatemala, relativa al descubrimiento de Copán.
Manuscript: 2 leaves, photoreproduction; 33 cm.
Original: British Museum, London.

C.A. 3 P 19
C.A. 3 R 476d

215. Pasion domini de Jesucristo en lengua maya, 1803.

Manuscript: 22 leaves, photoreproduction; 22 cm.
Original: Robert Garrett Collection, Princeton University.
Miscellaneous short documents concerning the pueblo of Teabo.

BYU, LC
C.A. 6 P 26

216. Peticiones de los principales del pueblo de San Francisco
[el Alto, jurisdicción de la alcaldia mayor] de Totonicapán.

Manuscript: 20 leaves, photoreproduction; 22 cm.
Original: Bibliothèque Nationale, Paris.
"A beautifully written document, in double column, Spanish
and Quiché, giving the official appeal of the Indians of
San Francisco [el Alto], near Totonicapán, in a dispute
with those of San Cristóbal" (Gates note).

AC/NL, BYU, LC
C.A. 6 V 82

217. Pop, Eugenio

Doctrina cristiana en lengua kekchí, escrita por padron del
pueblo de San Agustín Lanquín, en la Verapaz, por Eugenio Pop,
alcalde que fue en el año de 1795.
Manuscript: 19 leaves, photoreproduction; 22 cm.
Original: Bibliothèque Nationale, Paris.

BYU, LAL/TU, LC
C.A. 6 P 81d

218. Popol Vuh

Empiezan las historias del origen de los indios de esta provincia
de Guatemala; traducida de la lengua quiché en la castellana para
más comodidad de los ministros del Santo Evangelio, por el R.P.F.
Francisco Ximénez, cura doctrinero por el pueblo de Santo Tomás
Chuilá.
Manuscript: 56 leaves, photoreproduction; 32 cm.
Original: Bibliothèque Nationale, Paris.
                              BYU, LC
                              C.A. 4 Xi 44h

219. Escolios a las historias del origin de los indios escoliadores
por el R.P.F. Francisco Ximénez, cura doctrinero por el Real
Patronato del pueblo de Santo Tomás Chichicastenango, del
sagrado orden de Predicadores, para mayor noticia a los ministros
de los indios.
Manuscript: 6 leaves, photoreproduction; 32 cm.
                              BYU, LC
                              C.A. 4 Xi 44h

220. Historia de la gentilidad americana traducida al castellano.
Manuscript: 64 leaves, photoreproduction; 33 cm.
Original: Bibliothèque Nationale, Paris.
Translation only of leaves 172 to 236.
                              AC/NL, BYU, LC
                              C.A. 4 Xi 44h 3

221. [Pozarenco, Juan (d.1771)]

Arte de lengua zoque para la mayor gloria de dios nuestro señor,
17 cent.
Manuscript: 16 leaves, photoreproduction; 22 cm.
Original: Bibliothèque Nationale, Paris.
"A manuscript of the XVII century. The only Zoque manuscripts
known are those of Pozarenco, and a vocabulary by Gonzáles of
about the same date" (Gates note).
                              AC/NL, BYU, LAL/TU, LC
                              MEX 6 P 879a

222. Doctrina cristiana en lengua tzoque, seguida de un confesionario
y del modo de dar el viático a los enfermos, en la misma lengua;
obra del Rdo. padre maestro fray Juan Pozarenco, quien la acabo
en veinte y dos de agosto del año de 1696.
Manuscript: 32 leaves, photoreproduction; 22 cm.
Original: Bibliothèque Nationale, Paris.
"The last 14 pages contain a brief vocabulary" (Gates note).
The original was found by Brasseur de Bourbourg in the Dominican
monastery at Ciudad Real in Chiapas.
                              AC/NL, BYU
                              MEX 6 P 879a

223. Pozarenco, Juan (d.1771)

Vocabulario de la lengua tzoque, 1733.
Manuscript: 176 leaves, photoreproduction; 22 cm.
Original: John Carter Brown Library, Brown University
"This vocabulary has been for more than fifty years in the
possession of a Catholic priest, Clemente Castillejos, who
got it from his predecessor in the curate of Tecpatlán, and
left it to his nephew. the licentiate don Mariano Rodríguez,
in the city of Tuxtla Gutiérrez, who told me that it had on a
blank leaf, only lately lost, the words 'año de 1733'. It
contains a careful elaborated Spanish-Zoque dictionary and
was, it seems, forming a part of a larger work before it was
bound up as it is now. The preceding 55 leaves might have
contained a grammar or a doctrina cristiana" (Berendt note).
BBC/UP
MEX 6 P 879v

224. Quaderno del idioma mazateca de las cosas y términos más comunes
y usuales para instrucción de principiantes, año de 1827.

Manuscript: 50 leaves, photoreproduction; 22 cm.
"This is one of the few Mazatec in existence" (Gates note).
Arranged in double column Spanish and Mazatec.
AC/NL, BYU, LAL/TU, LC
MEX 6 Qu 2

225. Relación individual de los gobiernos, alcaldias mayores, y
corregimientos que compredido el distrito de la Real Audiencia
y Capitanía General del reino de Goathemala, sus respectivos
goces de sueldos, utilidades que lo gran por los frutos que
producen sus provincias y bajo este respecto la cantidad en
que puede S.M. en casos de urgencia del erario beneficiarlos a
excepción de los que están situados en puertos del mar, costas
y territorios fronterizos a indios bárbaros e infieles para
proveer los en personas de experiencias militares.

Manuscript: 4 leaves, photoreproduction; 29 cm.
C.A. 4 Xi 44
C.A. 4 Xi 44h 3

226. Requena, Francisco Xavier de

Relación de meritos y servicios de don Francisco Xavier de
Requena, capitán, alcalde castellano del presidio del Petén
Itzá, 1685.
Manuscript: 22 leaves, photoreproduction; 33 cm.
Interesting for primary information on the Itzá and Manché
Maya.
C.A. 2 L 11

227. Reyes, Antonio de los

Arte en lengua mixteca; compuesta por el padre fray Antonio de
los Reyes, de la orden de Predicadores, vicario de Tepuzculula ...
México : En Casa de Pedro Balli, 1593.
Printed: 69 leaves, photoreproduction; 15 cm.
"Of the greatest importance from its early date and excessive
rarity" (Gates note).

BYU, LC
MEX 6 R 33

228. Riveiro, Tomás

Explicación de la doctrina cristiana en lengua kekchí; sermones
en lengua kekchí; traducción del español por don Tomás Riveiro,
1798-1799.
Manuscript: 40 leaves, photoreproduction; 32 cm.
Original: Robert Garrett Collection, Princeton University.
"An exquisitely written manuscript of the XVIII century; Spanish
and Kekchí in parallel columns" (Gates note).

BYU, LAL/TU, LC
C.A. 6 Ex 73r 2

229. Roca, Augusto

Carta del padre dominico maestro Roca, desde el convento de
Santo Domingo de Guatemala, a don José Miguel de San Antonio,
relativa al descubrimiento de Palenque y primeras gestiones
realizadas para su desescombra y teoria sobre sus habitaciones,
noviembre 27 de 1792.
Manuscript: 2 leaves, photoreproduction; 33 cm.
Original: British Museum, London.

C.A. 3 P 19
C.A. 3 R 476d

230. Rocha, Juan Eligio de la

Apuntamientos de la lengua mangue, 1842.
Manuscript: 3 leaves, photoreproduction; 22 cm.
Original: Berendt-Brinton Collection, University of Pennsylvania.
"Manuscript, copied in Granada, 1874. Rocha was author of a
Spanish grammar and teacher of French and Spanish grammar in the
University of León, where he died in 1873. His brother placed
his notes on the Mangue tongue at Dr. Berendt's disposal, who
copied from them the above pages" (Brinton 1900:27).

BYU
C.A. 6 B 452m

231. Ruano Suárez, Alberto

Vocabularios de las lenguas pokomán y chortí, 1892.
Manuscript: 61 leaves, photoreproduction; 33 cm.
Original: Robert Garrett Collection, University of Pennsylvania.
Includes separate vocabularies for San Luis Jilotepeque and

Chiquimula. For Chortí, "of the greatest ethnographic and linguistic value. This manuscript contains some 1600 words, and was taken at Chiquimula in 1892, at a time when the dialect [Chortí] had entirely died out save for old natives over 50 years of age; it is therefore a complete salvage" (Gates note).
AC/NL, BYU, LC
C.A. 6 R 82

232. Ruz, [José] Joaquín [Francisco Carrillo de]

Análisis del idioma yucateco al castellano, por el R.P. fray Joaquín Ruz ... Mérida de Yucatán : Impreso por Mariano Guzmán, 1851.
Printed: 16 leaves, photoreproduction; 13 cm.
"This is a word-for-word translation of two articles of the Roman catechism into Maya" (Brinton 1900:7).
BBC/UP
C.A. 6 R 94

233. Catecismo historico, o compendio de la historia sagrada, y de la doctrina cristiana; con preguntas, y respuestas, y lecciones seguidas, por el Abad Fleury; y traducidas del castellano al idioma yucateco, con un breve exortación para el entrego del Santo Cristo a los enfermos, por el P.P.Fr. Joaquín Ruz, de la orden de San Francisco, para la instrucción de los naturales ... Mérida de Yucatán : En la Oficina a Cargo de Domingo Cantón, 1822.
Printed: 94 leaves, photoreproduction; 22 cm.
A translation into Yucatec of the *Catécisme historique* (Paris, 1690) of the Abbé Claude Fleury in an abbreviated form. This is a Gates reproduction of a copy in the Berendt-Brinton Collection at the University of Pennsylvania.
BBC/UP, BYU, LC
C.A. 6 R 94

234. Vía sacra del divino amante corazón de Jesús; dispuesta por las cruces del calvario, por el presbítero José de Herrera Villa-vicencio; traducida al idioma yucateco por el R.P.Fr. Joaquín Ruz ... Mérida de Yucatán : Impreso por Nazario Novelo, 1849.
Printed: 34 leaves, photoreproduction; 13 cm.
A Gates reproduction of a copy in the Berendt-Brinton Collection at the University of Pennsylvania.
BBC/UP, BYU
C.A. 6 R 94

235. Sacramentos en lengua kekchí.

Manuscript: 5 leaves, photoreproduction; 33 cm.
BYU, LC
C.A. 6 D 65
C.A. 6 D 659 G Microfilm

236. Sahagún, Bernardino de [c.1499-1590]

Comienza un ejercicio en lengua mexicana, sacado del Santo Evango.
y distribuido por todos los días de la semana contiene meditaciones
devotas muy provechosas para cualquier Xpiano. que se quiere llegar
a Dios, 1574.
Manuscript: 43 leaves, photoreproduction; 22 cm.
Original: Ayer Collection, Newberry Library, Chicago.
BYU, LC
MEX 6 Sa 19e

237. Doctrina en la lengua mexicana, ca. 1575.
Manuscript: 44 leaves, photoreproduction; 33 cm.
"The Doctrina, which bears his signature twice, was once
followed by a section on Indian customs, etc., now lost" (Gates
note).
AC/NL, BYU, LC
MEX 6 Sa 19d

238. Siguense unos sermones de dominicas y de santos en lengua
mexicana; no traducidos de sermonario alguno sino compuestos
nuevamente a la medida de la capacidad de los indios; breves
en materia y en lenguaje congruo venusto y llano fácil de
entender para todos los que le oyeran altos y bajos principales
y macehuales hombres y mujeres; compusiera el año de 1540
anse comenzado a corregir y añadir este año de 1563, en este
mes de julio infraoctava visitationis; el autor los somete a
la correctio de la madre sancta iglesia romana co todas las
otras que en esta lengua mexicana a compuesto.
Manuscript: 112 leaves, photoreproduction; 33 cm.
"This wonderful manuscript is one of the finest in existence,
on great heavy maguey paper sheets, not quite complete, but
probably still in the original binding" (Gates note).
AC/NL, BYU
MEX 6 Sa 19s

239. Vocabulario en lengua mexicana, ca. 1590.
Manuscript: 155 leaves, photoreproduction; 22 cm.
"The Náhuatl in the original is in red; the manuscript appears
beautifully and regularly written. Sahagún's name does not
appear, but it was identified as by him by Sr. Alfredo Chávez"
(Gates note).
AC/NL, BYU, LC
MEX 6 Sa 19v

240. Salazar, Gabriel de

Informe del M.Rdo. padre fray Gabriel de Salazar, prior del
convento de Cobán al rey, escrito en 20 del mes de diciembre
del año de 1636, sobre los asuntos y misiones de la Verapaz.
Manuscript: 3 leaves, photoreproduction; 32 cm.
Original: Bibliothèque Nationale, Paris.
Includes a discussion on navigation of the Río Usumacinta and

entradas from Cobán to Laguna de Términos. On the verso of
the first leaf is given: "Informe de Gabriel de Salazar,
prior de Cobán sobre averse huido los indios del Chol al
monte." Handwritten copy of the original by Brasseur de
Bourbourg.
                                    BL/UC
                                    C.A. 6 D 660 G
                                    C.A. 6 D 660 G Microfilm

241. San Juan, José Miguel

Carta de Joseph Miguel de San Juan al coronel Philipe de Sesina
relativa a una 'medalla' hallada en Palenque, 2 de diciembre de
1792.
Manuscript: 6 leaves, photoreproduction; 33 cm.
Original: British Museum, London.
                                    C.A. 3 P 19
                                    C.A. 3 R 476d

242. Sánchez de la Baquera, Juan

Modo breve de aprender a leer, escribir, pronunciar, y hablar
el idioma otomí, en el cual se contiene su ortografía, arte,
y modo de conjugar, y un confesionario con examen de conciencia;
dispuesto por Juan Sánchez de la Baquera, español natural, y
vecino del pueblo de Tula, quien reverente lo dedica a los
dulcimos nombres de Jesús, María, y Joseph, año de 1747.
Manuscript: 55 leaves, photoreproduction; 22 cm.
Original: Bancroft Library, University of California, Berkeley.
"The writer says most of the many who wrote for Otomí had in
mind only to learn the prayers and doctrina, and not the far
more important knowledge of how to read and write the language;
this he [Sánchez de la Baquera] took for his purpose in writing"
(Gates note).
                                    AC/NL, BYU, LC
                                    MEX 6 B 22

243. [Sánchez Viscayno, José Antonio]

Doctrina cristiana en la lengua utlateca, o quiché, del uso de
fray Josef Antonio Sánchez Viscayno, año de 1790.
Manuscript: 12 leaves, photoreproduction; 22 cm.
Original: Bibliothèque Nationale, Paris.
"A beautifully written manuscript in double columns, Spanish and
Quiché" (Gates note).
                                    AC/NL, BYU, LAL/TU, LC
                                    C.A. 6 V 82

244. Sá[nche]z, José Antonio del

Marial sacro y santoral; sermones en la lengua quiché, escritos
por varios autores, principalmente por un indio, por lo cual
hay mucho que corregir, o enmendar en todos los textos latinos;

pertenece al uso del P.F. A. Sz., hijo de la Santa Provincia
de Dulcísimo Nombre de J.H.S. de Guatemala, año de 1796.
Manuscript: 160 leaves, photoreproduction; 23 cm.
Original: Bibliothèque Nationale, Paris.
"It is a mere copy (made in a different hand) of a manuscript
that was in possession of Father Saz" (Tozzer note).
AC/NL, BYU, LC
C.A. 6 Sa 9

245. [Pláticas] compuesto en lengua cakchiquel por el padre
Predicador fray Antonio del Saz, hijo de esta provincia
del Sanctísimo Nombre de Jesús de Guatemala, 1662.
Manuscript: 155 leaves, photoreproduction; 15 cm.
AC/NL, BYU, LAL/TU, LC
C.A. 6 Sa 9

246. [Sandalia, Domingo]

Escrituras varias de testamento en lengua quiché, 1750-1777.
Manuscript: 22 leaves, photoreproduction; 21 cm.
Documents concerning the lands of Domingo Sandalia.
BYU
C.A. 6 Es 1

247. Santo Domingo, Tomás de [d.1729]

Vocabulario en la lengua cakchiquel [y castellano], richin
fratris Thomae a Sto. Dominico e coetu fratrum sacri ordinis
predicatorum superopidi de Zumpan animarum curam intendentis,
1693.
Manuscript: 139 leaves, photoreproduction; 22 cm.
Original: Bibliothèque Nationale, Paris.
"A very handsome manuscript of the XVII century; all the
initials of the words are Gothic letters, in red" (Gates note).
AC/NL, BYU, LAL/TU, LC
C.A. 6 Sa 59v

248. Santo Viacrucis

El ejercicio del Santo Viacrucis puesto en lengua maya y copiado
de un antiguo manuscrito; lo da a la prensa con superior permiso
el Dr. José Vicente Solís y Rosales, quien desea se propague esta
devoción entre los fieles principalmente de la clase indígena;
va corregida por M. Antonio Peralta ... Mérida de Yucatán :
J.D. Espinosa e Hijos, 1869.
Printed: 16 leaves, photoreproduction; 16 cm.
C.A. 6 C 28

249. Sermonario grande en lengua mexicana, 16 cent.

Manuscript: 328 leaves bound in 2 vols., photoreproduction; 22 cm.
Original: British Museum, London.
"This beautiful manuscript I considered of enough importance and

early enough to make one of our selected Aztec list. As
Mrs. Nuttall confirms me, all this is very early Náhuatl,
so archaic as to be almost unintelligible to modern experts"
(Gates note).

AC/NL, BYU, LC
MEX 6 L 50

250. Sermones en lengua maya, copiados de un manuscrito anciano, ca. 1775.

Manuscript: 56 leaves, photoreproduction; 20 cm.
Original: Berendt-Brinton Collection, University of Pennsylvania.
"Copied from the library of Rev. Crescencio Carrillo, Mérida.
The paper and writing of the original date from the last half
of the XVIII century. The language is clear and correct 'muy
común y muy inteligible por todos los yucatecos'"(Brinton 1900:
12-13).

AC/NL, BYU, LC
C.A. 6 P 69

251. Sermones en lengua maya [de Sotutá], ca. 1750.

Manuscript: 72 leaves, photoreproduction; 33 cm.
BYU
C.A. 6 Se 6

252. Sermones en lengua pokonchí, ca. 1575.

Manuscript: 186 leaves, photoreproduction; 22 cm.
Original: Tozzer Library, Harvard University.
AC/NL, BYU, LC
C.A. 6 Se 6

253. Sermones sobre los evangelios y fiestas del año en la lengua
matlazinque de las indias.

Manuscript: 285 leaves bound in 2 vols., photoreproduction; 22 cm.
Original: Bibliothèque Nationale, Paris.
"The handwriting in the latter part of this volume is very like
indeed to Gilberti's, only somewhat more slanting" (Gates note).
Leaf 63 states "Este cartapacio de la lengua matlatzinque es del
uso de fray Antonio de Villanueva" and leaves 69 and 285 give
"Es de la librería de S. Luca. P. Francisco Vergar".

AC/NL, BYU, LC
MEX 6 Se 6

254. Sermones y oraciones en lengua pokonchí, ca. 1550.

Manuscript: 377 leaves bound in 3 vols., photoreproduction; 32 cm.
Original: Robert Garrett Collection, Princeton University.
"This volume, with the former Viana, Zúñiga, and Ximeno, can be
counted the two greatest Poconchí manuscripts known" (Gates note).

AC/NL, BYU, LC
C.A. 6 V 654s

255. [Serra, Angel]

Vocabulario, arte, y confesionario en lengua tarasca, ca. 1695.
Manuscript: 129 leaves, photoreproduction; 22 cm.
"The Serra is undoubtedly an independent compilation. The
writing is scrawly, and the whole not easy to use" (Gates
note). "It is evidently of an early date" (Gates 1940).
AC/NL, BYU, LC
MEX 6 Se 6

256. [Sierra, Bernardo]

Para ayudar a bien morir en lengua yucateca, traducida del
Ramillete de divinas flores, y fue compuesto por don Bernardo
Sierra, expurgado del Santo oficio del Real Consejo de
Castilla.
Manuscript: 38 leaves, photoreproduction; 22 cm.
Original: Robert Garrett Collection, Princeton University.
Miscellaneous short documents.
AC/NL, LC
C.A. 6 Or lt

257. [Solano, Félix]

Vocabulario en lengua castellana y guatemalteca, que se llama
cak-chi-quel-chi, ca. 1578.
Manuscript: 305 leaves, photoreproduction; 33 cm.
Original: Robert Garrett Collection, Princeton University.
A note states: "Este diccionario fue escrito por el R.P.Fr.
Félix Solano, religioso de San Francisco". Cakchiquel and
Spanish are in parallel columns.
C.A. 6 So 41v 2 F

258. Manuscript: 250 leaves bound in 2 vols., photoreproduction; 33 cm.
Original: Bibliothèque Nationale, Paris.
Handwritten copy of the original by E.G. Squier.
AC/NL, BYU, LC
C.A. 6 So 41v 2

259. Sonora, Marqués de

Comunicación del marqués de Sonora a don Juan Bautista Muñoz,
de marzo 1 de 1786, en que anuncia por orden del rey el envió
de unas cartas y planos relativos al descubrimiento de Palenque
y que habian sido remitidos por el presidente de Guatemala.
Manuscript: 2 leaves, photoreproduction; 33 cm.
Original: British Museum, London.
C.A. 3 P 19
C.A. 3 R 476d

260. Tapia Zentano, Carlos de

Paradigma, apologética, arte, vocabulario, y doctrina en lengua
huasteca, ca. 1750.

Manuscript: 81 leaves, photoreproduction; 22 cm.
Original: Ayer Collection, Newberry Library, Chicago.
"The only Haustec manuscript known ... contains matter not
published in his printed grammar of 1767" (Gates 1924).
Contents include: Paradigma apologético que desea persuadir
ingenuo escribiendo desapasionado la notica de la lengua
huasteca, Noticia de la lengua huasteca, Diccionario
huasteco, and Catecismo y doctrina cristiana.
AC/NL, BYU, LC
MEX 6 T 16

261. [Temporal, Bartolomé de]

Libro de comparaciones y de moral cristiana en lengua tzendal;
escrito por el P.Fr. Bartholomé Temporal, ca. 1600.
Manuscript: 171 leaves, photoreproduction; 22 cm.
Original: Bibliothèque Nationale, Paris.
"This Tzental manuscript belonged to Brasseur, and he named it
for Temporal whose name appears; but Temporal's writing is very
different from that of the text, which is clearly XVI century,
much like that of Father Ara, and also the note only says
these 'comparaciones son del padre Temporal', which is more
likely to mean ownership of the volume, than authorship. But
the manuscript is another first grade document in the almost
hopeless scarcity of Tzental-Tzotzil material of any kind,
especially early" (Gates note).
AC/NL, BYU, LC
C.A. 6 C 73

262. Testamento de Chimolab en lengua kekchí, 1565.

Manuscript: 3 leaves, photoreproduction; 33 cm.
AC/NL, LAL/TU, LC
C.A. 6 D 65
C.A. 6 D 659 G Microfilm

263. Theologia indorum de Zacapulas, ca. 1650.

Manuscript: 296 leaves bound in 3 vols., photoreproduction; 22 cm.
Original: Robert Garrett Collection, Princeton University.
AC/NL, BYU, LC
C.A. 6 T 34z

264. Theologia indorum o sermones de pasión en lengua quiché.

Manuscript: 199 leaves bound in 2 vols., photoreproduction; 22 cm.
Original: Robert Garrett Collection, Princeton University.
AC/NL, BYU, LC
C.A. 6 P 26

265. Toro, Francisco

Sermones en lengua tzoque, 1709.

-94-

Manuscript: 176 leaves, photoreproduction; 34 cm.
Original: Robert Garrett Collection, Princeton University.
"A manuscript copied from one written in 1709, and later destroyed" (Gates note).

BYU
MEX 6 T 63

266. Torralba, Juan Francisco

Arte zapoteco, confesionario, administración de los santos sacramentos, y otras curiosidades, que en él se contienen; perteneciente al muy R.P.Fr. Juan Francisco Torralba, religioso presbítero del sagrado orden de Predicadores de la provincia de Santo Ypólito Martír, de la ciudad de Oaxaca; A.M.D.G.; sacado de su original en esta cabeza de Ocotlán, año de 1800.
Manuscript: 155 leaves, photoreproduction; 22 cm.
Original: Ayer Collection, Newberry Library, Chicago.
Includes terms for numerals, units of time by years, months, weeks, and days, kinship terminology, and parts of the body.

AC/NL, BYU
MEX 6 T 63

267. Torresano, Estevan

Arte de la lengua cakchiquel, por fray Estevan Torresano; modo de contar en esta lengua, paralelo de la lengua quiché, cakchiquel, y tzutuhil, 1754.
Manuscript: 74 leaves, photoreproduction; 17 cm.
Original: Bibliothèque Nationale, Paris.
"The Torresano Arte is from the original of 1754, from which Squier's copy was made, and from Squier's the Berendt in the DGB [Daniel G. Brinton Collection]. It is one of the handsomest manuscripts we have, almost like print, in its Roman and Italic" (Gates note).

AC/NL, BBC/UP, BYU, LAL/TU, LC
C.A. 6 T 66

268. Tres cédulas reales dirigidas a los oidors de la Audiencia Real de la ciudad de México y al gobernador y capitán general presidente de Guatemala, años de 1677-1680.
Manuscript: 3 leaves, photoreproduction; 32 cm.
Original: Bibliothèque Nationale, Paris.
Two copies of a royal decree, dated November 30, 1680, on provision of friars for the conversion and pacification of the Chol Indians, addressed to Lopé de Sierra Osorio, acting governor of Guatemala, and to Navas y Quevedo, acting bishop of Guatemala; also a copy of a letter, dated October 13, 1677, from the king of Spain to Sebastián de Olivera y Angulo, alcalde mayor of Verapaz, also relating to the work of pacification in the Verapaz region.

BL/UC
C.A. 6 D 660 G
C.A. 6 D 660 G Microfilm

269. Tum, Miguel

Frases en castellano y en lengua quiché.
Manuscript: 14 leaves, photoreproduction; 33 cm.
Original: Robert Garrett Collection, Princeton University.
"The work of a native of one of the old chief priestly families,
one Miguel Tum, and another writer in a different hand, to whom
we owe also the fragments of bilingual testament translation
at the end" (Gates note).
AC/NL, BYU, LC
C.A. 6 T 83

270. Tupeus, José Mariano

Vocabulario, doctrina, y oraciones en lengua mixteca, ca. 1800.
Manuscript: 74 leaves, photoreproduction; 22 cm.
Original: Latin American Library, Tulane University.
"With the possible exception of one unpublished manuscript
in Mexico no longer known to exist, the only Mixtec manuscript.
Contains an extensive vocabulary, confesionario, and other
matters in Mixtec" (Gates note).
BYU, LC
MEX 6 T 83

271. Urbano, Alonso

Arte breve de la lengua otomí compuesto por el padre fray
Alonso Urbano de la orden de N.P.S. Agustín; de las letras
A.B.C., 1605.
Manuscript: 35 leaves, photoreproduction; 22 cm.
Original: Bibliothèque Nationale, Paris.
"This is a short well written Otomí arte which from its very
early origin seemed worth including. It is a copy made for
Squier, from the original in Paris, and evidently most carefully
done" (Gates note).
AC/NL, BYU, LAL/TU, LC
MEX 6 Ur 1

272. Utzolan u xocot

Manuscript: 4 leaves, photoreproduction; 22 cm.
Original: Berendt-Brinton Collection, University of Pennsylvania.

BYU
C.A. 6 B 452m

273. Valdespino, Andrés

Breve explicación del arte zapoteca [del Levanto], 18 cent.
Manuscript: 7 leaves, photoreproduction; 22 cm.
Original: Latin American Library, Tulane University.
LC
MEX 6 L 575a

-96-

274. Valdés, Sebastián

Vocabulario de la lengua pocomám de Mita, por don Sebastián Valdés, cura de Jutiapa, 1868.
Manuscript: 4 leaves, photoreproduction; 22 cm.
Original: Berendt-Brinton Collection, University of Pennsylvania.
Includes about 80 words with equivalents in Pocomám and Pokonchí; copied by Karl Berendt in Guatemala, 1875.
BYU
C.A. 6 452vo

275. Valle, Blas del

Informe sobre la provincia de Verapaz, escrito por el Rdo. padre fray Blas del Valle de la orden de Predicadores, ca. 1690.
Manuscript: 2 leaves, photoreproduction; 32 cm.
Original: Bibliothèque Nationale, Paris.
Description of the Verapaz region and its indigenous population.
Handwritten copy of the original by Brasseur de Bourbourg.
BL/UC
C.A. 6 D 660 G
C.A. 6 D 660 G Microfilm

276. Varea, Francisco de [d.1636]

Calepino en lengua cakchiquel, por fray Francisco de Varea, hijo de esta S. Provincia del S.S. Nombre de Jesús de Religiosos de N.P.S. Francisco de Goathemala.
Manuscript: 238 leaves bound in 3 vols., photoreproduction; 22 cm.
Original: American Philosophical Society, Philadelphia.
"Copy of dictionary of late 16th century missionary made by fray Francisco Ceron 4000 Cakchiquel words (Parra's orthography) with equivalents" (Freeman 1966:87). A gift of Mariano Gálvez to the Society in September of 1834.
AC/NL, BYU, LC
C.A. 6 V 42

277. Vargas, Melchior de

Doctrina cristiana muy útil y necesaria en castellano, mexicano y otomí; traducida en lengua otomí por el muy R. padre fray Melchior de Vargoy de la orden del San Agustín, prior de Actopán, ordenada por mandado del Ilmo. y Rev. Sr. don Pedro de Moya de Contreras, arzobispo de México de Consejo de S.M. y con licencia impresa ... México : En Casa de Pedro Balli, 1576.
Manuscript: 37 leaves, photoreproduction; 22 cm.
Original: Latin American Library, Tulane University.
Handwritten copy of the printed text by Augustin Fischer, ca. 1866.
AC/NL, BYU, LC
MEX 6 D 65

278. Viana, Francisco de [d.1608]

Relación de la provincia de la Verapaz, hecha por los
religiosos de Santo Domingo de Cobán, 7 de diciembre de
1574, por fray Francisco Prior de Viana, fray Lucas Gallego
y fray Guillermo Cadena.
Manuscript: 10 leaves, photoreproduction; 33 cm.
Original: Real Academia de la Historia, Madrid.
Handwritten copy of the original document in the Muñoz
Collection by Buckingham Smith, March 1857.
BL/UC
C.A. 6 C 6

279. Sermones en lengua pokonchí, por padre fray Francisco de Viana
y el padre fray Gonzáles Ximeno, arregados por el padre fray
Dionisio de Zúñiga, ca. 1550.
Manuscript: 214 leaves bound in 2 vols., photoreproduction; 32 cm.
Original: Robert Garrett Collection, Princeton University.
"At the beginning of the seventeenth century Zúñiga collected an
early ca. 1550 volume of sermons by Viana and inserted the
missing sections from Ximeno, and had the volume rebound. By 1750
it belonged to Morales, the fiscal, whose grammar Berendt found
and copied. The document subsequently passed into the hands of a
Pokonchí family, the Caals" (Gates note).
AC/NL, BYU
C.A. 6 V 654p

280. [Vico, Domingo de (d.1555)]

Sermones en lengua achí, o tzutuhil; compuesto para el uso de los
padres de la orden de Santo Domingo de Guatemala, a principios del
siglo XVII, conforme al estilo del Ven. P.F. Domingo de Vico.
Manuscript: 174 leaves, photoreproduction; 22 cm.
Original: Bibliothèque Nationale, Paris.
Comprises 33 sermons in Tzutujil with emphasis on the principal
feasts of the saints and of the year.
AC/NL, BYU, LC
C.A. 6 V 66

281. Theología indorum de Cunen en lengua quiché, ca. 1550.
Manuscript: 144 leaves, photoreproduction; 23 cm.
Original: Robert Garrett Collection, Princeton University.
"This manuscript seems to be a mere copy of a Vico-type
theologia" (Tozzer note).
AC/NL, BYU, LC
C.A. 6 T 3

282. Theología indorum de los indios o instrucción de ellos en la fe
católica, por sermones sobre la vida de Christo, evangelios, y
fiestas de santos, en lengua indiana, [Cakchiquel], ca. 1550.
Manuscript: 275 leaves, photoreproduction; 22 cm.
Original: Bibliothèque Nationale, Paris.

AC/NL, BYU
C.A. 6 V 66a

283. [Vico, Domingo de (d.1555)]

Theología indorum en lengua cakchiquel.
Manuscript: 208 leaves bound in 2 vols., photoreproduction; 22 cm.
C.A. 6 V 66

284. Theología indorum en lengua quiche, ca. 1550.
Manuscript: 252 leaves bound in 2 vols., photoreproduction; 22 cm.
Original: Robert Garrett Collection, Princeton University.
"No other title or information. The manuscript begins with no chapter heading. The rest is entirely in Quiché and is divided into topics every three or four pages. It is dated in the 16th century by Gates" (Gates 1940). Also known as 'Vico G'.
AC/NL, BYU
C.A. 6 T 34c

285. Theología indorum en lengua quiché, 1553.
Manuscript: 104 leaves, photoreproduction; 22 cm.
Original: Bibliothèque Nationale, Paris.
"I am inclined to rest on attributing the Theologia indorum manuscript definitely to Vico. He has the primary credit it seems for this series of Bible stories in the different languages; he was a wonderful linguist and later writers used to translate these stories into other dialects, and to add others 'al estilo del Rdo. padre Vico'. The manuscript is dated 1553, two years before Vico's death among the Lacandones, and there is every reason, I think, to assign it to him" (Gates note). Also known as 'Vico D'.
AC/NL, BYU
C.A. 6 V 66

286. Theología indorum ubinaam en lengua quiché, ca. 1650.
Manuscript: 185 leaves, photoreproduction; 22 cm.
Original: Bibliothèque Nationale, Paris.
A note gives "De la librería del convento de N.P. San Francisco de Guatemala". Also known as 'Vico C'.
AC/NL, BYU, LC
C.A. 6 V 66

287. Theología indorum en lengua tzutuhil, ca. 1550.
Manuscript: 188 leaves, photoreproduction; 22 cm.
Original: Bibliothèque Nationale, Paris.
AC/NL, BYU, LC
C.A. 6 V 66

288. Theología indorum para los indios en lengua [quiché] de Verapaz, 1605.
Manuscript: 198 leaves, photoreproduction; 22 cm.
Original: Bibliothèque Nationale, Paris.

AC/NL, BYU, LC
C.A. 6 V 66

289. [Vico, Domingo de (d.1555)]

Vae rucam ru vuhil rumac vutz, theologia indorum ru binaam,
tihobal quichim indio cristiano pa ru chabal; Dios rumac, ahau
pa cakchiquel chicovi, auctore P.Fr. Dominco de Vico.
Manuscript: 131 leaves, photoreproduction; 22 cm.
Original: Bibliothèque Nationale, Paris.
Also known as 'Vico E'.

AC/NL, BYU
C.A. 6 V 66

290. Vocabulario cakchiquel y quiché.
Manuscript: 285 leaves bound in 2 vols., photoreproduction; 22 cm.
Original: Bibliothèque Nationale, Paris.
"Evidently a copy of some earlier pattern, perhaps a manuscript
of the Vico type" (Tozzer note). Brasseur de Bourbourg (1925)
gives the following title: Vocabulario de la lengua cakchiquel,
con advertencia de los vocablos de las lenguas quiché y tzutuhil,
se traslado de la obra compuesta por el Ilmo. padre el venerable
fray Domingo de Vico.

AC/NL, LC
C.A. 6 V 66

291. Villacañas, Benito [1547-1610]

[Arte y] vocabulario en lengua cakchiquel, por el P. fray Benito
de Villacañas, ornis. Prery. hecho después de aver tratado cuarenta
anos con los indios de esta lengua sin interrupción con ejemplo y
zelo de las ánimos muy singular cuyo fruto y premio goza ahora en
los jardines de la gloria, traslado 10 de noviembre de 1692.
Manuscript: 173 leaves, photoreproduction; 22 cm.
Original: Berendt-Brinton Collection, University of Pennsylvania.
This is a Berendt copy of the original; an arte occupies leaves
1-20, and the vocabulario the remainder of the volume.

BBC/UP, BYU, LC
C.A. 6 V 71

292. Vocablos de la lengua huave colectados por el abate Brasseur de
Bourbourg, comparados con los equivalentes en las principales
lenguas de la América del Sur, y en las lenguas vecinas de
Oaxaca y Chiapas, 1859.

Manuscript: 7 leaves, photoreproduction; 22 cm.
Original: Berendt-Brinton Collection, University of Pennsylvania.
"Manuscript, compiled by Dr. Berendt. It contains also the Huave
words collected by Mr. E.A. Fuertes, in 1870, for the Smithsonian"
(Brinton 1900:25).

BYU
C.A. 6 B 452m

293. Vocabulario breve y manual de la lengua [tarasca] de Michoacán, 1647.

Manuscript: 75 leaves, photoreproduction; 21 cm.
The vocabulary extends from A to X.
AC/NL, BYU
MEX 6 V 85

294. Vocabulario castellano y cakchiquel, 1732.

Manuscript: 228 leaves bound in 2 vols., photoreproduction; 22 cm.
Original: Bibliothèque Nationale, Paris.
"A complete vocabulary. A to TZ, written in a small, fine hand.
On the last page is some very bad writing which may mean that
the manuscript was compiled and written in 1732" (Gates 1940).
AC/NL, BYU, LC
C.A. 6 V 85

295. Vocabulario de la lengua cakchiquel.

Manuscript: 359 leaves bound in 3 vols., photoreproduction; 17 cm.
"The anonymous Cakchiquel vocabulary of 718 pages is a manuscript
I was myself fortunate to unearth some years ago, and it is a
very handy volume" (Gates note).
AC/NL, BYU, LC
C.A. 6 V 85

296. Vocabulario de la lengua cakchiquel, 1704.

Manuscript: 92 leaves, photoreproduction; 12 cm.
Original: Bibliothèque Nationale, Paris.
"Have not studied this at all; it is early enough to be worthwhile"
(Gates note). Brasseur de Bourbourg (1871:109) gives the
following title: Noticia breve de los vocablos más usuales de la
lengua cakchiquel.
AC/NL, BYU, LAL/TU, LC
C.A. 6 V 85

297. Vocabulario de la lengua mazateca y castellano, ca. 1830.

Manuscript: 10 leaves, photoreproduction; 22 cm.
AC/NL, BYU, LAL/TU, LC
MEX 6 V 85a

298. Vocabulario en lengua mazahua [i.e., Otomí].

Manuscript: 300 leaves bound in 2 vols., photoreproduction; 32 cm.
"The writing is not easy, and the ink faded very irregularly
making a good reproduction very trying; but to date it is our
only Otomí-Mazahua dictionary of any size" (Gates note).
BYU
MEX 6 V 85

299. Vocabulario en lengua quiché y castellana, ca. 1750.

Manuscript: 186 leaves, photoreproduction; 22 cm.
Original: Robert Garrett Collection, Princeton University.
"The vocabulary runs from A to M; a second volume was apparently
written, but no trace of its whereabouts" (Gates note).
AC/NL, BYU, LC
C.A. 6 V 85

300. Vocabulario en el idioma totonaca, 1780.

Manuscript: 46 leaves, photoreproduction; 22 cm.
Original: Latin American Library, Tulane University.
BYU
MEX 6 T 64

301. Vocabulario grande en lengua cakchiquel y quiché, 18 cent.

Manuscript: 353 leaves bound in 2 vols., photoreproduction; 22 cm.
Original: Bibliothèque Nationale, Paris.
AC/NL, BYU, LC
C.A. 6 C 13

302. Vocabulario maya y castellano.

Manuscript: 49 leaves, photoreproduction; 22 cm.
"This is a little modern working vocabulary" (Gates note).
C.A. 6 V 85

303. Vocabularios de la lengua xinca de Sinacantan por don Juan Gavarrete,
1868, y de Yupiltepeque y Jalapa por don Sebastián Valdés, cura
de Intiapa, 1868.

Manuscript: 5 leaves, photoreproduction; 22 cm.
Original: Berendt-Brinton Collection, University of Pennsylvania.
Handwritten copies of the original documents made by Karl Berendt,
1875.
BYU
C.A. 6 B 452m

304. Ximénez, Francisco [1666-c.1722]

Arte de las tres lenguas cakchiquel, quiché, y tzutuhil; escrito
por el R.P.F. Francisco Ximénez, cura doctrinero por el Real
Patronato del pueblo de Santo Tomás Chuilá, ca. 1710.
Manuscript: 119 leaves, photoreproduction; 33 cm.
Original: Bibliothèque Nationale, Paris.
"Much of the writing is clear and plain, but the ink is pale
and brown through the whole volume, and at places is almost
wholly illegible. Taken right through the photographs are
much easier to read than the original. The volume contains
quite a few extra notations in later hands, some apparently
Brasseur's to whom the volume belonged" (Gates note).
AC/NL, BYU, LC
C.A. 6 X 1

305. Ximénez, Francisco [1666-c.1772]

Primera parte del tesoro de las lenguas cakchiquel, quiché, y
tzutuhil, en que las dichas lenguas se traducen en la nuestra
española compuesto por el R.P.F. Francisco Ximénez, del sagrado
orden de Predicadores, cura doctrinero por el Real Patronato
del pueblo de Santo Tomás Chichicastenango, ca. 1710.
Manuscript: 204 leaves bound in 2 vols., photoreproduction; 33 cm.
Original: Bibliothèque Nationale, Paris.
AC/NL, BYU, LC
C.A. 6 X 4

306. Xiu Chronicles

Manuscript: 82 leaves, photoreproduction; 32 cm.
Original: Tozzer Library, Harvard University.
"The Xiu chronicles are a compilation of documents, ca. 1608-1817,
relating to the authority of the Xiu family, preconquest and
colonial rulers of the province of Maní in Yucatán" (Glass and
Robertson 1975:390).
AC/NL, BYU, LC
C.A. 7 X 4 F

307. Zakicoxol, o baile de la conquista en lengua quiché.

Manuscript: 213 leaves bound in 2 vols., photoreproduction; 22 cm.
Original: Robert Garrett Collection, Princeton University.
"This volume comprises six different versions of the Dance of the
Conquest. One of them appears to be in Uspantec" (Gates note).
AC/NL, BYU, LC
C.A. 6 D 79

308. Manuscript: 16 leaves, photoreproduction; 22 cm.
Original: Robert Garrett Collection, Princeton University.
AC/NL, BYU, LC
C.A. 6 Z 1

309. Zakicoxol, o baile de Cortés, en quiché y castellano, escrito
memoria por Pedro Torres, 1875.

Manuscript: 3 leaves, photoreproduction; 22 cm.
Original: Berendt-Brinton Collection, University of Pennsylvania.
"This is a modern drama written by a native, in Quiché and Spanish,
the plot based on the conquest of Mexico. It is one of the few
correct specimens of the native drama which have been preserved,
and although not possessing the claim of antiquity, presents the
general style and manner of treatment adopted in the primitive
scenic representations" (Brinton 1900:14-15).
BYU
C.A. 6 B 452m

310. Zambrano Bonilla, Joseph

Arte de lengua totonaca, conforme a el arte de Antonio
Nebrija, compuesto por don Joseph Zambrano Bonilla, cura
beneficiado, vicario y juez eclesiástico de San Andrés
Hueitlalpan, dedicado al Ilmo.Sr.Dr.D. Domingo Pantaleón
Alvarez de Abreu, dignisimo arzobispo obispo de esta diocesi,
lleva añadido una doctrina de la lengua de Naolingo, con algunas
voces de la lengua de aquella sierra, y de esta de aca ...
Puebla : Imprenta de la Viuda de Miguel de Ortega, 1752.
Printed: 137 leaves, photoreproduction; 22 cm.
"Original very scarce, material almost none, and all the
manuscripts now locked up in Hispanic [Foundation]
(Gates note).

·   BYU
                             MEX 6 B 64

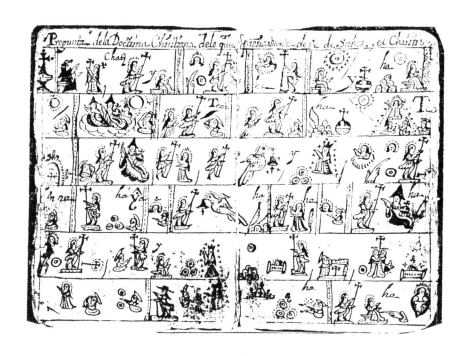

Testerian catechism
acquired in Mérida by Edward H. Thompson (no. 546)

311. Alzate y Ramírez, José Antonio [1738-1799]

Descripción de Xochicalco antigüedades mexicana, registrada en 12 de noviembre 1777.
Manuscript: 10 leaves, handwritten; 31 cm.
MEX 3 A1 98d 2

312. Anales de Cuauhtitlán

Annals of Cuauhtitlán. Historical notes of Mexico and its environs, compiled by José Fernando Ramírez and translated by Faustino Galicia Chimalpopoca, Gumesindo Mendoza, and Felipe Sánchez Solís ... México : Imprenta de Ignacio Escalante, 1865.
Manuscript: 102 leaves, typewritten; 28 cm.
Chronological annals and historical sequences in Náhuatl from Toltec and Chichimec to Spanish periods, composed ca. 1570. English translation of the Spanish original.
MEX 7 C 44 E

313. Andrews, Edward Wyllys IV [1916-1971]

Excavations at Dzibilchaltún, northwestern Yucatán, Mexico, 1959.
Manuscript: 19 leaves, typewritten; 28 cm.
C.A. 3 An 26e F

314. The Maya supplementary series, 1938.
Manuscript: 89 leaves, typewritten; 28 cm.
C.A. 9 An 26m

315. Table of all supplementary series of the Maya area.
Manuscript: 5 leaves, typewritten; 28 cm.
PAM A

316. Apuntaciones para la estadística de la provincia de Yucatán, que formaron de orden superior en 20 de marzo de 1814 los señores Calzadilla, Echanove, Bolio y Zuaznavar ... Mérida : Imprenta de J.D. Espinosa e Hijos, 1871.

Manuscript: 19 leaves, typewritten; 28 cm.
Includes extracts in Spanish on subdelegaciones de pueblos and general population in Yucatán.
L.SOC.77.90.1

317. Asociación conservadora de los monumentos arqueológicos de Yucatán; copia de los documentos relativos a su fundación primeros trabajos ofrecida a la Carnegie Institution of Washington, como un recuerdo de la visita a Yucatán de varios de sus principales miembros, Mérida, Yucatán, México, 1923.

Manuscript: 140 leaves, typewritten; 22 cm.
Spanish and English text; includes letters by Alfred M. Tozzer
on pages 87 and 107.

C.A. 9 As 57

318. Atwood, Rollin S. [b. 1903]

Geographic survey of the highlands of Guatemala, 1932.
Manuscript: 15 leaves, typewritten; 28 cm.
"The central object of the report is the village of Santo Tomás
Chichicastenango."

C.A. 1 C 215f

319. Atwood, Wallace W. [1872-1949]

The physiographic provinces of the highlands of Guatemala, 1932.
Manuscript: 12 leaves, typewritten; 28 cm.
"Centers particularly on the Lake Atitlán region."

C.A. 1 C 215f

320. Avendaño y Loyola, Andrés de [d.1705]

Relación of two trips to the Petén, Guatemala, 1697.
Manuscript: 132 leaves, handwritten; 28 cm.
An important early account of the Petén Itzá and the site
of Tayasal. English translation of the Spanish text by
Charles P. Bowditch with revisions by G. Rivera.

C.A. 2 Av 3r

321. Manuscript: 135 leaves, typewritten; 28 cm.

C.A. 2 Av 3r

322. Manuscript: 143 leaves, typewritten; 28 cm.

C.A. 2 Av 3r 2

323. Baile de los diablos, en lengua kekchí.

Manuscript: 7 leaves, typewritten; 28 cm.
"Esta historia fué arreglado y corregido por Leoncio
Rivera, 19 de octubre de 1812; copiado [por] Pedro Xi,
Carchá, 1 de septiembre de 1922" (McDougall note).

C.A. 4 M 147d F

324. Manuscript: 7 leaves, typewritten; 28 cm.
"Copy of a text in the possession of Domingo Caal, Cobán,
Alta Verapaz. The writing was that of his father, Tiburius
Caal, who had it copied in 1885" (McDougall note).

C.A. 4 M 147d F

325. Baile de los micos, en lengua kekchí.

Historia de micos y monos para festijar a nuestro patrón
Domingo de Guzmán.
Manuscript: 10 leaves, typewritten; 28 cm.

"Hecho en el año 1829; copiado 1 enero 1875" (McDougall note).
C.A. 4 M 147d F

326. Baile de los venados, en lengua kekchí.

Historia de mazate llamada en el dialecto kekchí, Caxlan Quej,
dedicalo a San Pedro y San Pablo.
Manuscript: 5 leaves, typewritten; 28 cm.
"Copied in Carchá, September 18, 1901, by Pedro Xi" (McDougall
note).
C.A. 4 M 147d F

327. Bandelier, Adolph Francis [1840-1914]

Alphabetical index of Notes on the bibliography of Yucatán and
Central América, comprising Yucatán, Chiapas, Guatemala (the
ruins of Palenque, Ocosingo, and Copán), and Oaxaca (ruins of
Mitla), 1881.
Manuscript: 7 leaves, typewritten; 27 cm.
C.A. 10 B 221a

328. Baughman, J.L.

An early account of marine fisheries of the Mayas as given in
Diego de Landa's Relación de las cosas de Yucatán, with notes
on the probable identification of the fishes.
Manuscript: 50 leaves, typewritten; 28 cm.
C.A. 4 B 326e

329. Berendt, Karl Hermann [1817-1878]

[Extract from Berendt's preface to his copy of the Motul Maya
dictionary].
Manuscript: 4 leaves, handwritten; 24 cm.
Translation from the Spanish.
C.A. 6 B 772c

330. Notes on the antiquities of Nicaragua, 1874.
Manuscript: 3 leaves, typewritten; 28 cm.
C.A. 3 B 452n

331. Berlin, Brent [b. 1936]

Diccionario del tzeltal de Tenejapa, Chiapas, por Brent Berlin
y Terrence Kaufman, 1962.
Manuscript: 138 leaves, typewritten; 28 cm.
MEX 6 B 455d

332. Blom, Frans Ferdinand [1893-1963]

Report on the ruins of Uaxactun, and other ruins in the
department of Petén, Guatemala: Carnegie Institution of
Washington Guatemala Expedition, 1924.
Manuscript: 173 leaves, typewritten; 28 cm.

Introduction signed by Sylvanus G. Morley.
                                    C.A. 3 B 621r

333. Bourgeois, Julia F.

The true Mexican chronology as proved by manuscripts in
the Archives of the Indies in Seville and the Royal
Academy of History in Madrid, years 1579-1582, 1935.
Manuscript: 45 leaves, typewritten; 28 cm.
Includes her *The Codex Sierra calendar or the true
equivalent for the Aztec calendar*, and correspondence
with Alfred M. Tozzer regarding these papers.
                                    MEX 9 B 666t F

334. Bowditch, Charles Pickering [1842-1921]

Books photographed by William E. Gates; copies given by
Charles P. Bowditch to the Peabody Museum.
Manuscript: 498 leaves bound in 3 vols., typewritten; 28 cm.
                                    C.A. 6 B 674b F
                                    C.A. 6 B 674b Microfilm
                                    C.A. 6 C 280 Microfilm

335. Collection of volumes in Berendt's Linguistic Collection.
Manuscript: 93 leaves, handwritten; sizes vary.
Includes photographs of illustrations from the *Chilam Balam
of Chumayel*.
                                    C.A. 6 B 46b

336. Index of inscriptions in Seler's [1899] article on the
monuments of Copán and Quiriguá, ca. 1913.
Manuscript: 1 leaf, typewritten; 28 cm.
                                    MEX 1 Se 48g E 2 F
                                    MEX 1 Se 48g E 2 Microfilm
                                    MEX 1 Se 48g E 3 F

337. Maya manuscripts.
Manuscript: 110 leaves, handwritten; 25 cm.
Unpublished study of the *Codex Dresden* and Maya writing in
general.
                                    C.A. 7 B 674m

338. Notes on the Gates photograph collection.
Manuscript: 64 leaves, handwritten and photoreproduction;
various sizes.
                                    C.A. 6 G 223b

339. The Numeration, calendar systems, and astronomical knowledge
of the Mayas ... Cambridge, Massachusetts : The University Press, 1910.
Printed: 346 p.; 26 cm.
Privately printed for the use of the Peabody Museum of American
Archaeology and Ethnology, Harvard University.
                                    C.A. 9 B 674n

340. Brasseur de Bourbourg, Charles Etienne [1814-1874]

Antigüedades de Centro-América.
Manuscript: 2 leaves, typewritten; 28 cm.
Transcript of an article in *La Gaceta de Guatemala*, San José,
Costa Rica, November 19, 1853.
C.A. 3 An 87

341. Antigüedades de Centro-América.
Manuscript: 4 leaves, typewritten; 28 cm.
Transcript of an article in *La Gaceta de Guatemala*, San José,
Costa Rica, September 17, 1856.
C.A. 3 B 736a

342. Antigüedades guatemaltecas.
Manuscript: 11 leaves, typewritten; 28 cm.
Transcript of articles in *La Geceta de Guatemala*, San José,
Costa Rica, February 23, 1856 and June 2, 1856.
C.A. 3 B 736ag

343. Interesting discoveries in Guatemala; ruins of unknown
ancient cities, traces of early migrations from the north.
Manuscript: 10 leaves, typewritten; 28 cm.
Transcript of a correspondence to the *New York Tribune*, November
21, 1855.
C.A. 3 B 736i

344. [Preface and introductory material to Brasseur de Bourbourg's
1861 edition of the *Popol Vuh*].
Manuscript: 33 leaves, typewritten; 28 cm.
English translation of the French by Charles P. Bowditch of
*Popol Vuh: le livre sacré et les mythes de l'antiquité Américaine,
avec les livres héroiques et historiques des Quichés* ... Paris :
Arthus Bertrand, 1861.
C.A. 6 4 P 814 F B E

345. Breton, Adela Catherine [1849-1923]

Notes, transcripts, and translations of various Maya documents.
Manuscript: 153 leaves, handwritten; 28 cm.
Includes selections in English from the *Xiu Chronicles*, trans-
criptions in Maya from the *Libro de los Cocomes de Cacalchén*,
English and Spanish texts of the Cárdenas y Valencia *Relación*
of 1643 and the Del Río description of Palenque, and
excerpts in Spanish from the *Chilam Balam of Chumayel*.
C.A. 6 B 756m F

346. [Watercolor reproductions of wall paintings from Chichén Itzá,
ca. 1917].
Manuscript: 20 leaves, photoreproduction; sizes vary.
Includes color reproductions of mural paintings from Temple A,
the North Building, and the Casa de las Monjas. These are based
on photographs and drawings made between 1903 and 1907. Scales

-110-

indicated are 1:12 and 1:4.

C.A. 3 B 755r P

347. Bunzel, Ruth

Report on fieldwork done in Chichicastenango, Guatemala, submitted to the Committee on Selection of the John Simon Guggenheim Memorial Foundation, 1930.
Manuscript: 12 leaves, typewritten; 28 cm.
Fieldwork conducted between August and October of 1930.

C.A. 4 B 887r

348. Cahabón Manuscript.

Manuscript: 35 leaves, handwritten; 32 cm.
This manuscript was purchased by Charles P. Bowditch from Robert Burkitt in 1901 and presented to the Peabody Museum on December 6, 1901. A note by Burkitt states "The manuscript contains no historical allusions. Its only value is philological."

C.A. 6 C 12

349. Manuscript: 73 leaves, photoreproduction; 33 cm.
Original: Tozzer Library, Harvard University.

C.A. 6 C 12 c.2

350. Cano, Agustín [1650-1719]

[Informe sobre la entrada de la Verapaz al Petén en el año de 1695].
Manuscript: 20 leaves, typewritten; 28 cm.
An important early account of the Petén region. Cano taught at the Universidad de Guatemala and served several administrative positions until he was appointed cura of Jocotenango in 1687.
He had earlier helped to reestablish the mission at San Lucas Tzalec (or Salac) near the present Río Sarstoon in Belize.
Transcript of the original document in Spanish.

C.A. 2 C 16

351. Manuscript: 20 leaves, handwritten; 28 cm.
English translation of the Spanish by Adela C. Breton, ca. 1915.

C.A. 2 C 16

352. Manuscript: 86 leaves, handwritten; 22 cm.
Corrections and suggestions by Charles P. Bowditch regarding the Breton translation.

C.A. 2 C 16

353. Manuscript: 4 leaves, handwritten; 28 cm.
Correspondence of Charles P. Bowditch with Adela C. Breton regarding Breton's translation of the Cano manuscript. Two letters, dated March 30, 1915 and April 2, 1915.

C.A. 2 C 16

354. Cárdenas y Valencia, Francisco de

   Relación historial eclesiástica de la provincia de Yucatán de
   la Nueva España, que se hizo en ella en virtud de cédula real
   del año de 1635, por el bachiller Francisco de Cárdenas y
   Valencia, clérigo de ella, para enviar al Consejo de Indias
   me remitió el mismo, y la recibí en 10 de noviembre de 1643.
   Manuscript: 68 leaves, photoreproduction; 29 cm.
   Original: British Museum, London.
                                            C.A. 2 C 178r

355. Carter, James R.

   The Presentation copy of Maya artifacts, photographed by James
   R. Carter, 1931 ... Cleveland : Privately printed by Louise
   Klein Miller and James R. Carter.
   Printed: 50 mounted photographs; 56 cm.
   Photographs of Maya pottery made in Mérida, Yucatán. With few
   exceptions, vessels photographed are from the collections of
   Julia Peón de Camara and Rafael de Regil C. Some were originally
   collected by Teobert Maler. Sites represented include Aké,
   Campeche, Chilib, Hochob, Itzincab, Jaina, Maxcanú, Peto, Sotutá,
   and Uxmal.
                                            C.A. 3 C 245p P

356. Carter, Wilbert K.

   A secondary ethnography of the Sierra Popoluca of Veracruz,
   1949.
   Manuscript: 173 leaves, typewritten; 28 cm.
                                            MEX 4 C 246s F

357. Case, Henry A.

   Views on and of Yucatán; besides notes upon parts of the
   State of Campeche and the territory of Quintana Roo ... Mérida
   de Yucatán : Published by Henry A. Case, 1911.
   Printed: 237 p.; 24 cm.
   Handwritten annotations throughout by Teobert Maler.
                                            C.A. 3 C 266v

358. Castellanos, Abraham

   Análisis y lectura del lienzo mixteco de Santa Maria Yolotepec,
   distrito de Juquilá, Oaxaca, México, 1917.
   Manuscript: 12 leaves, typewritten; 28 cm.
                                            MEX 3 C 276a

359. Chamberlain, Robert Stoner

   History of the conquest of Yucatán.
   Manuscript: 45 leaves, typewritten; 28 cm.
                                            C.A. 2 C 355h

360. Chavero, Alfredo [1841-1905]

    Calendario o rueda del año de los antiguos indios: estudio
    cronológicos por Alfredo Chavero ... México : Imprenta de
    Museo Nacional, 1901.
    Printed: 13 p.; 47 cm.
    Study of the falsified pictorial manuscript known as
    Colección Chavero no. 3. Many pencil notes throughout by
    Charles P. Bowditch.
                                            C.A. 6 X 49 E F

361. Copy-book containing drawings from various known Mexican
    Indian pictorial manuscripts, drawings of Mexican pyramids, and
    Egyptian, East Indian, and Javanese iconographic motifs and
    buildings; also contains copies of six pages of the Tonalamatl
    Aubin, a manuscript in the Bibliothèque Nationale, Paris,
    possibly by José Fernando Ramírez.
    Manuscript: 41 leaves; 30 cm.
    Contains the bookplate and stamp of Alfredo Chavero; some
    drawings have been cut out and removed.
                                            MEX 7 C 39c

362. Chilam Balam of Chumayel

    Manuscript: 107 leaves, photoreproduction; 26 cm.
    Copy made by Teobert Maler, ca. 1887, from the original in
    Mérida.
                                            C.A. 7 C 436ch

363. Manuscript: 9 leaves, typewritten; 28 cm.
    Photographs relative to Chichén Itzá from the manuscript of
    Chumayel, translated into Spanish by Ermilio Solís Acalá, 1926.
                                            C.A. 1 R 423b

364. Manuscript: 20 leaves, 60 cm.
    Galley-proof of the Maya text from the files of Alfred M. Tozzer.
                                            C.A. 7 C 436ch Tg P

365. Chilam Balam of Tusik

    Manuscript: 17 leaves, photoreproduction; 28 cm.
    Partially similar to the *Chilam Balam of Chumayel*; also contains
    legends and prayers. From negatives made for the Carnegie
    Institution in Washington in 1936 (Gibson and Glass 1975:387).
                                            PAM B

366. Clark, Charles Upson

    Manuscript notebooks containing excerpts copied from European
    archives in 1952-1953, relating to Spanish America.
    Manuscript: 1142 leaves bound in 6 vols., handwritten; 21 cm.
    Notes on historical material from archives in Barcelona, London,
    Madrid, and Seville.
                                            SPAN AM C 547m

367. Cline, Howard F.

A Provisional author list of Luis Vargas Rea publications,
1943-1955.
Manuscript: 30 leaves, typewritten; 28 cm.
Vargas Rea published more than 400 titles of historical
and literary interest, several uniquely published. Many
issues are of direct concern to Mexican ethnohistory.
MEX 10 C 615p F

368. Codex Borbonicus

Manuscript: 36 leaves, photoreproduction; 10 cm.
Original: Bibliothèque de l'Assemblée Nationale Française, Paris.
A preconquest or early 16th century ritual-calendrical screenfold
from Central Mexico. Includes four major sections: a tonalpohualli
or 260 day divinatory almanac, the association of the 9 Lords
of the Night with the year-bearer days for a 52-year period, an
18 month festival calendar for a New Fire ceremony year, and
additional month ceremonies. Photographed and mounted to form
a screenfold by Salvador Mateos H. (Glass and Robertson 1975:97-98).
MEX 7 B 644m

369. Codex Colombino [Falsified version]

Manuscript: 28 leaves, color facsimile; 36 cm.
A watercolor copy of 1912 and a five-page description dated
1916 by Manuel de Velasco. (Glass 1975:304).
MEX 7 C 717 F

370. Codex Cospi

Manuscript: 26 leaves, photoreproduction; 20 cm.
Original: Biblioteca Universitaria, Bologna.
Preconquest ritual-calendrical screenfold of the Borgia Group.
Includes aspects of the 260-day tonalamatl. Photographed and
mounted to form a screenfold by Salvador Mateo H. (Glass
and Robertson 1975:113).
MEX 7 C 821m

371. Codex Dresden

Manuscript: 74 leaves, color facsimile; 23 cm.
Original: Sächsische Landesbibliothek, Dresden.
Preconquest ritual-calendrical screenfold from the lowland Maya
region. Includes divinatory almanacs, multiplication tables
for synodical revolutions of the planet Venus, representations
of various ceremonies and deities, and other matters (Glass and
Robertson 1975:125-126).
C.A. 7 D 81

-114-

372. Codex Hemenway

Manuscript: 40 leaves, photoreproduction; 26 cm.
Original: Peabody Museum of Archaeology and Ethnology, Harvard
    University.
A techialoyan manuscript from San Antonio Huixquilucan, Mexico,
dated 1532. Original manuscript is of bark fiber and comes from
the collection of Zelia Nuttall, as of 1893 (Robertson and
Robertson 1975:273).

MEX 7 H 372h

373. Codex Kingsborough

Manuscript: 70 leaves, photoreproduction; 33 cm.
Original: British Museum, London.
Related to a lawsuit held before the Council of the Indies between
the Indians of Tepetlaoztoc and the encomendero, Juan Velásquez
de Salazar. Includes four major sections: introductory material
relating to the preconquest history, tribute, genealogy, and social
organization of Tepetlaoztoc, a yearly record of tribute and other
goods and services provided to various encomenderos by the
Indians from 1522 to 1554, and a textual conclusion to the
document and a petition (Glass and Robertson 1975:151).

MEX 7 T 26

374. Manuscript: 70 leaves, color facsimile; 38 cm.
A watercolor copy of the original by Annie G. Hunter, made ca.
1917-1918.

MEX 7 K 61t

375. Manuscript: 115 leaves, handwritten; 28 cm.
Spanish transcription of the original by Adela C. Breton.

MEX 7 K 61tr

376. Codex Laud

Manuscript: 46 leaves, color facsimile; 16 cm.
Original: Bodleian Library, Oxford.
Preconquest ritual-calendrical screenfold of the Borgia Group.
Most of its 11 sections develop aspects of the tonalpohualli,
the 260-day augural cycle (Glass and Robertson 1975:152-153).
A watercolor copy of the original by Annie G. Hunter.

MEX 7 L 363h

377. Codex Madrid

Manuscript: 14 leaves, photoreproduction; 21 cm.
Original: Museo de América, Madrid.
Preconquest ritual-calendrical screenfold from the lowland Maya
region. The content of the *Codex Madrid* appears to be primarily
concerned with divination. Photographed and mounted to form a
screenfold by Salvador Mateo H. (Glass and Robertson 1975:153-
155).

C.A. 7 C 818m

378. Codex Magliabecchiano XIII.3

    Manuscript: 13 leaves, typewritten; 28 cm.
    Original: Biblioteca Nazionale Centrale, Florence.
    Early 16th century ritual-calendrical document from the
    Valley of Mexico. Spanish text and English translation by
    Howard F. Cline of sections on death rituals.
                                        MEX 7 M 27bc

379. Codex Mexicanus (BNP 23-24)

    Manuscript: 53 leaves bound in 2 vols., photoreproduction; 53 cm.
    Original: Bibliothèque Nationale, Paris.
    Calendrical, historical, and genealogical document from the Valley
    of Mexico. Most of the codex contains pictorial annals from
    1168 through 1571, with some emphasis on the Tenochca-Mexica
    (Glass and Robertson 1975:165-166).
                                        MEX 7 M 574

380. Codex Nuttall

    Manuscript: 86 leaves, photoreproduction; 13 cm.
    Original: British Museum, London.
    Preconquest historical screenfold from western Oaxaca. Includes
    genealogical and historical sections on Tilantongo, Teozacoalco,
    and Cuilapan, and an incomplete history of 8 Deer from the
    marriage of his parents in 1009 and his birth in 1011 to the
    1050. Photographed and mounted as a screenfold by Salvador Mateos
    Higuera (Glass and Robertson 1975:176-177).
                                        MEX 7 N 963m

381. Codex Pérez

    Manuscript: 200 leaves, photoreproduction; 28 cm.
    Nineteenth century ritual-calendrical manuscript concerning Maní
    and other localities in Yucatán. Contains copies and extracts by
    Juan Pío Pérez of various Maya texts of the sort known as Books
    of Chilam Balam as well as several other documents. Includes
    correlations of Maya and Christian calendars, astrological and
    zodiacal material, almanacs, prophecies, historical data, and
    the *Chronicle of Maní* as well as an introduction by Crecencio
    Carrillo y Ancona (Glass and Robertson 1975:180-181; Gibson and
    Glass 1975:384-385).
                                        C.A. 7 P 416 P

382. Codex Xolotl

    Manuscript: 17 leaves, photoreproduction; 33 cm.
    Original: Bibliothèque Nationale, Paris.
    Sixteenth century historical and genealogical manuscript from
    the Texcoco region of Mexico. Includes a detailed Texcocan
    history of events in the Valley of Mexico from the arrival of
    the Chichimecs of Xolotl in a year 5 Tecpatl through events
    leading up to the Tepanec War (1427)(Glass and Robertson

1975:241).

                                                    MEX 7 X 74

383. Compendio en la lengua quiché.

    Manuscript: 226 leaves, handwritten; 21 cm.
    Includes a short Quiché vocabulary of 39 leaves, A through Sa.
    Acquired by Charles P. Bowditch through Robert Burkitt.
                                                    C.A. 6 Q 73

384. Conant, Kenneth

    Maya architecture.
    Manuscript: 9 leaves, typewritten; 28 cm.
                                                    C.A. 3 C 742m

385. Cooke, C. Wythe

    A possible solution of a Mayan mystery.
    Manuscript: 4 leaves, typewritten; 28 cm.
    A radio presentation made August 4, 1933 under the auspices
    of Science Service (Washington, D.C.) over the Columbia
    Broadcasting System outlining the geological causes of the
    Classic Maya collapse.
                                                    C.A. 3 C 774p

386. Cordy, N.

    The Maya year at the inauguration of the calendar, 1940.
    Manuscript: 14 leaves, typewritten; 28 cm.
                                                    C.A. 9 C 812m F

387. Coronel, Juan [1569-1651]

    Arte en lengua de maya.
    Manuscript: 47 leaves, typewritten; 28 cm.
    English translation of *Arte en lengua de maya* ... México :
    Imprenta de Diego Garrido por Adriano Cesar, 1620.
                                                    C.A. 6 C 81a 2

388. Cruz Cohuatzincatl, Francisco de la

    Pièce justificative d'un procès, entre Francisco de la Cruz
    Cohautzincatl, indio natural de Xochimilco, et Joachim Teocplatl,
    relativement à des immeubles, des champs et des loyers, México,
    13 octubre 1571.
    Manuscript: 30 leaves, photoreproduction; 33 cm.
    Original: Bibliothèque Nationale, Paris.
    Genealogical and economic (property plans) document, in Náhuatl,
    from Xochimilco (Glass and Robertson 1975:238).
                                                    MEX 7 C 889 F

389. Diccionario pocomchí-castellano y castellano-pocomchí de San
Cristóbal Cahcoh, ca. 1575.

Manuscript: 515 leaves, photoreproduction; 35 cm.
Original: Berendt-Brinton Collection, University of Pennsylvania.
"This is the work of a Dominican missionary, written about
the end of the sixteenth century. The whole appears to have
covered at least 900 leaves. These valuable remains were
presented to Dr. Berendt by the cura of San Cristóbal Cahcoh
in Guatemala. The writing is small but legible" (Brinton
1900:16). Photoreproduction for Charles P. Bowditch by the
Massachusetts Historical Society.

C.A. 6 D 5 F
C.A. 6 D 659 G Microfilm

390. Dieseldorff, Erwin Paul [1868-1940]

Ancient land titles of the Kekchí Indians, Cobán, 1903.
Manuscript: 8 leaves, typewritten; 28 cm.

C.A. 6 D 566 F

391. [Correspondence with Franz Boas and Frederick Ward Putnam
regarding publication of ancient Kekchí land titles, 1903].
Manuscript: 3 leaves, typewritten; 28 cm.
Includes three letters.

C.A. 6 D 566 F

392. Dimick, John M.

Zaculeu: su restauración por la United Fruit Company.
Manuscript: 28 leaves, typewritten; 28 cm.

C.A. 3 Un 3z S F

393. Dixon, Roland Burrage [1875-1934]

The heart and blood offering in Mexican sunworship, 1897.
Manuscript: 12 leaves, typewritten; 28 cm.

MEX 4 D 646h

394. Doctrina en lengua quiché.

Manuscript: 166 leaves, photoreproduction; 24 cm.
"The original of the volume belongs to Prof. Marshall E. Saville
of New York. He has allowed it to be copied by the Massachusetts
Historical Society. It is practically the same as the doctrina
in Quiché which was reproduced by William E. Gates in 1913,
Boston" (Bowditch note).

BBC/UP, LC
C.A. 6 D 65

395. Emerson, Harold

Interpretation of the Mayan calendar, parts 1 and 2, 1945.
Manuscript: 15 leaves, typewritten; 28 cm.
Issued by The Mayan Temple, Brooklyn, New York
C.A. 9 Em 34m F

396. The Mayan calendar for 1946, 1945.
Manuscript: 8 leaves, typewritten; 28 cm.
Issued by The Mayan Temple, Brooklyn, New York
C.A. 9 Em 34m F

397. Field, Henry

The Indians of Tepoztlán, Morelos, Mexico, 1949.
Manuscript: 131 leaves, typewritten; 28 cm.
"This statistical material supplements the anthrogeographical
study based on my researches in Morelos during 1945-1946."
MEX 5 F 445i

398. Förstemann, Ernst Wilhelm [1822-1906]

[Letter to Charles Pickering Bowditch from Ernst W. Förstemann
regarding the Codex Dresden, dated August 28, 1905, Charlottenburg,
Germany].
Manuscript: 3 leaves, typewritten; 28 cm.
C.A. 1 F 77 E F

399. Fowler, Henry

A Narrative of a journey across the unexplored portion of
British Honduras, with a short sketch of the history and
resources of the Colony ... Belize : Government Press, 1879.
Manuscript: 136 leaves, typewritten; 28 cm.
Transcription in English of the printed edition.
C.A. 1 F 82 F

400. Fuentes y Guzmán, Francisco Antonio de [c.1643-1700]

Recordación florida, discurso historial, natural, militar y
politica del reino de Guatemala.
Manuscript: 15 leaves, handwritten; 27 cm.
Translation into English of Volume II, Book III, Chapters 11-12,
relating to the hieroglyphic writing of the Pipil of Guatemala;
includes six leaves of facsimile.
C.A. 3 F 95

401. Manuscript: 14 leaves, photoreproduction; 27 cm.
Reproduction of Volume II, Book IV, Chapters 10-11, relating to
the ruins of Copán.
C.A. 3 F 95

402. Galindo, Juan [1802-1840]

    [Papers, plans, sketches, etc., relating to the archaeology, ethnology, geography, and history of Guatemala in the 1830's].
    Manuscript: 1 reel, 35mm microfilm.
    Original: Bibliothèque Nationale, Paris.
    Collection of Galindo papers originally from the Société de Géographie in Paris.
                           C.A. 1 G 133p

403. Gamio, Manuel [1883-1960]

    Excavaciones en Teotihuacán, Santa Lucía y Azcapotzalco.
    Manuscript: 10 leaves, typewritten; 36 cm.
    Includes 12 photographic plates of excavation views and 16 charcoal drawings of pottery fragments.
                           MEX 3 G 146e F

404. Gann, Thomas William Francis [1867-1938]

    The contents of some ancient mounds in Central America.
    Manuscript: 6 leaves, typewritten; 28 cm.
    Transcript of an article in *Proceedings of the Society of Antiquaries of London* 16:308-317, 1895.
                           C.A. 3 G 155c

405.   Exploration of two mounds in British Honduras.
    Manuscript: 3 leaves, typewritten; 28 cm.
    Transcript of article in *Proceedings of the Society of Antiquaries of London* 15:430-434, 1893.
                           C.A. 3 G 155e

406. Gaspar, Joseph

    The Merchant: an Aztec comedia.
    Manuscript: 38 leaves, typewritten; 28 cm.
    Translation by John Hubert Cornyn of original 1627 text by Joseph Gaspar of San Juan Bautista Tolancingo.
                           MEX 1 G 213m

407. Gates, William Edmund [1863-1940]

    Circumstances of Gates' acquisition and publishing of the Gomesta [manuscript], 1934-1935.
    Manuscript: 8 leaves, typewritten; 28 cm.
    Includes extracts of correspondence between W.E. Gates and Alfred M. Tozzer.
                           C.A. 9 G 585g S

408.   [Drawings of shoe vases in the Berendt and Sarg collections].
    Manuscript: 11 leaves, handwritten; 28 cm.
    Line drawings of shoe vessels from San Roque, Omtepe Island, Nicaragua, and Cobán, Guatemala.
                           MEX 1 M 68 F

409. Gates, William Edmund [1863-1940]

The published treatise in the Mayance and southern Mexican
languages, 1915.
Manuscript: 25 leaves, typewritten; 28 cm.
MEX 6 G 223u

410. Génin, Alexis Manuel Auguste

Mexican collections of Auguste Génin, 1920.
Manuscript: 73 leaves, typewritten; 29 cm.
Génin was director general of the Compañia Nacional Mexicana de
Dinamita y Explosivos and amassed a large collection of
archaeological and ethnographic objects from central and
southern Mexico. Volume includes photographs of Huichol Indians
and archaeological specimens from Mexico, Hidalgo, and Oaxaca.
MEX 1 G 28

411. Gerrodette, F.H.

The linguistic status of the Indians of Mexico and Central
America, 1891-1892.
Manuscript: 353 leaves, handwritten; 28 cm.
MEX 6 G 32

412. Goodman, Joseph T. [1838-1917]

[Working notes and drawings on Maya hieroglyphic writing].
Manuscript: 26 leaves, handwritten; 54 cm.
"Goodman charts. Apparently manuscript work of Joseph Goodman, left
by him to T.T. Waterman, literary executor. Transferred with all
Goodman manuscripts to the Peabody Museum by A.L. Kroeber.
A.M. Tozzer, August 1, 1922".
C.A. 3 G 622m P

413. Hamp, Eric

Linguistics.
Manuscript: 78 leaves, typewritten; 28 cm.
Descriptive sketches of the following languages: Chañabal, Chico-
muceltec, Chiapanec, Chinantec, Chol, Chontal, Cuicatec, Huave,
Lacandón, Mazatec, Mixe, Popoluca, Tojolabal, Tzeltal, Tzotzil,
Zapotec, Zoque, and proto-Zoquean.
C.A. 6 H 186i F

414. Hanke, Lewis

Proposal submitted to the Hakluyt Society in regard to publication
of Las Casas, 1933.
Manuscript: 9 leaves, typewritten; 28 cm.
"Contains a copy of a letter from Edward Lynam of the Hakluyt
Society to Hanke and a handwritten letter from the latter to
Professor Roland Dixon, concerning the above proposal".
SPAN AM H 194p

415. Harrison, Margaret W.

Bibliography of Afred V. Kidder, 1901-1946.
Manuscript: 8 leaves, typewritten; 28 cm.
REF K 538h 1947

416. Bibliography of Alfred V. Kidder, 1910-1943.
Manuscript: 7 leaves, typewritten; 28 cm.
REF K 538h

417. Healey, Giles Grenville

Photographs of the Lacandons, 1953.
Manuscript: 67 mounted plates in 2 portfolios; 66 cm.
Stills from a United Fruit Company motion picture entitled
The Living Maya. Includes photographs of Lacandón Maya from
Petha, Lagos Miramar, and El Cedro settlements. Subjects
include manufacture of bark cloth, corn planting, Miramar
settlement architecture, incense burners, flutes, and dug-out
canoes. Also in the collection are views of Structures 1 and
2 at Bonampak, and Structure 11 at Yaxchilán.
C.A. 4 H 349p E F

418. [Hernández, Magdalena]

Will of the widow of Luis Caal Hernández in the Kekchí
language, with a translation by Erwin P. Dieseldorff, 1903.
Manuscript: 5 leaves, typewritten; 28 cm.
C.A. 6 H 43w

419. Herrera y Tordesillas, Antonio de [1559-1625]

Historia general de los hechos de los castellanos en las islas
y Tierra Firme del mar oceano.
Manuscript: 17 leaves, typewritten; 28 cm.
Translation into English of Libro 10, Decada 55, Chapter 1,
relating to the siege by Montejo at Chichén Itzá, by O.G.
Ricketson.
C.A. 1 R 423b

420. Historia del pueblo de [San Pedro] Yolox en su congregación, en el
año de 1603.

Manuscript: 9 leaves, typewritten; 30 cm.
"The following 'history' refers to the village of San Pedro Yolox.
It is the unofficial capital of the nine towns forming the Upper
Chinantla or Chinantla Serrano, in the Sierra de Juárez, state of
Oaxaca, Mexico. This document was one among several copied from
the village archive during a residence in Yolox in 1942-43".
Transcript by Howard F. Cline in 1942.
MEX 2 Sa 58

421. Historia tolteca-chichimeca.

Manuscript: 50 leaves, photoreproduction; 33 cm.
Original: Bibliothèque Nationale, Paris.
Early 16th century historical manuscript from Cuauhtinchan,
Puebla. Recounts the migration of Nonoalca-Chichimeca and
Tolteca-Chichimeca peoples from Tula, the foundation of
Cuauhtinchan, their struggles with the Aztecs, and a history
of Cuauhtinchan during the early Spanish regime (Gibson and
Glass 1975:375; Glass and Gibson 1975:220-221).
MEX 7 H 629

422. Manuscript: 143 leaves, photoreproduction; 33 cm.
MEX 7 H 630 F

423. Hunter, Annie C.

[A short paper on native Mexican numeral values, 1920].
Manuscript: 2 leaves, typewritten; 28 cm.
Bound with *Codex Kingsborough*.
MEX 7 K 61tr

424. Jaramillo, Manuel Vicente

Gramática descriptiva y vocabulario del lenguaje mam, con las
pruebas y los materiales comparativos del quiché, 1918.
Manuscript: 569 leaves, typewritten; 28 cm.
C.A. 6 J 280g
C.A. 6 J 280g Microfilm

426. Kempton, J.H.

Preliminary report on the agricultural survey of Yucatán in 1935.
Manuscript: 10 leaves, typewritten; 28 cm.
C.A. 1 K 329p F

427. Kingsborough, Lord (King, Edward, Lord Kingsborough) [1795-1837]

Antiquities of Mexico comprising facsimiles of ancient Mexican
paintings and hieroglyphics, preserved in the royal libraries of
Paris, Berlin, and Dresden, in the Imperial Library of Vienna, in
the Vatican Library, in the Borgian Museum at Rome, in the Library
of the Institute at Bologna, and in the Bodleian Library at Oxford;
together with the monuments of New Spain, by M. Dupaix, with their
respective scales of measurements and accompanying descriptions;
the whole illustrated by many valuable inedited manuscripts, by
Lord Kingsborough; the drawings, on stone, by A. Aglio ...
London : Printed by James Moyes, 1831-1848.
Printed: 9 vols.; 57 cm.
Extensive pencil notes by Charles P. Bowditch.
MEX 3 K 58 P

428. LaFarge, Oliver [1901-1963]

> Chols, Chortis, and Putuns, ca. 1932-1933.
> Manuscript: 64 leaves, typewritten; 28 cm.
> C.A. 6 L 121c

429. [Correspondence with Ernest Noyes regarding Chol Maya linguistics, 1932-1933].

> Manuscript: 77 leaves, typewritten; 28 cm.
> C.A. 6 L 121c

430. Landa, Diego de [1524-1579]

> Relación de las cosas de Yucatán, sacada de lo que escribió el padre fray Diego de Landa, de la orden de San Francisco, ca. 1566.
> Manuscript: 69 leaves, photoreproduction; 24 cm.
> Original: Real Academia de la Historia, Madrid.
> Probably the most important source for the lowland Maya, history of the Spanish discovery, the conquest, ecclesiastical and native history, and Maya hieroglyphic writing.
> C.A. 4 L 23r 3
> C.A. 4 L 23r 5 P
> C.A. 4 L 23r 6 Microfilm

431. Manuscript: 162 leaves, typewritten; 28 cm.

> English translation by Charles P. Bowditch of the 1864 French translation of Brasseur de Bourbourg, and corrected from the 1881 Spanish edition issued by Juan de Dios de la Rada y Delgado (Rosny 1881).
> C.A. 4 L 23r E B

432. Manuscript: 24 leaves, photoreproduction; 23 cm.

> Photographs of illustrations from Landa.
> C.A. 4 L 23r 9

433. Lanz Trueba, Joaquín

> Algo de arqueología campechana, 1915.
> Manuscript: 9 leaves, typewritten; 35 cm.
> MEX 3 L 297r

434. [Letter to the Carnegie Institution of Washington submitting three papers which were published in a local Campeche, Mexico, newspaper, 1932].

> Manuscript: 2 leaves, typewritten; 28 cm.
> MEX 3 L 297r

435. [Letter from Frank F. Bunker recommending that three papers be forwarded to Alfred V. Kidder, 1932].

> Manuscript: 1 leaf, typewritten; 28 cm.
> MEX 3 L 297r

436. Lanz Trueba, Joaquín

La escritura jeroglífica maya, 1930.
Manuscript: 8 leaves, typewritten; 35 cm.
MEX 3 L 297r

437. Ruinas de la civilización maya en el estado de Campeche, de la
républica de México.
Manuscript: 9 leaves, typewritten; 35 cm.
MEX 3 L 297r

438. Lebrón de Quiñones, Lorenzo

Sumaria relación de la visita hecha por el Lic. Lorenzo
Lebrón de Quiñones, oidor alcalde mayor de Nueva Galicia
a Colima, 1554.
Manuscript: 165 leaves, typewritten; 28 cm.
MEX 2 L 493s

439. Lecocq, M.

Contributions à l'histoire de la civilisation dans l'Amérique
pré-Colombienne et faits connexes, 1890.
Manuscript: 18 leaves, handwritten; 28 cm.
C.A. 3 L 51c

440. León, Nicolás

Datos referentes a una especie nueva de escritura jeroglífica
en México, ca. 1905.
Manuscript: 29 leaves, handwritten; 28 cm.
General remarks about Mixtec and Zapotec pictorial manuscripts.
Pencil notes by Charles P. Bowditch.
MEX 9 L 55d

441. Lienzo de San Pedro Ixcatlan

Manuscript: 1 leaf, facsimile; 256 cm.
Original: Robert Garrett Collection, Princeton University.
Cartographic and historical map from San Pedro Ixcatlán, Tuxtepec
district, northern Oaxaca. This is an ink tracing on linen of the
original.
MEX 7 T 894

442. Lincoln, Jackson Steward [d. 1949]

An ethnological study of the Ixil Indians of the Guatemala
highlands.
Manuscript: 224 leaves, typewritten; 28 cm.
Includes miscellaneous handwritten notes on calendrics and
cofradía organization, extracts from the Nebaj parish register
1835-1856, draft of a manuscript entitled "A newly recorded old
Quiché calendar among the Ixil of Guatemala in 1939-1940."
C.A. 4 L 638e

443. Lincoln, Jackson Steward [d. 1949]

    [Field notes on the Ixil Indians of the Guatemala highlands,
    1939-1941].
    Manuscript: 6 vols., handwritten; 16 cm.
                                                    C.A. 4 L 638f

444. Lizana, Bernardo de [1581-1631]

    History of Yucatán.
    Manuscript: 147 leaves, typewritten; 28 cm.
    Translation into English of 1893 (México : Museo Nacional de
    México) edition with pencil notes by Charles P. Bowditch.
                                                    C.A. 2 L 768h E P

445. Manuscript: 15 leaves, typewritten; 28 cm.
    Translation into English of Chapters I-IV, and partial translation
    of Chapter VI, relating to the foundation and history of Izamal,
    by O.V. Klock.
                                                    C.A. 2 L 768h E
                                                    C.A. 2 L 768h E K

446. Lothrop, Samuel Kirkland [1892-1965]

    Notes on Guatemalan textiles, 1928.
    Manuscript: 29 leaves, typewritten; 28 cm.
                                                    C.A. 4 L 914n

447. The southeastern frontier of the ancient Maya, ca. 1939.
    Manuscript: 20 leaves, typewritten; 28 cm.
                                                    C.A. 3 L 914s

448. McBryde, Felix Webster

    Summary of field work done in Sololá, Guatemala, 1932.
    Manuscript: 3 leaves, typewritten; 28 cm.
    "The emphasis of this report is laid on the products sold in
    the Sololá market, their origin, distribution, and use".
                                                    C.A. 1 C 215f

449. McDougall, Elsie

    [Letter to Alfred M. Tozzer regarding Paul Wirsing and his
    Kekchí linguistic research, 1932].
    Manuscript: 3 leaves, handwritten; 28 cm.
                                                    C.A. 6 W 748m

450. Maldonado de Matos, Manuel

    Arte de la lengua szinca, con algunas reflexiones críticas al
    arte cakchiquel; compuesto por el Mtro.Dn. Manuel Maldonado
    de Matos, cura proprio del partido de Santiago Sacatepéquez,
    dedícalo al Ilmo. Señor Dor.Dn. Pedro Cortés y Larraz, del
    consejo de Su Majestad, dignísimo arzobispo de Guathemala, 1770.

Manuscript: 153 leaves, handwritten; 27 cm.
Original: Tozzer Library, Harvard University.
"The present manuscript was found in the city of Guatemala
during the winter of 1917 in the hands of a priest, and was
acquired during the winter of 1918 ... it is thus far the
only work on the language to come to light" (Saville note).
"The original must have been in the possession of the former
Franciscan Father Daniel Sánchez García who published the
Gramatica de la lengua cakchiquel [of Carlos J. Rosales,
1748], 1920" (pencil note by Charles P. Bowditch). Includes
108 leaves of the *Arte* and 45 leaves of the *Vocabulario*.
C.A. 6 M 29a
C.A. 6 M 29a Microfilm

451.   Manuscript: 153 leaves, photoreproduction; 27 cm.
Original: Tozzer Library, Harvard University.
Photoreproduction for Charles P. Bowditch by the Massachusetts
Historical Society, Boston.
C.A. 6 M 29a 1918

452. Maler, Teobert [1842-1917]
Chichén.
Manuscript: 15 leaves, typewritten; 28 cm.
English translation of an article in *Revista de Yucatán*, Mérida,
July 21-28, 1926; comprises a criticism of the work of Edward
H. Thompson at Chichén Itzá.
C.A. 3 M 293c

453.   Historia de las ruinas de Chichén Itzá.
Manuscript: 63 leaves, typewritten; 28 cm.
"This copy from a typewritten copy made in Mérida from the
article as republished in a pamphlet; original in *La Prensa*,
Mérida, 1910 and republished as a pamphlet of 34 leaves, 1926".
C.A. 3 M 293h
C.A. 3 M 293yu

454.   Impressions of a trip to the ruins of Cobá and Chichén
Itzá.
Manuscript: 7 leaves, typewritten; 28 cm.
A summarized and abridged translation of *Impresiones de
viaje a las ruinas de Cobá y Chichén Itzá* ... Mérida : Imprenta
José E. Rosaldo, 1932.
C.A. 3 M 293i E

455. Manuscrito nahua del siglo XVI; redactado entre los años 1572 y 1585,
siendo papa Gregorio XIII; empastado probablemente a fines del
siglo XIX o principio del XX; maltratado después de empastado,
empieza con las palabras izcatqui yca quiztica; tratase de un
libro relacionado con reformas al calendario y temas conexos
(medicina y agricultura) relacionados con los estudios astronómicos.

Manuscript: 1 reel, 35 mm microfilm
Contents include: Explicación de la bula de la Santa Cruzada
y lista de las días en que se alcanza indulgencia plenaria,
Reportorio, Sobre la caridad, Anatomía y medicina, De los
vientos, De las horas, días y noches, manera de contar en el
reportorio, Horóscopo según los meses, Anatomía y medicina,
Agricultura, Calendario y astrología, Medicina, Horoscopo según
las planetas, Hierbas medicinales, and Calendario y astrología.
Original manuscript comprises 105 leaves.
MEX 4 M 319 Microfilm

456. Mapa de Cuauhtlantzinco

Manuscript: 1 leaf, color facsimile; 357 cm.
A 17th or 18th century historical document from San Juan
Cuauhtlantzinco, Puebla, Mexico. A complete watercolor copy,
presumably a copy of the Ramírez copy (Glass and Robertson
1975:120-121).
MEX

457. Mappa Reinisch

Manuscript: 2 leaves, photoreproduction; 48 cm.
Original: Bibliothèque Nationale, Paris.
A genealogical document, glossed in Náhuatl, from the
Oxtoticpac-Texcoco region of Mexico, ca. 1586 (Glass and
Robertson 1975:186).
MEX 8 M 322m

458. Martínez Hernández, Juan [1866-1959]

[Papers regarding Maya calendrics and historical manuscripts,
1910-1928].
Printed: 167 p.; 24 cm.
Includes offprints of the following: Los grandes ciclos de la
historia maya según el manuscrito de Chumayel (*Reseña de la
segunda sesion del XVII Congreso Internacional de Americanistas,
México*, 1912), Tabla astronómica del codice de Dresden (*Boletín
de la Universidad Nacional del Sureste*, 1926), Paralelismo entre
los calendarios maya y azteca, su correlación con la calendario
juliano (*Diario de Yucatán*, 1926), Crónicas maya: crónicas de
Yaxkukul (*Diario de Yucatán*, 1926), Crónicas mayas (*Diario
de Yucatán*, 1927), Crónica de Maní (*Boletín de la Universidad
Nacional del Sureste*, n.d.), Significación cronológica de los
ciclos mayas (*Proceedings of the XIII International Congress
of Americanists, New York*, 1928). Extensive pencil notes by
Alfred M. Tozzer; also a letter from Juan Martínez Hernández
to Alfred M. Tozzer regarding Maya calendrics, March 30, 1926.
MEX 8 M 366p

459. [Maya catechism, 1887]

Manuscript: 90 leaves, handwritten; 22 cm.

Yucatec-Spanish catechism from Ticul, Yucatán.
MS S 451

460. Mayas: antiquities and culture,a bibliographical list, 1927.
Manuscript: 8 leaves, typewritten; 28 cm.
Prepared by W.A. Slade, Chief Bibliographer, Library of
Congress, March 29, 1927.
C.A. 1 Un 3m 2

461. Mayas: antiquities and culture, a list of recent references,
supplementing list of March 29, 1927.
Manuscript: 12 leaves, typewritten; 28 cm.
Prepared by Florence S. Hellman, acting Chief Bibliographer,
New York Public Library.
C.A. 1 Un 3m 3

462. [Miscellaneous land documents from Maní, Yucatán, 1557-1813]
Manuscript: 5 leaves, photoreproduction; 26 cm.
Original: Archivo General de la Conquista, Mexico
Photographic copies made by Franz Blom in 1927 and deposited in
the Middle American Research Institute (Latin American Library)
at Tulane University. Partially published by John L. Stephens
(1841:2:263-268), 1843.
C.A. 6 Ar 2

463. Molé, Harvey E.

The Abbé Brasseur de Bourbourg.
Manuscript: 28 leaves, typewritten; 28 cm.
Paper read at the residence of Reginald L. Jones, The Monday
Night Club, Summit, New Jersey, May 21, 1945.
C.A. 1 B 736m

464. Morán, Francisco

Arte en lengua choltí que quiere decir lengua de milperos, 1695.
Manuscript: 24 leaves, typewritten; 28 cm.
Anonymously edited and copied from a photographic copy in the
Gates Collection, library of the Middle American Research
Institute, Tulane University; includes comparative notes by
Oliver LaFarge.
C.A. 6 M 793a 4

465. Confesionario en lengua choltí, escrito en el pueblo de San
Lucas Salac del Chol, 1685.
Manuscript: 59 leaves, typewritten; 28 cm.
Text and English translation by Oliver LaFarge and Ernest
Noyes, ca. 1932-1933.
C.A. 6 L 121c

466. Morán, Francisco

Vocabulario en lengua choltí de Francisco Morán, 1695.
Manuscript: 110 leaves, typewritten; 28 cm.
Transcript by Ernest Noyes of a photoreproduction of the
original text in the library of the Middle American Research
Institute, Tulane University, 1932.
C.A. 6 M 793vo

467. Manuscript: 38 leaves, typewritten; 28 cm.
Spanish-Chol vocabulary rearranged from Morán by J.E.S.
Thompson, 1945.
C.A. 6 M 793v

468. Morley, Sylvanus Griswold [1883-1948]

The Ancient Maya ... Stanford : Stanford University Press, 1946
Printed: 520 p.; 24 cm.
Annotations throughout by Alfred M. Tozzer.
C.A. 3 M 827an

469. Anthropology 9 notes: Middle American archaeology, Harvard
University.
Manuscript: 44 leaves, handwritten; 27 cm.
Class notes from 45 lectures delivered by Alfred M. Tozzer
between October 3, 1907 and January 22, 1908.
ANT M 827a

470. Check-list of the Corpus Inscriptionum Mayarum and check-list
of all initial and supplementary series. 1948.
Manuscript: 97 leaves, typewritten; 28 cm.
"Includes all known examples of the Maya hieroglyphic texts
carved upon stone or wood, or moulded with stucco, as well as
all known Initial Series (449); it does not contain, except in
the case of Initial Series and the two Period Ending dates
(no. 69 and 125), those texts which are either painted upon
pottery or frescoes, or those engraved upon jade, bone, shell,
or metal, a very much smaller group" (Morley note).
C.A. 7 M 827c F

471. Deluge myths of Central America and Mexico, 1904.
Manuscript: 29 leaves, handwritten; 27 cm.
ANT M 827d

472. Field diaries of the east coast of Yucatán and Honduras, 1918 and
1922.
Manuscript: 149 leaves, typewritten; 28 cm.
Includes a letter of transmittal of entree for 1922 from the
Carnegie Institution of Washington to Samuel K. Lothrop. Entries
for 1918 relate to Honduras and 1922 material to a trip up the
east coast of Yucatán.
C.A. 3 M 827di

-130-

473. Morley, Sylvanus Griswold [1883-1948]

The four principal gods of the Maya codices and their name glyphs, 1908.
Manuscript: 168 leaves, handwritten; 35 mm microfilm
Morley's A.M. thesis submitted to Harvard University.
C.A. 9 M 827f Microfilm

474. The occurrence and representation of the death deity in the Maya codices, 1908.
Manuscript: 25 leaves, typewritten; 28 cm.
C.A. 9 M 827o

475. Muñoz, Juan Bautista

Cópia de los manuscritos que recogió en sus viajes don Juan Bautista Muñoz y se entregaron en su muerte a Su Majestad; sacada de la Biblioteca Valenciana de don Justo Pastor Fustér, Valencia, 1827.
Manuscript: 557 leaves, handwritten; 21 cm.
Handwritten copy of the original two folio volumes; compiled by José Fernando Ramírez.
MS M 92

476. Noticias de varias plantas [de Yucatán] y sus virtudes.
Manuscript: 13 leaves, typewritten; 28 cm.
C.A. 4 N 845

477. Nuttall, Zelia María Magdalena [1857-1933]

Fresh light on ancient American civilizations and calendars: a summary, ca. 1925.
Manuscript: 4 leaves, typewritten; 28 cm.
C.A. 9 N 963f

478. [Ossado, Ricardo]

Libro de judío [medicina] en lengua maya.
Manuscript: 78 leaves, handwritten; 16 cm.
This manuscript was given to A. LePlongeon by Apolonia Tibaja in Mérida, April 18, 1883.
C.A. 6 Os 7 L

479. Medicina dómestica y descripción de los nombres y virtudes de las yerbas indígenas de Yucatán y las enfermadades a que se aplican, que dejó manuscrito el famoso médico romano don Ricardo Ossado, el judío, que vivió en el pueblo de Valladolid en el siglo diez y siete; siendo ésta copia fiel del original manuscrito que dejó la señora doña Petrona Carrillo de Valladares de Ticul.
Manuscript: 34 leaves, typewritten; 28 cm.
C.A. 4 Os 7m

480. Oviedo y Valdés, Gonzalo Fernández de [1478-1557]

Historia general y natural de las Indias, Islas y Tierra
Firme del Mar Oceano.
Manuscript: 147 leaves, typewritten; 28 cm.
Translation into English of Part III, Book IV, Chapters I-III
and XI-XIII, relating to Nicaragua by Alice Gillespie of 1851
(Madrid : Imprenta de la Real Academia de la Historia) edition.
SPAN AM Ov 4hi
SPAN AM Ov 4hi Microfilm

481. Papers of Itzcuintepec

Manuscript: 12 leaves, photoreproduction; 26 cm.
Original: British Museum, London.
A 16th century historical and genealogical document from
northern Puebla in Mexico. Comprises an incomplete set of
photographs of the papers (together with photographs of the
Lienzo de Tecciztlán y Tequatepec), attributed to Teobert Maler
(Glass and Robertson 1975:143-144).
MEX 7 T 82

482. Paso y Troncoso, Francisco del [1842-1916]

Pictorial writing: the Codex Kingsborough and what it teaches
us.
Manuscript: 8 leaves, typewritten; 28 cm.
English translation from the Spanish by Eduardo Noguera.
MEX 7 K 61tr

483. Pasquelle

Drawings of Copán pottery in the Peabody Museum [of Archaeology
and Ethnology, Harvard University].
Manuscript: 33 plates, handwritten; 41 cm.
Partially colored line drawings.
C.A. 3 P 265d F

484. Paxbolon, Pablo

Relación of don Pablo Paxbolon in the Chontal language of
Acalán-Tixchel, Campeche, México, 1614.
Manuscript: 17 leaves, photoreproduction; 18 cm.
Original: Archivo General de Indias, Seville.
The Chontal text provides valuable data relating to the
political organization and religion of Acalán and to various
historical events.
C.A. 6 P 289r
MEX 6 P 289r

485.   Manuscript: 26 leaves, typewritten; 28 cm.
Typewritten transcript of original; includes notes by J.E.S.
Thompson.
C.A. 6 P 289r

486. Payne, A.W.

[Letter to Oliver G. Ricketson regarding the prehispanic population of Yucatán, June 20, 1932].
Manuscript: 10 leaves, typewritten; 28 cm.
Includes several leaves on the indigenous population of Yucatán from 1549, 1609, 1639, and 1757 enumerations, summary population figures from Cárdenas y Valencia's *Relación historial eclesiástica* of 1643, and population figures from the 1757 summary of Ignacio Padilla.
C.A. 5 P 292p F

487. [Letter to France V. Scholes regarding the prehispanic population of Yucatán, March 7, 1932].
Manuscript: 7 leaves, typewritten; 28 cm.
Includes several leaves on population figures based upon Vásquez de Espinosa and the Yucatán tax list of 1551.
C.A. 5 P 292p F

488. Pérez, José Pío

Cronología de Yucatán.
Manuscript: 20 leaves, handwritten; 23 cm.
Transcription of an original manuscript made by Pérez and later owned by Brasseur de Bourbourg. The original apparently existed in Yucatán about 1840; this version was purchased in Guatemala ca. 1860-1880 by Helen J. Sanborn.
C.A. 8 P 41

489. Pinart, Alfonso L. [1852-1911]

Vocabulario castellano-cuna, compuesto por el Sr. don Alfonso L. Pinart, 1882.
Manuscript: 20 leaves, typewritten; 31 cm.
C.A. 6 P 65v

490. Pláticas de la historia sagrada en lengua kekchí del siglo XVII.

Manuscript: 126 leaves, photoreproduction; 26 cm.
Original: Berendt-Brinton Collection, University of Pennsylvania. "Several of the leaves are nearly destroyed, and the whole is much stained" (Brinton 1900:18). Reproduction of the original made for Charles P. Bowditch by the Massachusetts Historical Society.
C.A. 6 P 69

491. Popenoe, Dorothy Hughes [1899-1932]

The pre-Columbian bells of Mexico and Central America, ca. 1927.
Manuscript: 23 leaves, typewritten; 28 cm.
SPAN AM P 811c

492. Popol Vuh

Popol Vuh o libro sagrado.
Manuscript: 124 leaves, handwritten; 23 cm.
Transcription, in Spanish, of a manuscript in Guatemala,
possibly by Brasseur de Bourbourg; purchased in Guatemala
by Helen J. Sanborn ca. 1860-1880.
C.A. 8 P 41

493. Prokosch, Eric

Chamula government.
Manuscript: 35 leaves, typewritten; 28 cm.
MEX 4 P 943c F

494. Quaderno de idioma zapoteco del valle, que contiene algunas
reglas las más comunes del arte, un vocabulario algo copioso,
un confesionario, y otras cosas que verá el cristiano lector;
se ha escrito procurando todo lo posible imitar la pronunciación
natural de los indios; sacado lo más de los autores antiguos
que escribieron de este idioma; sea todo a mayor honra y gloria
de Dios Ntro. Señor alivio de los ministros y utilidad de las
almas, señor Martin Filcapete y juno. 22, 1793.

Manuscript: 288 leaves bound in 2 vols., photoreproduction; 26 cm.
Original: John Carter Brown Library, Brown University.
Photoreproduction made for Charles P. Bowditch by the
Massachusetts Historical Society.
MEX 6 G 93 1918

495. [Quaderno de los naturales del pueblo de Santa María Magdalena
en lengua tzotzil].

Manuscript: 3 leaves, photoreproduction; 18 cm.
Photoreproduction of the original manuscript in Chiapas made
by Giles Healey, 1950.
C.A. 4 Sa 59c

496. Quaderno en que constan los documentos de tierras de la
hacienda [de] San Juan Bautista Tabí en idioma maya o
yucateca, 1569-1808.

Manuscript: 7 leaves, photoreproduction; 28 cm.
Original: Latin American Library, Tulane University.
Includes translations in Spanish and Yucatec Maya.
C.A. 6 T 19

497. [Quiché-Cakchiquel religious chants].

Manuscript: 54 leaves, handwritten; 17 cm.
"Presented to the Peabody Museum by V.M. Cutter, December 19,
1925" (pencil note). Includes only pages 21 through 135.
C.A. 8 Q 40

-134-

498. Ramos, Félix

    Vocabulario español-paya, ca. 1945.
    Manuscript: 49 leaves, handwritten; 22 cm.
    C.A. 6 R 147v

499. Ransome, Jack C.

    A survey of southern Mexico, ca. 1945.
    Manuscript: 60 leaves, typewritten; 28 cm.
    "A small part of a project organized by cultural anthropologists
    to investigate the cultural continuity of seventeen Indian
    linguistic groups of southern Mexico."
    MEX 4 R 174s F

500. Relación de Michoacán

    Relación de las ceremonias y ritos y población y gobernación
    de los indios de la provincia de Michoacán, hecha al ilustrísimo
    Sr. don Antonio de Mendoza, virrey y gobernador de esta Nueva
    España por Su Majestad, ca. 1540.
    Manuscript: 147 leaves, photoreproduction; 37 cm.
    Original: Biblioteca de Monasterio de El Escorial, Madrid.
    An important ethnographic and historical report on pre-Spanish
    Tarascan Michoacán; includes written text and illustrations
    (Gibson and Glass 1975:325; Glass and Robertson 1975:167-168).
    MEX 4 R 279t F

501. Relaciones de Yucatán

    Manuscript: 233 leaves, typewritten; 28 cm.
    Translation into English of *Relaciones de Yucatán I. Colección
    de Documentos inéditos relativos al descubrimiento, conquista
    y organización de las antiguas posesiones españolas de ultramar*,
    tomo 11 ... Madrid : Tipográfico Sucesores de Rivadeneyra, 1898.
    SPAN AM c 671 (v.11) E

502. Ricketson, Oliver Garrison [1894-1952]

    A brief history of Chichén Itzá.
    Manuscript: 8 leaves, typewritten; 28 cm.
    C.A. 1 R 423b

503. Chichén Itzá in the Spanish era.
    Manuscript: 5 leaves, typewritten; 28 cm.
    C.A. 1 R 423b

504. Data bearing on the water supply of Yucatán.
    Manuscript: 5 leaves, typewritten; 28 cm.
    C.A. 1 R 423b

505. Index of ruins in the Maya area, compiled by O.G. Ricketson, Jr.
    and F. Blom, 1924-1925.
    Manuscript: 92 leaves, typewritten; 28 cm.

C.A. 3 R 42.1 ind

506. Ricketson, Oliver Garrison [1894-1952]

Information for expeditions based in Belize, by O.G. Ricketson,
Jr., E.B. Ricketson, and A.L. Smith, 1931.
Manuscript: 8 leaves, typewritten; 28 cm.
"The information herein contained describe the local and
hence highly specialized conditions to be met by expeditions
into the Maya area when based in Belize, British Honduras."
C.A. 3 R 42.1 inf

507. Rivard, Jean-Jacques

Modern Yucatec Maya-Spanish vocabulary, 1968.
Manuscript: 1316 leaves bound in two vols., typewritten; 30 cm.
Contains about 40,000 entries.
C.A. 6 R 522m

508. Riveiro, Tomás

Explicación de la doctrina cristiana en lengua kekchí;
sermones en lengua kekchí; traducción del español por don
Tomás Riveiro, 1798-1799.
Manuscript: 68 leaves, typewritten; 28 cm.
Typewritten translation of the original manuscript by William
E, Gates; contains a few passages in the original Kekchí with
Spanish translations.
C.A. 6 Ex 73r 4

509. [Rockstroh, Edwin]

Los indígenas de la América Central y sus idiomas.
Manuscript: 17 leaves, photoreproduction; 22 cm.
"Probably by Dr. Rockstroh, Guatemala, 1877 or 78, under
the direction of Dr. Berendt" (Gates note).
C.A. 6 B 452m

510. Rosny, León de

Repertoire biographique et bibliographique de la litterature
Yucateque, composé d'après des notes inédites extraits des
papiers de Lucien de Rosny.
Manuscript: 137 leaves, handwritten; 29 cm.
C.A. 10 R 733r

511. Roys, Ralph Loveland [1879-1965]

Critical Maya text of the katun prophecies in the Books of
Chilam Balam, series I.
Manuscript: 20 leaves, typewritten; 28 cm.
C.A. 7 R 816c

512. Roys, Ralph Loveland [1879-1965]

Guide to the Codex Pérez, ca. 1945.
Manuscript: 41 leaves, typewritten; 28 cm.
C.A. 7 R 816g

513. [Historical source material for the history of Mayapán].
Manuscript: 53 leaves, typewritten; 28 cm.
C.A. 2 R 816h F

514. [Letter to A.V. Kidder regarding work in Yucatán during the winter of 1935].
Manuscript: 19 leaves, typewritten; 28 cm.
Includes two maps of northern Yucatán.
C.A. 1 R 8161 F

515. Ruppert, Karl [1895-1960]

Album of unpublished photographs of monuments and rubbings of inscriptions at Calakmul, La Muñeca, Río Bec II, Río Bec V, Alta Mira, Naachtun, Oxpemul, Balakbal, Uxul, Pasión del Cristo, y y Pechal, ca. 1934.
Manuscript: 53 mounted photographs; 37 cm.
The monuments are described in *Archaeological reconnaissance in Campeche, Quintana Roo, and Petén*, by Karl Ruppert and John H. Denison, Jr., Carnegie Institution of Washington, Publication 543, 1943.
C.A. 3 R 878a F

516. Field diary of the Seventeenth Central American Expedition of the Carnegie Institution of Washington, 1934.
Manuscript: 295 leaves bound in 2 vols., typewritten; 24 cm.
Describes Carnegie Institution of Washington fieldwork in Campeche, Quintana Roo, and Petén; sites include Aguada Las Tuchas, Aguada Piu, Aguada Tres Marías, Aguada Venado, Alta Mira, Aurora, Balakbal, Becan, Carmelita, Delicia, Marihuana, Pasadita, Placeres, San Lorenzo, and Victoria.
C.A. 3 R 878s

517. Ruz Lhullier, Alberto [1906-1979]

Maya zone, January 1948: archaeological investigations in Kabáh and Uxmal, Yucatan, financed by Benjamin B. Félix, 1948.
Manuscript: 87 leaves, typewritten; 28 cm.
Includes both English and Spanish versions.
MEX 3 R 949m

518. Sahagún, Bernardino de [1499-1590]

Historia general de las cosas de Nueva España.
Manuscript: 314 leaves, typewritten; 32 cm.
English translation by Sara Jay Parker of Books I and II of Bustamente's (México : Imprenta de Galván, 1829-1830) translation

Sahagún; concerned with deities, feasts, and sacrifices of the Aztecs.

MEX 4 Sa 19hg E P

519. Sahagún, Bernardino de [1499-1590]

Historia general de las cosas de Nueva España.
Manuscript: 160 leaves of mounted plates; 34 cm.
Incomplete collection of colored plates made by J. Cooper Clark, with a manuscript list of illustrations. "These plates made from original illustrations in the Florentine manuscript of Sahagún at the expense of Charles Pickering Bowditch". Includes a typewritten letter from Alfred M. Tozzer to Ingersoll Bowditch regarding the collection, April 15, 1926, and a separate notebook of 80 leaves listing individual illustrations by Sahagún chapter.

MEX 7 Sa 19h 2 F

520. Sánchez de Aguilar, Pedro [1555-1648]

Informe contra idolorum cultores del obispado de Yucatán, 1639.
Manuscript: 26 leaves, typewritten; 28 cm.
Miscellaneous extracts from the 1639 (Madrid : Viuda de Juan González) edition regarding the Cucul and Xiu families, Yucatec calendrics, history, and so forth.

MEX 1 M 68 E F
MEX 1 M 68 E Microfilm

521. [Sánchez Salazar, Manuel]

How St. Helen found the Holy Cross; Aztec text by Manuel Sánchez Salazar.
Manuscript: 42 leaves, typewritten; 35 mm microfilm.
Translated into English in 1932 by John Hubert Cornyn. "Seventy years after the conquest, all plays written by Náhuatl-speech Indians were in Aztec metre, written for memorizing by rhythm; Cornyn had Indians dance the Lord's Prayer in Aztec while reciting it ... priest complained".

MEX 1 Sa 55h Microfilm

522. Scholes, France Vinton

[Letter to Alfred V. Kidder regarding the relación of don Pablo Paxbolon, June 21, 1943].
Manuscript: 1 leaf, typewritten; 28 cm.

MEX 6 P 289r

523. [Letter to Oliver G. Ricketson regarding the prehispanic population of Yucatán, May 5, 1932].
Manuscript: 3 leaves, typewritten; 28 cm.
Discussion of 1549 and 1570 tax lists and relevant materials in Spanish archives.

C.A. 5 P 292p F

524. Scholes, France Vinton

[Letter to Oliver G. Ricketson regarding the prehispanic
population of Yucatán, August 31, 1932].
Manuscript: 1 leaf, handwritten; 28 cm.
Discussion of primary sources, including Yucatán tax lists
and López de Velasco.

C.A. 5 P 292p F

525. Schuller, Rudolf R. [d. 1932]

Antiquities of Nicaragua.
Manuscript: 2 leaves, typewritten; 28 cm.

C.A. 3 Sch 81a

526. Extracts from a comparative and analytic dictionary of the
Maya-Quiché-Carib-Arawák languages, 1919-1929.
Manuscript: 284 leaves, typewritten; 28 cm.
Comparative wordlists for Cakchiquel, Chaneabal, Choltí,
Chortí, Kekchí, Mam, Pokomám, Pokonchí, Popoluca, Quiché,
Tzeltal, Tzotzil, and Tzutuhil, compiled from various written
dictionaries.

C.A. 6 Sch 8 F

527. Materials for vocabularies and bibliographies of Central
American and South American languages, compiled by R.R. Schuller,
from the works of Thiele, Sapper, Morán, etc.
Manuscript: 20 packages of typewritten notes in two metal
boxes; 22 cm.

C.A. 6 Sch 81m

528. On the Bowditch-Gates Collection of photostat reproductions
of Central American manuscripts in the Peabody Museum library,
ca. 1931.
Manuscript: 225 leaves, handwritten; 21 cm.
C.A. 6 C 280 Microfilm
C.A. 6 Sch 8o F

529. En torno del libro Popol Vuh, 1928.
Manuscript: 29 leaves, typewritten; 28 cm.
Transcription of an article in *Nuestro Diario*, Guatemala,
November 13, 1928.

C.A. 4 Sch 8 F

530. Sermones en lengua pokonchí, ca. 1575.

Manuscript: 192 leaves, handwritten; 25 cm.
Important for its early date and general lack of available
Pokonchí material.

C.A. 6 Se 6

531. Souls and testamentary executors [an Aztec dance text].

Manuscript: 24 leaves, typewritten; 35 mm microfilm.
Translated into English in 1931 from the Aztec by John
Hubert Cornyn. Note on manuscript states "Copied by the
undersigned from the original which was in his possession,
July 1899, [signed] Lic. Faustino Chimalpopoca Galicia Y.".
MEX 1 So 83 Microfilm

532. Spinden, Herbert Joseph [1879-1967]

A digest of recent work in Maya astronomy, 1935.
Manuscript: 13 leaves, typewritten; 28 cm.
A critique of Ludendorff's Palenque research.
C.A. 9 Sp 46di F

533. A final word on the Maya correlation, ca. 1940.
Manuscript: 4 leaves, typewritten; 36 cm.
The supplementary series as a count of solar eclipses with an
cumulative error.
C.A. 9 Sp 46f P

534. The historical position of the Toltecs.
Manuscript: 9 leaves, typewritten; 28 cm.
Incomplete manuscript.
C.A. 3 Sp 46h

535. History of the study of Mayan hieroglyphs, ca. 1930.
Manuscript: 31 leaves, typewritten; 28 cm.
"This unsigned manuscript was found in the office files of
Professor A.M. Tozzer after the latter's death. Internal references
clearly identify the author as H.J. Spinden. One such reference
is that on page 20, to the 13 months of 28 days. The date of
the manuscript is later than 1928 as there is a reference to
the Genet edition of Landa. The absence of references to Ludendorff
suggests a date of about 1930. The manuscript appears never
to have been completed or published."
C.A. 9 Sp 46h F

536. The status of the Olmeca.
Manuscript: 4 leaves, typewritten; 28 cm.
C.A. 4 Sp 46s

537. The Totonacs.
Manuscript: 4 leaves, typewritten; 28 cm.
C.A. 1 Sp 46t

538. Weaknesses of Mexican chronology, ca. 1940.
Manuscript: 4 leaves, typewritten; 28 cm.
MEX 1 Sp 46w

539. Spinden, Herbert Joseph [1879-1967]

The zodical calendar of the Maya, 1941.
Manuscript: 7 leaves, typewritten; 28 cm.
C.A. 9 Sp 46z F

540. Squier, Ephraim George [1821-1888]

Tongues from tombs.
Printed: 2 leaves, photoreproduction; 52 cm.
Original published in *Frank Leslie's Illustrated*, New York,
June 26, 1869 and July 7, 1869; description of the site of
Tenampua in Honduras and Pánuco, Palenque, and Ocosingo in
Mexico.
C.A. 3 Sq 44t P

541. Stanton, G.R.

[Correspondence from G.R. Stanton, curator for anthropology,
and F.S. Wallis, director of the Bristol City Museum,
regarding the Breton Collection, 1950].
Manuscript: 12 leaves, typewritten; 34 cm.
C.A. 3 B 756b

542. Stone, Doris Zemurray

A delimitation of cultures of northern and central pre-Columbian
Honduras, ca. 1941.
Manuscript: 20 leaves, typewritten; 28 cm.
C.A. 3 St 71d

543. Suárez, José

Vocabulario en lengua tepehua que se habla en el estado de
Hidalgo, 1893.
Manuscript: 8 leaves, handwritten; 28 cm.
Includes letters written in 1902 to Antonio Peñafiel by Fidencio
Morales and Manual P. Noblo regarding the vocabulary.
MEX 6 Su 11v

544. Swadesh, Morris [1909-1967]

La lingüística de las regiones entre los civilizaciones
mesoamericanas y andinas, 1959.
Manuscript: 5 leaves, typewritten; 34 cm.
PAM S

545. Tasaciones de la provincia de Yucatán, hechas en la Real Audiencia
de los confines que reside en la ciudad de Santiago de Guatemala,
1549.

Manuscript: 66 leaves, typewritten; 28 cm.
Original: Archivo General de Indias, Seville.
This 1549 tribute roll for Yucatán was made provisionally by
Francisco de Montejo and Franciscans in 1548, and confirmed

by the Audiencia of Guatemala in February of 1549; the
systematic and general assessment made for Yucatán.

SPAN AM Sp 14t

546. Testerian catechism

A Mexican catechism in Testerian hieroglyphs.
Manuscript: 50 leaves, handwritten; 16 cm.
Original: Tozzer Library, Harvard University.
This manuscript was purchased by Edward H. Thompson in Mérida
who presented it to Charles P. Bowditch. It contains the dates
1791 and 1801 written by an anonymous owner. "It has Spanish
headings and a few glosses in a native language, presumably
Otomi" (Glass 1975:294).

MEX 6 M 57
MEX 6 M 57 Microfilm

547. Manuscript: 50 leaves, photoreproduction; 22 cm.
A photographic copy made for Charles P. Bowditch by the
Massachusetts Historical Society.

MEX 6 M 57

548. Manuscript: 20 leaves, photoreproduction; 29 cm.
Original: John Carter Brown Library, Brown University.
A small volume of prayers with some glosses in Spanish
(Glass 1975:293).

MEX 8 T 28

549. Thompson, Edward Herbert [1865-1935]

Antiquities of Yucatán.
Manuscript: 172 leaves, handwritten; 59 cm.
Handcolored pencil drawings of pottery, lithics, and architecture
from Labna, Loltún, Uxmal, and other locations in northern
Yucatán.

C.A. 3 T 372at E F

550. [Letters to Stephen Salisbury, American Antiquarian Society,
Worcester, Massachusetts, regarding excavations at Chichén Itzá,
June 7, 1899 and May 29, 1900].
Manuscript: 7 leaves, handwritten; 28 cm.

C.A. 3 T 372r

551. The Maya pottery of Yucatán.
Manuscript: 27 leaves, typewritten; 28 cm.
Includes 29 photographic plates.

C.A. 4 T 372m

552. Newly discovered inscribed tablets of Chichen Itzá.
Manuscript: 17 leaves, typewritten; 34 cm.
Includes 10 photographic plates.

C.A. 3 T 372n

553. Thompson, Edward Herbert [1865-1935]

Photographs of Yucatán, 1885-1888.
Manuscript: 61 mounted photographic plates; 45 cm.
A collection of archaeological and ethnographic photographs.
Prehispanic architecture illustrated includes Chun-kat-zin,
Izamal, Kichmoo, Kabáh, Labna, Sabacche, Sayil, and Uxmal;
an unprovenienced incense burner is also given. Ethnographic
plates include views of Mérida, Izamal, and Valladolid. In
addition, other plates illustrate a tunkul or Maya drum,
henequen production, beehives, and several views of
mestizos and Indians; also Thompson as a young man.
C.A. 3 T 372p P

554. Religion of the Mayas, 1902.
Manuscript: 25 leaves, handwritten; sizes vary.
C.A. 4 T 372r

555. Report on excavations at Chichén Itzá, 1899-1900.
Manuscript: 33 leaves, handwritten; 27 cm.
Includes 50 photographic plates of Structures 3B-8, 3D-14,
Md-2, Md-9, and Las Monjas. Note on manuscript states:
"Examined by K. Ruppert. Reports many pages missing from
text. He has marked on margin designations in the Carnegie
system (Kilmartin map) of various buildings discussed. Second
part of report (1900) complete."
C.A. 3 T 372r

556. Thompson, John Eric Sidney [1898-1975]

Memorandum on the Gates Collection of Middle American books,
manuscripts, photostats, etc., 1941.
Manuscript: 3 leaves, typewritten; 28 cm.
C.A. 6 T 374m

557. Thompson, Raymond H.

A preliminary study of the Testerian catechism in the library
of the Peabody Museum, Harvard University, 1949.
Manuscript: 26 leaves, typewritten; 28 cm.
"This is a preliminary picture by picture interlinear type
translation of about the first third of the manuscript from
the Todo Fiel through El Credo."
MEX 6 T 377p F

558. Título de Cristóbal Melchor Ba en lengua kekchí, 1539.

Manuscript: 7 leaves, typewritten; 28 cm.
Land title from San Pedro Carchá transcribed in Kekchí and
English by Erwin P. Dieseldorff.
C.A. 6 D 566 F

559. Título de Poncio Tux en lengua kekchí, 1539.

> Manuscript: 5 leaves, typewritten; 28 cm.
> Land title from San Miguel Tucurú transcribed in Kekchí and
> English by Erwin P. Dieseldorff.
>> C.A. 6 D 566 F

560. Título de Tontem de Diego Zeb en lengua kekchí, 1779.

> Manuscript: 3 leaves, typewritten; 28 cm.
> Land title from San Pedro Carchá transcribed in Kekchí and
> English by Erwin P. Dieseldorff.
>> C.A. 6 D 566 F

561. Tonalamatl Aubin

> Manuscript: 20 leaves, handwritten facsimile; 35 cm.
> Original: Bibliothèque Nationale, Paris.
> Early 16th century ritual-calendrical screenfold from the
> Puebla region of Central Mexico (Glass and Robertson 1975:91).
>> MEX 7 T 61 F

562. Torquemada, Juan de

> Primera [segunda, tercera] parte de los veinte y un libros
> rituales y monarchia indiana.
> Manuscript: 19 leaves, typewritten; 28 cm.
> Notes on references to Yucatán from the 1723 (Madrid : Nicolas
> Rodríguez Franco) edition.
>> SPAN AM T 634v 2

563. Tozzer, Alfred Marston [1877-1954]

> Activity in proportion to physical equipment: comment upon
> Dr. Gamio's report.
> Manuscript: 3 leaves, typewritten; 28 cm.
> Discussion of Gamio's comments on the Archaic contact between
> the Maya and Central Mexicans. Published in *Art and Archaeology*
> 23:33-43, 1927.
>> C.A. 3 T 669p F

564. Archaeology and art.
> Manuscript: 2 leaves, typewritten; 28 cm.
> Description of a Peabody Museum, Harvard University, exhibition
> of objects from Copán, Piedras Negras, and Yucatán, at the
> Museum of Fine Arts in Boston. Published in *American Anthro-
> pologist* 14:206-207, 1912.
>> C.A. 3 T 669p F

565. Bibliography, 1948.
> Manuscript: 8 leaves, typewritten; 28 cm.
> Includes entries from 1900 through 1947.
>> C.A. 10 T 669b F

566. Tozzer, Alfred Marston [1877-1954]
      A classification of Maya verbs.
      Manuscript: 6 leaves, typewritten; 28 cm.
      Published in *Proceedings of the XVII International Congress
      of Americanists*, Mexico, pp. 233-237, 1912.
                                          C.A. 3 T 669p F

567. A Comparative Study of the Mayas and the Lacandones ...
      New York : Macmillan, 1907.
      Printed: 196 p.; 25 cm.
      Report of the Fellow in American Archaeology of the
      Archaeological Institute of America, 1902-1905. Handwritten
      notes by Tozzer and corrections between pages on separate
      leaves.
                                          C.A. 4 T 669c

568. Field diaries, Mexico, 1903-1905.
      Manuscript: 398 leaves bound in 3 vols., handwritten; 16 cm.
      Diaries of visits to Chichén Itzá, Valladolid, Yucatán, and
      the Usumacinta region (1903), and Yucatán (1904).
                                          C.A. 3 T 669f

569. [Introduction to Kelemen, Pál: Battlefield of the Gods ...
      London : George Allen and Unwin, 1937].
      Manuscript: 2 leaves, typewritten; 28 cm.
                                          C.A. 3 T 669p F

570. Introduction to the Bowditch photostat reproduction of the
      Tirado copy (1787) of a Quiché-Spanish dictionary, Peabody
      Museum, 1916.
      Manuscript: 3 leaves, typewritten; 28 cm.
                                          C.A. 3 T 669p F

571. [Letters from the field to the Tozzer family, 1900-1905].
      Manuscript: 748 leaves bound in 2 vols., typewritten; 28 cm.
      Includes 1900-1901 travels in California and New Mexico, and
      1902-1905 travels in Yucatán and Central Mexico.
                                          ANT T 669a

572. Maya art and architecture, 1936.
      Manuscript: 9 leaves, typewritten; 28 cm.
      A radio address presented March 26, 1936 on WAAB, Boston,
      in a series sponsored by the Museum of Fine Arts, Boston.
                                          C.A. 3 T 669p F

573. A Maya Grammar, with Bibliography and Appraisement of the
      Works Noted. Papers of the Peabody Museum of American
      Archaeology and Ethnology, Harvard University, vol. IX, 1921.
      Printed: 301 p.; 25 cm.
      Includes extensive handwritten notes and annotations by
      Tozzer.

C.A. 6 T 669m

574. Tozzer, Alfred Marston [1877-1954]

A Mexican catechism in Testerian hieroglyphs, 1919.
Manuscript: 3 leaves, typewritten; 28 cm.
C.A. 3 T 669p F

575. Middle America: archaeology, hieroglyphic writing, linguistics,
and physical anthropology.
Manuscript: 3 leaves, typewritten; 28 cm.
Published in *Handbook of Latin American Studies*, pp. 5-11, 1937.
C.A. 3 T 669p F

576. Notes on the Berendt Linguistic Collection, Philadelphia, 1905.
Manuscript: 154 leaves, handwritten; 28 cm.
C.A. 3 B 452t
C.A. 6 C 280 Microfilm

577. Notes on books and manuscripts on Middle America in the
Bancroft Library of the University of California, November
1917 to January 1918.
Manuscript: 83 leaves, typewritten; 28 cm.
C.A. 6 C 280 Microfilm
C.A. 10 T 669n

578. [Obituary: Charles Pickering Bowditch].
Manuscript: 3 leaves, typewritten; 28 cm.
C.A. 1 B 674t

579. The ruins of northeastern Guatemala.
Manuscript: 8 leaves, typewritten; 28 cm.
Published in *Proceedings of the XVII International Congress
of Americanists*, Mexico, pp. 400-405, 1912.
C.A. 3 T 669p F

580. Selected bibliography on the Aztecs: their ancient and
modern history.
Manuscript: 2 leaves, typewritten; 28 cm.
Includes 17 items, pre-1941.
C.A. 3 T 669p F

581. Survivals of ancient forms of culture among the Mayas of
Yucatán and the Lacandones of Chiapas.
Manuscript: 8 leaves, typewritten; 28 cm.
Published in : *Comte Rendu de la XVème Session du Congrès
International des Américanistes*, Québec, 2:283-288, 1906;
also read by F.W. Putnam at the International Congress of
Arts and Sciences, Department of Ethnology, St. Louis,
September 1904.
C.A. 3 T 669p F

582. Tozzer, Alfred Marston [1877-1954]

The Toltec architect of Chichén Itzá.
Manuscript: 17 leaves, typewritten; 28 cm.
Published in: *American Indian Life*, edited by E.C. Parsons,
pp. 265-271 ... New York : B.W. Huebsch, 1922.
C.A. 3 T 669p F

583. Tratado en la lengua otomí.

Manuscript: 138 leaves, photoreproduction; 22 cm.
MEX 6 T 68

584. Tschopik, Harry [1915-1956]

Textile motifs from Uloa Valley pottery, Honduras, 1937.
Manuscript: 18 leaves, typewritten; 28 cm.
C.A. 3 T 785t

585. [Unidentified Mexican village documents in Náhuatl and Spanish,
sixteenth and seventeenth centuries].

Manuscript: 1 reel, 35 mm microfilm
A very poor and largely illegible photographic copy made in
1969.
MEX 4 Un 3 Microfilm

586. Valentini, Philipp Johann Joseph [1822-1899]

Studies concerning the origin of ancient Mexican civilization,
1898.
Manuscript: 308 leaves, handwritten; 32 cm.
Includes some 35 drawings copied from various published
sources. Valentini argues for the Buddhist origins of Mesoamerican
civilization.
MEX 4 V 235s F

587. Villa Rojas, Alfonso

Breve reporte etnológico de un viaje a la zona tzeltal del
estado de Chiapas, 1938.
Manuscript: 108 leaves, typewritten; 28 cm.
MEX 4 V 711b F

588. Villacorta Calderón, José Antonio [1879-1964]

Codices mayas; reproducidos y desarrollados, por J. Antonio
Villacorta Calderón y Carlos A. Villacorta ... Guatemala :
Impreso en la Tipografía Nacional, 1930.
Printed: 450 p.; 27 cm.
Line drawings of the Dresden, Paris, and Madrid codices with
explanatory diagrams facing each reproduced page; extensive
marginal notes by Alfred M. Tozzer.
C.A. 7 D 816v

589. Villagutierre Soto-Mayor, Juan de

Historia de la conquista de la provincia de el Itzá, reducción
y progresos de la de el Lacandón, y otras naciones de indios
barbaros de la mediación de el reino de Guatemala, a las provincias
de Yucatán en la América septentrional.
Manuscript: 204 leaves, handwritten and typewritten; 30 cm.
Partial translation of Book I, Chapter VII, Book III, Book V,
Chapters I-XI, and Books VI and X from the 1701 (Madrid :
Imprenta de Lucas Antonio de Bedmor y Narvaez). Contents
include information of Cortés' journey to Lake Petén Itzá
from Mexico, the Dominican penetration into Chol and Manché
country from Guatemala and from Yucatán, and extensive data
on the Las Montañas mission system.
SPAN AM V 713h E

590. Vocabulario de lengua quiché, compuesto por el apostólico zelo
de los M.R.P. Franciscanos de esta santa provincia del dulcísimo
nombre de Jesús, del arzobispado de Guatemala; añadido por
él mismo autor otro diccionario corto de varios vocabo. que
faltaron y distintos nombres de diversas aves; copiado por
D. Fermin Joseph Tirado, sujeto instruído en dicho idioma, a
costa del P. Joseph Joachin Henriquez, clergio presbítero
domiciliario de dicho arzobispado, y teniente de cura de la
parroquia de Santo Domingo Zacualpa; se añadieron a esta copia
los arboles de consangd. y afinidad, año 1787.

Manuscript: 216 leaves, handwritten; 28 cm.
C.A. 6 V 85

591. Manuscript: 218 leaves bound in 2 vols., photoreproduction; 24 cm.
Original: Tozzer Library, Harvard University.
C.A. 6 V 85

592. Vocabulario de Mayathan por su abeceario.

Manuscript: 100 leaves, photoreproduction; 32 cm.
Original: Österreichische Nationalbibliothek, Vienna.
"This copy from S.G. Morley's negatives" (pencil note). Includes
only the Spanish to Maya portion of the vocabulary. The
original manuscript possibly by Diego Rejon.
C.A. 6 V 675

593. Whorf, Benjamin Lee

Notes on two recent findings from Central Mexico, 1940.
Manuscript: 7 leaves, typewritten; 28 cm.
Discussion of the Nahuatl dialect of Milpa Alta, Distrito
Federal, and relates certain carvings at Tepoztlán to the
Aztec deity Tepoztecatl.
MEX 6 W 620n

594. Wilson, R.W. [d. 1922]

Table of eclipses in the Dresden Codex.
Manuscript: 1 leaf, photoreproduction; 22 cm.
MEX 1 M 68 E F
MEX 1 M 68 E Microfilm

595. Wirsing, Paul

Balamqu'e-Po [en lengua kekchí].
Manuscript: 23 leaves, typewritten; 28 cm.
Contains Kekchí text with translation and vocabulary in
Kekchí, German, and English.
C.A. 6 B 182w

596. [Kekchí vocabulary, 1930].
Manuscript: 285 leaves, typewritten; 28 cm.
C.A. 6 W 748q

597. [Miscellaneous papers and drawings, some relevant to the
author's Kekchí vocabulary, ca. 1930-1935].
Manuscript: ca. 150 leaves, handwritten; 31 cm.
Includes a transcription of the Credo of Riveiro's *Explicación
de la doctrina cristiana* (1798), notes on the Kekchí calendar
and day names, agriculture, cosmology, and fragments of a
Kekchí to German vocabulary.
C.A. 6 W 748m

598. Xiu, Gaspar Antonio

[Relación sobre las costumbres de los indios de la provincia de
Yucatán, 1582].
Manuscript: 8 leaves, photoreproduction; 23 cm.
Original: Archivo General de Indias, Seville.
C.A. 4 C 43r

599. Manuscript: 18 leaves, typewritten; 28 cm.
Transcription of the Maya text and translation to English by
Ralph L. Roys, ca. 1940.
C.A. 4 C 43r E

600. Xiu Chronicles.

Manuscript: 82 leaves, handwritten; 32 cm.
C.A. 6 C 280 Microfilm
C.A. 7 X 4 F
C.A. 7 X 4 Microfilm

601. Manuscript: 177 leaves, photoreproduction; 37 cm.
Photoreproduction for Charles P. Bowditch by the Massachusetts
Historical Society; includes an introduction by Adela C. Breton.
C.A. 6 C 280 Microfilm
C.A. 8 X 49 2d ed.

602. Xiu Chronicles.

The Xiu Chronicles. Part I: The history of the Xiu, by
Sylvanus G. Morley, Part II: The Xiu Chronicle, by Ralph
L. Roys, 1941.
Manuscript: 813 leaves, typewritten; 35 cm.
Part I treats the history of the Xiu family; Part II includes
selected transcripts and a full English translation of the
chronicles. Included are the Maní Land Treaty of 1557, the
katun wheel of Maní, and the genealogical tree of the Xiu
family.
                          C.A. 8 X 49 F
                          C.A. 8 X 49 Microfilm

603.   Manuscript: 17 mounted photographic plates; 51 cm.
Includes a collection of preliminary and final plates to
illustrate the Morley and Roys study of the Xiu Chronicles.
Contents include genealogies of the former ruling houses
of Tenochtitlán and the cacicazgo of Acalán, and the Xiu family
from 1661 to 1934, and the Tutul Xiu of Uxmal from 987 to 1940;
also the Maní Land Treaty of 1557, a map of the Xiu region,
katun wheels from Cogolludo, and the Chilam Balam of Kaua and
Maní, and petitions of Pedro Xiu (1608), Salvador Xiu (1752),
and Pablo Xiu (1789), as well as a series of ethnographic
photographs of members of the Xiu family, the house of
Remesio Xiu in Ticul, and convents at Maní, Oxkutzcab, and
Mama.
                          C.A. 6 X 49 E F

604. Yde, Jens

Architectural remains along the coast of Quintana Roo; a report
of the Peabody Museum Expedition, 1913-1914, compiled from the
field notes of Raymond E. Merwin.
Manuscript: 44 leaves, typewritten; 28 cm.
Includes information on Cancun Island (Talmul and Groups I-III),
caves on the mainland, Isla de Mujeres, Nohku, and a reference
bibliography of sites in Quintana Roo; several architectural
plan and section drawings are in a pocket.
                          MUS 120.20.7.2.25

605. Yourison, Ruth Hitchner

Modern Chol texts collected by a Protestant missionary, ca. 1940-
1950.
Manuscript: 67 leaves, photoreproduction; 28 cm.
                          C.A. 6 M 720

606. Ziess, Emmanuel G.

Central American volcanoes in 1932.
Manuscript: 6 leaves, typewritten; 28 cm.
"Report is of particular interest in that he examined both

Santa María and Fuego volcanoes while in a period of
activity."

C.A. 1 C 215f

607. Zimmerman, Günter

Formen- und Begriffsanalyse der Hieroglyphen der drei Maya-
handschriften, mit besonderer Berucksichtigung der Dresdener
Handschrift, 1951.
Manuscript: 150 leaves, typewritten; 31 cm.
Doctoral dissertation from the University of Hamburg, West
Germany.

C.A. 9 Z 65f

608. Zumárraga, Juan [1468-1548]

[Miscellaneous manuscript regarding Indian affairs in Nueva
España.]
Manuscript: 2 leaves, photoreproduction; 44 cm.
Zumárraga was guardian of several convents in Yucatán and was
the first bishop of Mexico; he returned to Spain in 1534 and
was elevated by Pope Paul III to archbishop of Mexico in 1545.

MEX 1 Z 85 F

Libro de judio el lengua maya,
a Maya herbal acquired in Mérida
by A. LePlongeon (no. 478)

609. Ancient Mexican skulls.

   Manuscript: 1 leaf, typewritten; 28 cm.
   English translation of: Altmexikanische Schädel. *Globus* 73:
   83-84, 1898.

                          MEX 1 M 68 E F
                          MEX 1 M 68 E Microfilm

610. Ancient Mexican terra-cotta figurine.

   Manuscript: 2 leaves, typewritten; 28 cm.
   English translation of: Altmexikanische Terracottafigur.
   Globus 73:49-50, 1898.

                          MEX 1 M 68 E F
                          MEX 1 M 68 E Microfilm

611. Andrée, Richard [1835-1912]

   The Pleiades in mythology and their relation to the New Year
   and agriculture.
   Manuscript: 19 leaves, typewritten; 28 cm.
   English translation of: Die Pleiaden im Mythus und in ihrer
   Beziehung zum Jahresbeginn und Landbau. *Globus* 64:1-5, 1894.

                          MEX 1 M 68 E F
                          MEX 1 M 68 E Microfilm

612. [Review of] Maler, Teobert: Explorations in the department
   of Petén, Guatemala, and adjacent regions.
   Manuscript: 2 leaves, typewritten; 28 cm.
   English translation of: Maler, Teobert: *Explorations in the
   department of Petén, Guatemala, and adjacent regions.*
   Memoirs of the Peabody Museum of American Archaeology and
   Ethnology, Harvard University, vol. 4, no. 1-2 ... Cambridge,
   Massachusetts, 1908. *Globus* 95:177-178, 1909.

                          C.A. 3 An 2

613. Bastian, Adolf Philip Wilhelm [1826-1905]

   Stone sculptures from Guatemala.
   Manuscript: 59 leaves, typewritten; 28 cm.
   English translation of: *Steinsculpturen aus Guatemala* ...
   Berlin : Weidmannsche Buchhandlung, 1882

                          MEX 1 M 68 E F

614. Berendt, Karl Hermann [1817-1878]

The shoe vases of Central America.
Manuscript: 3 leaves, typewritten; 28 cm.
English translation of: Die Schuhvasen von Mittelamerika.
Petermann's Mitteilungen 59:132, 1913.
MEX 1 M 68 E F
MEX 1 M 68 E Microfilm

615. Berkhan, O.

On the development and explanation of the socalled Aztec
microcephalia.
Manuscript: 6 leaves, typewritten; 28 cm.
English translation of: Zur Entwicklung und Deutung der
sog. Azteken-Mikrocephalen. *Globus* 73:57-59, 1898.
MEX 1 M 68 E F
MEX 1 M 68 E Microfilm

616. Beyer, Hermann [1880-1942]

The day dates from the Maya altar in the National Museum of
Mexico.
Manuscript: 9 leaves, typewritten; 28 cm.
English translation of: Die Tagesdaten auf dem Maya-Altar des
Mexikanischen Nationalmuseums. *Zeitschrift für Ethnologie*
70:88-93, 1938.
C.A. 9 B 468t E F

617. The "dragon" of the Mexicans.
Manuscript: 5 leaves, typewritten; 28 cm.
English translation of: Der "Drache" der Mexikaner. *Globus*
93:157-158, 1908.
MEX 1 M 68 E F
MEX 1 M 68 E Microfilm

618. The glyph for twenty in the Maya inscriptions.
Manuscript: 8 leaves, typewritten; 28 cm.
English translation of: Das Zeichen für zwanzig in den Maya-
Inschriften. *El México Antiguo* 4:155-161, 1938.
C.A. 9 B 468z E F

619. The month of 28 days of the ancient Mexicans.
Manuscript: 6 leaves, typewritten; 28 cm.
English translation of: Die 28tägige Monat der alten Mexikaner.
Mitteilungen der Anthropologische Gesellschaft in Wien
40:238-240, 1910.
MEX 1 M 68 E F
MEX 1 M 68 E Microfilm

-154-

620. Beyer, Hermann [1880-1942]

The mythological monkeys of the Mexicans and the Maya.
Manuscript: 20 leaves, typewritten; 28 cm.
English translation of: Über die mythologischen Affen der Mexikaner und Maya. *Proceedings of the XVIII International Congress of Americanists*, London, pp. 140-154, 1912.

MEX 1 M 68 E F
MEX 1 M 68 E Microfilm

621. The polar constellation in the Mexican-Central American picture writings.
Manuscript: 7 leaves, typewritten; 28 cm.
English translation of: Die Polarkonstellation in den mexikanisch-zentralamerikanischen Bilderhandschriften. *Archiv für Anthropologie* 35:345-348, 1909.

MEX 1 M 68 E F
MEX 1 M 68 E Microfilm

622. Reduplication of forms in Maya writing.
Manuscript: 4 leaves, typewritten; 28 cm.
English translation of: Die Verdopplung in der Hieroglyphenschrift der Maya. *Anthropos* 21:581-582, 1926.

C.A. 6 B 468r F

623. The "series" of cosmic objects: a section from two Mexican picture writings.
Manuscript: 49 leaves, typewritten; 28 cm.
English translation of: Die "serie" der kosmischen Gegensätze: ein Abschnitt aus zwei mexikanischen Bilderhandschriften. *Archiv für Anthropologie* 9:293-319, 1912.

MEX 1 M 68 E F
MEX 1 M 68 E Microfilm

624. The south in the ideal world of ancient Mexico.
Manuscript: 8 leaves, typewritten; 28 cm.
English translation of: Der Süden in der Gedankenwelt Alt-Mexikos. *Mitteilungen der Anthropologischen Gesellschaft in Wien* 38:229-231, 1908.

MEX 1 M 68 E F
MEX 1 M 68 E Microfilm

625. Death masks on ancient American pottery.
Manuscript: 3 leaves, typewritten; 28 cm.
English translation of: Altamerikanische Totengesicht-Gefässe. *Globus* 71:328, 1896.

MEX 1 M 68 E F
MEX 1 M 68 E Microfilm

626. Dieseldorff, Erwin Paul [1868-1940]

Ancient painted pottery from Guatemala.
Manuscript: 8 leaves, typewritten; 28 cm.
English translation of: Alte bemalte Thongefässe von Guatemala. *Zeitschrift für Ethnologie* 25:547-550, 1893.
C.A. 3 D 56m

627. Classification of archaeological finds in northern Guatemala.
Manuscript: 19 leaves, typewritten; 28 cm.
English translation of: Klassifizierung seiner archäologischen Funde im nördlichen Guatemala. *Zeitschrift für Ethnologie* 41:862-876, 1909.
C.A. 3 D 56m

628. Excavations at Cobán.
Manuscript: 11 leaves, typewritten; 28 cm.
English translation of: Ausgrabungen in Cobán. *Verhandlungen der Berliner Anthropologischen Gesellschaft für Anthropologie, Ethnologie, und Urgeschichte* 25:374-382, 1893.
C.A. 3 D 56m

629. Jadeite and other ornaments of the Maya.
Manuscript: 5 leaves, typewritten; 28 cm.
English translation of: Jadeit und anderen Schmuck der Mayavölker. *Zeitschrift für Ethnologie* 37:408-411, 1905.
C.A. 3 D 56m

630. Ehrenreich, O.

On an archaeological trip to Mexico and Yucatán in October and November, 1906.
Manuscript: 5 leaves, typewritten; 28 cm.
English translation of: Uber einem archäologischen Ausflug nach Mexiko und Yukatan im October und November, 1906. *Zeitschrift für Ethnologie* 49:752-754, 1907.
MEX 1 M 68 E F
MEX 1 M 68 E Microfilm

631. Eichhorn, A.

The Hieroglyphic picture writing of the Maya.
Manuscript: 27 leaves, typewritten; 28 cm.
English translation of: *Die Hieroglyphen Bildschrift der Maya Völker in ihrer Stufenweisen entwicklung bis zur Ornamentszildschrift dargestellt und anden Hieroglyphen der 20 Monatstage Erlautert ...* Berlin : Georg Reimer, 1905.
A partial translation of only pp. 1-11 and 77-79.
MEX 1 M 68 E F
MEX 1 M 68 E Microfilm

632. Fischer, Heinrich H. [1817-1886]

An ancient Mexican stone figure.
Manuscript: 7 leaves, typewritten; 28 cm.
English translation of: Eine altmexikanische Steinfigur.
Globus 85:345-348, 1904.

MEX 1 M 68 E F
MEX 1 M 68 E Microfilm

633. Förstemann, Ernst Wilhelm [1822-1906]

The astronomy of the Maya.
Manuscript: 30 leaves, typewritten; 28 cm.
English translation of: Die Astronomie der Mayas. *Das*
Weltall 4:353-385, 1904.

C.A. 1 F 77 E F

634. Commentary on the Madrid Maya manuscript (Codex Tro-Cor-
tesianus).
Manuscript: 213 leaves, typewritten; 28 cm.
English translation of: *Commentar zur Madrider Mayahandschrift*
(Codex Tro-Cortesianus) ... Danzig : L. Saunders Buchhandlung
(G. Horn), 1902.

C.A. 7 F 685ct E F

635. Commentary on the Paris Maya manuscript (Codex Peresianus).
Manuscript: 44 leaves, typewritten; 28 cm.
English translation of: *Commentar zur Pariser Mayahandschrift*
(Codex Parisianus) ... Danzig : L. Saunders Buchhandlung
(G. Horn), 1903.

C.A. 7 F 685cp E F
C.A. 7 F 685cp E Microfilm

636. Comparison of the Dresden Maya manuscript with the Madrid.
Manuscript: 10 leaves, typewritten; 28 cm.
English translation of: Vergleichung der Dresdener Mayahand-
schrift mit der Madrider. *Globus* 86:269-271, 1904.

C.A. 1 F 77 E F

637. Connection of two Palenque inscriptions.
Manuscript: 14 leaves, typewritten; 28 cm.
English translation of: Zusammenhang zweier Inschriften von
Palenque. *Globus* 83:281-284, 1903.

C.A. 1 F 77 E F

638. The cross inscription at Palenque.
Manuscript: 36 leaves, typewritten; 28 cm.
English translation of: Die Kreuz-Inschrift von Palenque.
Zeitschrift für Ethnologie 34:105-121, 1902.

C.A. 1 F 77 E F

639. Förstemann, Ernst Wilhelm [1822-1906]
   An historical Maya inscription.
   Manuscript: 10 leaves, typewritten; 28 cm.
   English translation of: Eine historische Maya-Inschrift.
   Globus 81:150-153, 1902.
   C.A. 1 F 77 E F

640. Inscriptions of Yaxchilán.
   Manuscript: 13 leaves, typewritten; 28 cm.
   English translation of: Inschriften von Yaxchilán. *Globus*
   84:81-84, 1903.
   C.A. 1 F 77 E F

641. The Maya deity of the year end.
   Manuscript: 11 leaves, typewritten; 28 cm.
   English translation of: Das Mayagott der Jahresschlusses.
   Globus 80:189-192, 1901.
   C.A. 1 F 77 E F

642. Maya hieroglyphs as period designators.
   Manuscript: 19 leaves, typewritten; 28 cm.
   English translation of: Maya Hieroglyphen als Bezeichnung
   für Zeiträume. *Das Weltall* 6:13-23, 1905.
   C.A. 1 F 77 E F

643. Mercury among the Maya.
   Manuscript: 7 leaves, typewritten; 28 cm.
   English translation of: Der Merkur bei den Mayas. *Globus*
   79:298-299, 1901.
   C.A. 1 F 77 E F

644. The most recent Maya inscriptions.
   Manuscript: 6 leaves, typewritten; 28 cm.
   English translation of: Die spätesten Inschriften der Mayas.
   Globus 87:272-273, 1905.
   C.A. 1 F 77 E F

645. The nephrite slab at Leiden.
   Manuscript: 9 leaves, typewritten; 28 cm.
   English translation of: Die Nephritplatte zu Leiden.
   Zeitschrift für Ethnologie 35:553-557, 1903.
   C.A. 1 F 77 E F

646. The North Pole among the Aztec and Maya.
   Manuscript: 6 leaves, typewritten; 28 cm.
   English translation of: Der Nordpol bei Azteken und Mayas.
   Zeitschrift für Ethnologie 33:274-277, 1901.
   C.A. 1 F 77 E F

647. Förstemann, Ernst Wilhem [1822-1906]
     On the chronology of the Aztecs. 1905.
     Manuscript: 7 leaves, typewritten; 28 cm.
     English translation of: Zur Chronologie der Azteken. *Das Weltall* 5:373-377, 1905.
                                          C.A. 1 F 77 E F

648. On the Madrid Maya manuscript.
     Manuscript: 35 leaves, typewritten; 28 cm.
     English translation of: Zur Madrider Mayahandschrift.
     Zeitschrift für Ethnologie 35:771-790, 1903.
                                          C.A. 1 F 77 E F

649. Page 60 of the Dresden Maya manuscript: battle of some stars.
     Manuscript: 14 leaves, typewritten; 28 cm.
     English translation of: Blatt sechzig der Dresdener Maya-handschrift: Kampf einiger Gestorne *Das Weltall* 6:251-257, 1906.
                                          C.A. 1 F 77 E F

650. The position of the ahau among the Maya.
     Manuscript: 5 leaves, typewritten; 28 cm.
     English translation of: Die Lage der Agaus bein den Mayas.
     Zeitschrift für Ethnologie 36:138-141, 1904.
                                          C.A. 1 F 77 E F

651. [Preface to] Die Mayahandschrift der Königlichen Öffentlichen Bibliothek zu Dresden.
     Manuscript: 45 leaves, typewritten; 28 cm.
     English translation of: *Einleitung der Die Mayahandschrift der Königlichen Öffentlichen Bibliothek zu Dresden ...*
     Leipzig : A. Naumann'schen Lichtdrukerei, 1880.
                                          MEX 1 M 68 E F
                                          MEX 1 M 68 E Microfilm

652. The serpent numbers of the Dresden Maya manuscript.
     Manuscript: 9 leaves, typewritten; 28 cm.
     English translation of: Die Schlangenzahlen der Dresdener Mayahandschrift. *Das Weltall* 5:199-203, 1905.
                                          C.A. 1 F 77 E F

653. Stela J from Copán.
     Manuscript: 7 leaves, typewritten; 28 cm.
     English translation of: Die Stela J von Copán. *Globus* 85:361-363, 1904.
                                          C.A. 1 F 77 E F

654. Förstemann, Ernst Wilhelm [1822-1906]

The tenth cycle of the Mayas.
Manuscript: 12 leaves, typewritten; 28 cm.
English translation of: Der zehntecyklus der Mayas. *Globus* 82:140-143, 1902.

C.A. 1 F 77 E F

655. Three Maya hieroglyphs from Palenque.
Manuscript: 12 leaves, typewritten; 28 cm.
English translation of: Drei Inschriften von Palenque.
Zeitschrift für Ethnologie 32:215-221, 1900.

C.A. 1 F 77 E F

656. Two hieroglyph series in the Dresden Maya manuscript.
Manuscript: 17 leaves, typewritten; 28 cm.
English translation of: Zwei Hieroglyphenreihen in der Dresdener Mayahandschrift. *Zeitschrift für Ethnologie* 2:265-274, 1905.

C.A. 1 F 77 E F

657. Two Maya hieroglyphs.
Manuscript: 10 leaves, typewritten; 28 cm.
English translation of: Zwei Mayahieroglyphen. *Globus* 83:95-98, 1903.

C.A. 1 F 77 E F

658. What positions do the tonalamatls of the Maya manuscripts occupy during certain years?
Manuscript: 18 leaves, typewritten; 28 cm.
English translation of: Liegen die Tonalamatl der Mayahandschriften in bestimmten Jahren? *Zeitschrift für Ethnologie* 36:659-667, 1904.

C.A. 1 F 77 E F

659. Gatschet, Albert Samuel [1832-1907]

Exploration at the ruins of Copán in Honduras.
Manuscript: 2 leaves, typewritten; 28 cm.
English translation of: Die Erforschung der Ruinen von Copán in Honduras. *Globus* 71:99, 1897.

C.A. 3 G 22 E

660. Languages and dialects of Central America.
Manuscript: 16 leaves, typewritten; 28 cm.
English translation of: Central-Amerikas Sprachstämme und Dialekte. *Globus* 77:81-92, 1900.

MEX 1 M 68 E F
MEX 1 M 68 E Microfilm

661. Hartmann, Carl Vilhelm [1862-1941]

   Hartmann's archaeological and ethnographical research in
   Central America.
   Manuscript: 1 leaf, typewritten; 28 cm.
   English translation of: Hartmanns archäologische und ethno-
   graphische Forschungen in Mittelamerika. *Globus* 78:344, 1900.
                        MEX 1 M 68 E F
                        MEX 1 M 68 E Microfilm

662. Hissink, Karin [1907-1981]

   Masks as adornments on facades examined on the ancient
   structures of the Yucatán peninsula.
   Manuscript: 94 leaves, typewritten; 28 cm.
   English translation of: *Masken als Fassadenschmuck Untersucht
   an alten Bauten der Halbinsel Yukatan.* Akademische Abhandlungen zur Kulturgeschichte, Reihe 3, Band 2 ... Strassburg :
   Heitz, 1934.
                        C.A. 3 H 629m E

663. Jonghe, Edouard de [1878-1949]

   The ancient Mexican calendar.
   Manuscript: 45 leaves, typewritten; 28 cm.
   English translation of: Der altmexikanischer Kalender.
   Zeitschrift für Ethnologie 38:485-512, 1906.
                        MEX 1 M 68 E F
                        MEX 1 M 68 E Microfilm

664. Kreichgauer, Damian [1859-1940]

   The correlation of the Mayan and Julian calendars.
   Manuscript: 30 leaves, typewritten; 28 cm.
   English translation of: Anschluss der Maya-Chronologie an
   die Julianische. *Anthropos* 22:1-15, 1927.
                        C.A. 9 K 873a E

665. Krickeberg, Walter [1885-1962]

   An account of recent investigations into the history of the
   ancient cultures of Central America. II: Archaeological
   results.
   Manuscript: 76 leaves, typewritten; 28 cm.
   English translation of: Bericht über neuere Forschungen zur
   Geschichte der alten Kulturen Mittelamerikas. II: Archäologische Ergebnisse. *Das Welt als Geschichte* 3:194-230, 1937.
                        C.A. 3 K 892a E F
                        C.A. 3 K 892a E Microfilm

666. Lehmann, Walter

Ancient Mexican mosaics and King Motecuzoma's gifts to Cortés.
Manuscript: 17 leaves, typewritten; 28 cm.
English translation of: Altmexikanische Mosaiken und die
Geschenken König Motecuzomas an Cortés. *Globus* 90:318-322,
1906.

MEX 1 L 53 E F
MEX 1 L 53 E Microfilm

667. Ancient Mexican mosaics in the Ethnographical Museum in
Copenhagen.
Manuscript: 10 leaves, typewritten; 28 cm.
English translation of: Die altmexikanischen Mosaiken des
ethnographischen Museum in Kopenhagen. *Globus* 91:318-322,
1907.

MEX 1 L 53 E F
MEX 1 L 53 E Microfilm

668. Ancient Mexican shell ornaments in perforated work.
Manuscript: 8 leaves, typewritten; 28 cm.
English translation of: Altmexikanische Muschelzierate in
durchbrochener Arbeit. *Globus* 88:285-288, 1905.

MEX 1 L 53 E F
MEX 1 L 53 E Microfilm

669. The calendar of the Quiché Indians of Guatemala. A chapter
from the unpublished manuscript of Padre Ximénez on the
history of Chiapas and Guatemala.
Manuscript: 5 leaves, typewritten; 28 cm.
English translation of: Der Kalender der Quiché-Indianer
Guatemala. Ein Kapital aus dem unveröffentlichten Manuskript
des Padre Ximenez über die Geschichte von Chiapas und Guatemala.
Anthropos 11:403-410, 1911.

C.A. 9 X 4

670. Concerning Tarascan picture writing.
Manuscript: 11 leaves, typewritten; 28 cm.
English translation of: Uber Taraskische Bilderschriften.
Globus 88:410-412, 1905.

MEX 1 L 53 E F
MEX 1 L 53 E Microfilm

671. The five women of the west who died in childbirth and the
five gods of the south in Mexican mythology.
Manuscript: 34 leaves, typewritten; 28 cm.
English translation of: Die fünf im Kindbett gestorbenen Frauen
des Westens und die fünf Götter des Sudens in der mexikanischen
Mythologie. *Zeitschrift für Ethnologie* 37:848-871, 1905.

MEX 1 L 53 E F
MEX 1 L 53 E Microfilm

672.   Lehmann, Walter
        The Historia de los reinos de Colhuacan y de México.
        Manuscript: 15 leaves, typewritten; 28 cm.
        English translation of: Die Historia de los reinos de
        Colhuacan y de México. *Zeitschrift für Ethnologie*
        38:752-760, 1906.
                                MEX 1 L 53 E F
                                MEX 1 L 53 E Microfilm

673.   The Mexican greenstone figure in the Musée Guimet in Paris.
        Manuscript: 4 leaves, typewritten; 28 cm.
        English translation of: Die mexikanische Grünsteinfigur des
        Musée Guimet in Paris. *Globus* 90:60-62, 1906.
                                MEX 1 L 53 E F
                                MEX 1 L 53 E Microfilm

674.   Researches in Central America.
        Manuscript: 6 leaves, typewritten; 28 cm.
        English translation of: Forschungen in Mittelamerika.
        Globus 94:289-290, 1909.
                                MEX 1 L 53 E F
                                MEX 1 L 53 E Microfilm

675.   Results of a scientific expedition to Central America and
        Mexico, 1907-1909.
        Manuscript: 88 leaves, typewritten; 28 cm.
        English translation of: Ergebnisse einer Forschunsreise in
        Mittelamerika und Mexiko, 1907-1909. *Zeitschrift für
        Ethnologie* 42:688-749, 1910.
                                MEX 1 L 53 E F
                                MEX 1 L 53 E Microfilm

676.   [Review of] Prowe, Hermann: The knowledge of the Quiché
        Indians in mythical form.
        Manuscript: 3 leaves, typewritten; 28 cm.
        English translation of: Zu dem Aufsatz: Das Wissen der Quiché-
        Indianer in mythischer Form. *Globus* 90:274-275, 1906.
                                MEX 1 M 68 E F
                                MEX 1 M 68 E Microfilm

677.   A Toltec dirge.
        Manuscript: 61 leaves, typewritten; 28 cm.
        English translation of: Ein Tolteken-Klagesang. *Festschrift
        Eduard Seler*, pp. 281-319, Stuttgart, 1922.
                                MEX 4 L 528 E F

678. Lehmann, Walter

Traditions of the ancient Mexicans: edited text and
original in Náhuatl with Latin translation.
Manuscript: 21 leaves, typewritten; 28 cm.
English translation of: Traditions des anciens Mexicaines:
texte inédit et original en lengue Nahuatl avec traduction
en Latin. *Journal de la Société des Americanistes de Paris*
3:239-297, 1906.

MEX 4 L 528tr

679. Linné, Sigvald

The expedition to Mexico in 1934-35 sent out by the Ethno-
graphical Museum of Sweden: the archaeological investigations.
Manuscript: 24 leaves, typewritten; 28 cm.
English translation of: Statens etnografiska museums expedition
till Mexico 1934-35: de arkeologiska undersökningarna.
Ethnos 2:267-318, 1937.

MEX 3 L 649e

680. Lorenz-Liburnau, Ludwig von

Remarks on the feathers used [in the Mexican feather orna-
ment in the Imperial Museum of Natural History, Vienna].
Manuscript: 2 leaves, typewritten; 28 cm.
English translation of: Bemerkungen uber die verwendeten
Vogelfedern. *Verhandlungen des XVI. Internationalen Ameri-
kanistec-Kongresses*, Vienna, pp. 247-248, 1908. Also in:
Gesammelte Abhandlungen 5:177, 1915.

MEX 1 Se 48g E 2 F
MEX 1 Se 48g E 2 Microfilm
MEX 1 Se 48g E 3 F

681. Ludendorff, Hans

About the origin of the tzolkin-period in the calendar of
the Maya.
Manuscript: 27 leaves, typewritten; 28 cm.
English translation of: *Uber die Entstehung der Tzolkin-
Periode im Kalendar der Maya*. Untersuchungen zur Astronomie
der Maya, no. 1 ... Berlin : Preussischen Akademie der
Wissenschaften, 1930.

C.A. 9 L 965u E F
C.A. 9 L 965u E Microfilm

682. Ludendorff, Hans

About pages 51 and 52 of the Dresden-Codex and about some
astronomical inscriptions of the Maya.
Manuscript: 59 leaves, typewritten; 28 cm.
English translation of: *Über die Seiten 51 und 52 des
Dresdener Kodex und über einige astronomische Inschriften
der Maya.* Untersuchungen zur Astronomie der Maya, no. 6 ...
Berlin : Preussischen Akademie der Wissenschaften, 1933.
C.A. 9 L 965u E F
C.A. 9 L 965u E Microfilm

683. About the reduction of the Maya dates to our chronology.
Manuscript: 21 leaves, typewritten; 28 cm.
English translation of: *Über die Reduktion der Maya-Datierungen
auf unsere Zeitrechnung.* Untersuchungen zur Astronomie der
Maya, no. 2 ... Berlin : Preussischen Akademie der Wissen-
schaften, 1930.
C.A. 9 L 965u E F
C.A. 9 L 965u E Microfilm

684. The astronomical inscription from the Temple of the Cross
at Palenque.
Manuscript: 41 leaves, typewritten; 28 cm.
English translation of: *Die astronomische Inschrift aus dem
Tempel des Kreuzes in Palenque.* Untersuchungen zur Astronomie
der Maya, no. 9 ... Berlin : Preussischen Akademie der
Wissenschaften, 1936.
C.A. 9 L 965u E F
C.A. 9 L 965u E Microfilm

685. The astronomical inscriptions at Yaxchilán.
Manuscript: 33 leaves, typewritten; 28 cm.
English translation of: *Die astronomische Inschriften in
Yaxchilán.* Untersuchungen zur Astronomie der Maya, no. 7 ...
Berlin : Preussischen Akademie der Wissenschaften, 1933.
C.A. 9 L 965u E F
C.A. 9 L 965u E Microfilm

686. The astronomical meaning of the Maya inscriptions.
Manuscript: 40 leaves, typewritten; 28 cm.
English translation of: *Zur astronomischen Deutung der Maya-
Inschriften.* Untersuchungen zur Astronomie der Maya, no. 10 ...
Berlin : Preussischen Akademie der Wissenschaften, 1936.
C.A. 9 L 965u E F
C.A. 9 L 965e F Microfilm

687. Ludendorff, Hans
       The astronomical meaning of pages 51 and 52 of the Dresden
       Codex.
       Manuscript: 18 leaves, typewritten; 28 cm.
       English translation of: *Die astronomische Bedeutung der
       Seiten 51 und 52 des Dresdener Maya-Kodex.* Untersuchungen
       zur Astronomie der Maya, no. 3 ... Berlin : Preussischen
       Akademie der Wissenschaften, 1931.
                              C.A. 9 L 965u E F
                              C.A. 9 L 965u E Microfilm

688. Further astronomical inscriptions of the Maya.
       Manuscript: 22 leaves, typewritten; 28 cm.
       English translation of: *Weitere astronomische Inschriften
       der Maya.* Untersuchungen zur Astronomie der Maya, no. 8 ...
       Berlin : Preussischen Akademie der Wissenschaften, 1934.
                              C.A. 9 L 965u E F
                              C.A. 9 L 965u E Microfilm

689. The moon-age in the inscriptions of the Maya.
       Manuscript: 31 leaves, typewritten; 28 cm.
       English translation of: *Das Mondalter in den Inschriften
       der Maya.* Untersuchungen zur Astronomie der Maya, no. 4 ...
       Berlin : Preussischen Akademie der Wissenschaften, 1931.
                              C.A. 9 L 965u E F
                              C.A. 9 L 965u E Microfilm

690. The venus-table of the Dresden Codex.
       Manuscript: 11 leaves, typewritten; 28 cm.
       English translation of: *Die Venustafel des Dresdener Kodex.*
       Untersuchungen zur Astronomie der Maya, no. 5 ... Berlin :
       Preussischen Akademie der Wissenschaften, 1931.
                              C.A. 9 L 965u E F
                              C.A. 9 L 965u E Microfilm

691. Maler, Teobert [1842-1917]
       Explorations in the department of Petén, Guatemala: Tikal.
       Manuscript: 179 leaves, typewritten; 28 cm.
       English translation of an original manuscript in German.
       Later published as: Maler, Teobert: *Explorations in the
       department of Petén, Guatemala: Tikal.* Memoirs of the
       Peabody Museum of American Archaeology and Ethnology,
       Harvard University, vol. 5, no. 1 ... Cambridge, Massachusetts,
       1901.
                              C.A. 3 M 293 E

692.   Maler, Teobert [1842-1917]

Explorations in Yucatán [I].
Manuscript: 72 leaves, typewritten; 28 cm.
English translation of: Yukatekische Forschungen. *Globus*
68:247-259, 277-292, 1895.

                              C.A. 3 M 293m
                              C.A. 3 M 293yu

693.   Explorations in Yucatán [II].
Manuscript: 85 leaves, typewritten; 28 cm.
English translation of: Yukatekische Forschungen. *Globus*
82:197-230, 1902.

                              C.A. 3 M 293m
                              C.A. 3 M 293yu

694.   Recent expeditions for archaeological research in Yucatán.
Manuscript: 5 leaves, typewritten; 28 cm.
English translation of: Neue archäologische Forschungsreisen
in Yukatan. *Globus* 81:14-15, 1902.

                              C.A. 3 M 293m
                              C.A. 3 M 293yu

695.   Recently discovered ruins in Yucatán.
Manuscript: 14 leaves, typewritten; 28 cm.
A note by H.E.D. Pollock gives: "Maler mentions his article
in *Globus*, 1895, as 'recently published', and thus dates this
manuscript fairly closely. I have looked through the *American
Naturalist* from 1895 to 1910 but cannot find this article, so
suppose it was not published. There are however several
short articles by Maler and [Henry C.] Mercer. Mercer was
editor for the anthropology section of the *American Naturalist*.
In one article Maler promises to send the present manuscript
or at least one like it."

                              C.A. 3 M 293r
                              C.A. 3 M 293yu

696.   Meinshausen, Martin

Solar and lunar eclipses in the Dresden Maya manuscript.
Manuscript: 6 leaves, typewritten; 28 cm.
English translation of: Uber Sonnen- und Mondfinsternisse
in der Dresdener Mayahandschrift. *Zeitschrift für Ethnologie*
45:221-227, 1913.

                              MEX 1 M 68 E F
                              MEX 1 M 68 E Microfilm

697. Noll-Husum, Herbert

The basic factors in Maya chronology: a study in descriptive astronomy.
Manuscript: 22 leaves, typewritten; 28 cm.
English translation of: Grundlegendes zur Zeitbestimmung der Maya: eine Aufgabe der geschichtlichen Himmelskunde.
Zeitschrift für Ethnologie 69:53-63, 1937.
C.A. 9 N 72g E F

698. Palleske, R.

The journey of Carl Lumholtz in Mexico.
Manuscript: 4 leaves, typewritten; 28 cm.
English translation of: Die Reisen von Carl Lumholtz in Mexiko. *Globus* 71:225-226, 1896.
MEX 1 M 68 E F
MEX 1 M 68 E Microfilm

699. Preuss, Konrad Theodor [1869-1938]

Ancient Mexican vessels for sacrifical blood, explained by statements of Cora Indians.
Manuscript: 21 leaves, typewritten; 28 cm.
English translation of: Die Opferblutschale der alten Mexikaner nach den Angaben der Cora-Indianer. *Zeitschrift für Ethnologie* 43:293-306, 1911.
MEX 4 P 928o F

700. The ancient settlement of Chaculá (Guatemala).
Manuscript: 13 leaves, typewritten; 28 cm.
English translation of: Die alten Ansiedlungen von Chaculá (Guatemala). *Globus* 81:346-350, 1902.
MEX 1 P 92 E F
MEX 1 P 92 E Microfilm

701. The astral religion of Mexico in prehispanic times and at the present.
Manuscript: 10 leaves, typewritten; 28 cm.
English translation of: Die Astralreligion in Mexiko in vorspanischer Zeit und in der Gegenwart. *Transactions of the III International Congress for the History of Religions*, Oxford, England, vol. 1, pp.36-41, 1908.
MEX 1 M 68 E F
MEX 1 M 68 E Microfilm

702. The contest of the sun with the stars in Mexico.
Manuscript: 17 leaves, typewritten; 28 cm.
English translation of: Der Kampf der Sonne mit den Sternen in Mexiko. *Globus* 87:136-140, 1905.
MEX 1 P 92 E F
MEX 1 P 92 E Microfilm

703.   Preuss, Konrad Theodor [1869-1938]
        Cosmic hieroglyphs of the Mexicans.
        Manuscript: 75 leaves, typewritten; 28 cm.
        English translation of: Kosmische Hieroglyphen der Mexikaner.
        Zeitschrift für Ethnologie 33:1-47, 1901.
                        MEX 1 P 92 E F
                        MEX 1 P 92 E Microfilm

704.   Fantasies in regard to The Fundamental Principles of Civiliza-
        tion.
        Manuscript: 12 leaves, typewritten; 28 cm.
        English translation of: Phantastien über die Grundlagen der
        Kultur. *Globus* 80:9-12, 1903.
        A critique of Nuttall, Zelia: *The Fundamental Principles of
        Old and New World Civilizations* ... Cambridge, Massachusetts:
        Peabody Museum of American Archaeology and Ethnology, Harvard
        University, 1901.
                        MEX 1 P 92 E F
                        MEX 1 P 92 E Microfilm

705.   The fire god as a basis for the comprehension of the Mexican
        religion as a whole.
        Manuscript: 210 leaves, typewritten; 28 cm.
        English translation of: Die Feuergötter als Ausgangspunkt zum
        Verständnis der mexikanischen Religion in ihrem Zusammenhange.
        Mitteilungen der Anthropologischen Gesellschaft in Wien 33:
        129-233, 1903.
                        MEX 4 P 928 E F

706.   The fortune books of the ancient Mexicans.
        Manuscript: 13 leaves, typewritten; 28 cm.
        English translation of: Die Schicksalbücher der alten Mexikaner.
        Globus 79:261-264, 1901.
                        MEX 1 P 92 E F
                        MEX 1 P 92 E Microfilm

707.   The XIV International Congress of Americanists at Stuttgart,
        August 18-24, 1904.
        Manuscript: 15 leaves, typewritten; 28 cm.
        English translation of: Der XIV Internationale Amerikanisten-
        kongress in Stuttgart, 18 bis 23 August, 1904. *Globus* 86:199-
        202, 1904.
                        MEX 1 P 92 E F
                        MEX 1 P 92 E Microfilm

708. Preuss, Konrad Theodor [1869-1938]
The glyph for war in the Mexican picture writings.
Manuscript: 48 leaves, typewritten; 28 cm.
English translation of: Die Hieroglyphe des Krieges in den
mexikanischen Bilderhandschriften. *Zeitschrift für Ethnologie*
32:109-145, 1900.
MEX 1 P 92 E F
MEX 1 P 92 E Microfilm

709. Mexican pottery figurines.
Manuscript: 19 leaves, typewritten; 28 cm.
English translation of: Mexikanische Thonfiguren. *Globus*
79:85-91, 1901.
MEX 1 P 92 E F
MEX 1 P 92 E Microfilm

710. The monkey in Mexican mythology.
Manuscript: 13 leaves, typewritten; 28 cm.
English translation of: Der Affe in der mexikanische Mythologie.
Ethnologisches Notizblatt 2:66-76, 1901.
MEX 1 P 92 E F
MEX 1 P 92 E Microfilm

711. The origin of human sacrifice in Mexico.
Manuscript: 49 leaves, typewritten; 28 cm.
English translation of: Der Ursprung der Menschenopfer in
Mexiko. *Globus* 86:108-119, 1904.
MEX 1 P 92 E F
MEX 1 P 92 E Microfilm

712. The origin of religion and art.
Manuscript: 143 leaves, typewritten; 28 cm.
English translation of: Der Ursprung der Religion und Kunst.
Globus 86:321-327, 335-363, 388-392, 1904; 87:333-337, 347-
350, 380-384, 394-400, 1905.
MEX 4 P 928u E F

713. Parallels between the ancient Mexicans and the modern Huichol
Indians.
Manuscript: 5 leaves, typewritten; 28 cm.
English translation of: Parallelen zwischen den alten
Mexikanern und den heutigen Huichol indianern. *Globus* 80:
314-315, 1901.
MEX 1 P 92 E F
MEX 1 P 92 E Microfilm

714.   Preuss, Konrad Theodor [1869-1938]
        The relief representing a Mexican death deity in the Royal
        Museum of Ethnology at Berlin.
        Manuscript: 37 leaves, typewritten; 28 cm.
        English translation of: Das Reliefbild einer mexikanischen
        Todes-Gottheit im Königliches Museum für Volkerkunde zu
        Berlin. *Verhandlungen der Berliner Gesellschaft für Anthro-
        pologie, Ethnologie, und Urgeschichte* 34:445-467, 1902.
                        MEX 1 P 92 E F
                        MEX 1 P 92 E Microfilm

715.   A ride through the country of the Huichol Indians in the
        Mexican Sierra Madre.
        Manuscript: 40 leaves, typewritten; 28 cm.
        English translation of: Ritte durch das Land der Huichol-
        Indianer in der mexikanischen Sierra Madre. *Globus* 92:155-
        161, 167-177, 1907.
                        MEX 1 P 92 E F
                        MEX 1 P 92 E Microfilm

716.   Sin in the ancient Mexican religion.
        Manuscript: 19 leaves, typewritten; 28 cm.
        English translation of: Die Sunde der mexikanischen Religion.
        Globus 83:253-257, 268-273, 1903.
                        MEX 1 P 92 E F
                        MEX 1 P 92 E Microfilm

717.   A visit among the Mexicano (Aztec) in the western Sierra
        Madre.
        Manuscript: 18 leaves, typewritten; 28 cm.
        English translation of: Ein Besuch bei den Mexicanos (Azteken)
        in der Sierra Madre Occidental. *Globus* 93:189-194, 1908.
                        MEX 1 P 92 E F
                        MEX 1 P 92 E Microfilm

718.   Prowe, Hermann
        The knowledge of the Quiché Indians in mythical form.
        Manuscript: 14 leaves, typewritten; 28 cm.
        English translation of: Das Wissen der Quiché-Indianer in
        mythischer Form. *Globus* 90:157-160, 1906.
                        MEX 1 M 68 E F
                        MEX 1 M 68 E Microfilm

719.   Quiché myths [a reply to Lehmann 1906]
        Manuscript: 6 leaves, typewritten; 28 cm.
        English translation of: Quiché-Sagen (Entgenung von Dr. H.
        Prowe). *Globus* 91:305-306, 1907.
                        MEX 1 M 68 E F
                        MEX 1 M 68 E Microfilm

720. Recent researches at Chichén Itzá.
     Manuscript: 19 leaves, typewritten; 28 cm.
     English translation of: Neuere Forschungen in Chichén-Itzá.
     Globus 72:200-206, 1897.
                                        MEX 1 M 68 E F
                                        MEX 1 M 68 E Microfilm

721. Recent researches in the ruins of Uxmal (Yucatán)
     Manuscript: 14 leaves, typewritten; 28 cm.
     English translation of: Neue Forschungen in den Ruinen von
     Uxmal (Yukatan). *Globus* 71:220-224, 240-242, 1897.
                                        MEX 1 M 68 E F
                                        MEX 1 M 68 E Microfilm

722. Sapper, Karl [1866-1945]
     Aztec place names in Central America.
     Manuscript: 11 leaves, typewritten; 28 cm.
     English translation of: Aztekische Ortsnamen in Mittelamerika.
     Zeitschrift für Ethnologie 37:1002-1007, 1905.
                                        C.A. 1 Sa 69m E F
                                        C.A. 1 Sa 69m E Microfilm

723. Caecilie Seler on ancient roads in Mexico and Guatemala.
     Manuscript: 8 leaves, typewritten; 28 cm.
     English translation of: Cäcilie Seler auf alten Wegen in
     Mexiko und Guatemala. *Globus* 78:389-392, 1900.
                                        C.A. 1 Sa 69m E F
                                        C.A. 1 Sa 69m E Microfilm

724. The Central American Exhibition at Guatemala, 1897.
     Manuscript: 13 leaves, typewritten; 28 cm.
     English translation of: Die Mittelamerikanische Ausstellung
     in Guatemala, 1897. *Globus* 72:325-328, 1897.
                                        C.A. 1 Sa 69m E F
                                        C.A. 1 Sa 69m E Microfilm

725. Central American weapons in modern use.
     Manuscript: 28 leaves, typewritten; 28 cm.
     English translation of: Mittelamerikanische Waffen im modernen
     Gebrauche. *Globus* 83:53-65, 1903.
                                        C.A. 1 Sa 69m E F
                                        C.A. 1 Sa 69m E Microfilm

726. The character of Central American Indians.
     Manuscript: 16 leaves, typewritten; 28 cm.
     English translation of: Der Charakter der mittelamerikanischen
     Indianer. *Globus* 87:128-131, 1905.
                                        C.A. 1 Sa 69m E F
                                        C.A. 1 Sa 69m E Microfilm

727. Sapper, Karl [1866-1945]

Food and drink of the Kekchí Indians.
Manuscript: 16 leaves, typewritten; 28 cm.
English translation of: Speise und Trank der Kekchi Indianer.
Globus 75:259-263, 1901.

C.A. 1 Sa 69m E F
C.A. 1 Sa 69m E Microfilm

728. The future of the Indian tribes of Central America.
Manuscript: 55 leaves, typewritten; 28 cm.
English translation of: Die Zukunft der mittelamerikanischen
Indianerstämme. *Archiv für Rassen und Gesellschafts Biologie*
2:383-412, 1905.

C.A. 1 Sa 69m E F
C.A. 1 Sa 69m E Microfilm

729. An Indian insurrection at San Juan Ixcoy, Huehuetenango,
Guatemala.
Manuscript: 2 leaves, typewritten; 28 cm.
English translation of: Ein Indianer Aufstand in San Juan
Ixcoy, Huehuetenango, Guatemala. *Globus* 74:199, 1898.

C.A. 1 Sa 69m E F
C.A. 1 Sa 69m E Microfilm

730. The influence of man on the formation of the Mexican-
Central American landscape.
Manuscript: 14 leaves, typewritten; 28 cm.
English translation of: Der Einfluss des Menschen auf die
Gestaltung des mexikanische-mittelamerikanischen Landschafts-
bildes. *Globus* 89:149-152, 1906.

C.A. 1 Sa 69m E F
C.A. 1 Sa 69m E Microfilm

731. Journey in Honduras.
Manuscript: 2 leaves, typewritten; 28 cm.
English translation of: Reise in Honduras. *Globus* 74:119,
1898.

C.A. 1 Sa 69m E F
C.A. 1 Sa 69m E Microfilm

732. The Mexican territory of Quintana Roo.
Manuscript: 9 leaves, typewritten; 28 cm.
English translation of: Das mexikanische Territorium
Quintana Roo. *Globus* 88:165-167, 1905.

C.A. 1 Sa 69m E F
C.A. 1 Sa 69m E Microfilm

733. Sapper, Karl [1866-1945]
Mushroom-shaped idols from Guatemala and San Salvador.
Manuscript: 2 leaves, typewritten; 28 cm.
English translation of: Pilzförmige Götzenbilder aus Guatemala und San Salvador. *Globus* 73:327, 1898.
C.A. 1 Sa 69m E F
C.A. 1 Sa 69m E Microfilm

734. Northern Central America with a trip to the highlands of Anahuac. Travels and studies of the years 1888-1895.
Manuscript: 215 leaves, typewritten; 28 cm.
English translation of: *Das nördliche Mittel-Amerika nebst einem Ausflug nach dem Hochland von Anahuac. Reisen und Studien aus den Jahren 1888-1895* ... Braunschweig : Friedrich Vieweg, 1897.
C.A. 1 Sa 69n E

735. An old Indian land law-suit in Guatemala.
Manuscript: 6 leaves, typewritten; 28 cm.
English translation of: Ein altindianischer Landstreit in Guatemala. *Globus* 72:94-97, 1897.
C.A. 1 Sa 69m E F
C.A. 1 Sa 69m E Microfilm

736. Old Indian settlements in Guatemala and Chiapas.
Manuscript: 21 leaves, typewritten; 28 cm.
English translation of: Altindianische Ansiedlungen in Guatemala und Chiapas. *Veröffentlichungen aus dem Königlichen Museum für Völkerkunde* 4:13-20, 1895.
C.A. 1 Sa 69m E F
C.A. 1 Sa 69m E Microfilm

737. The Payas in Honduras, written after a visit in 1898.
Manuscript: 13 leaves, typewritten; 28 cm.
English translation of: Die Payas in Honduras, geschildert nach einem Besuche im Jahre 1898. *Globus* 75:80-83, 1899.
C.A. 1 Sa 69m E F
C.A. 1 Sa 69m E Microfilm

738. A pictorial catechism of the Mazahua in Mexico.
Manuscript: 6 leaves, typewritten; 28 cm.
English translation of: Ein Bilderkatechismus der Mazahua in Mexiko. *Globus* 80:125-126, 1901.
C.A. 1 Sa 69m E F
C.A. 1 Sa 69m E Microfilm

739. Sapper, Karl [1866-1945]

The present status of our ethnographical knowledge of Central America.
Manuscript: 97 leaves, typewritten; 28 cm.
English translation of: Der Gegenwärtige Stand der ethnographischen Kenntnis von Mittelamerika. *Archiv für Anthropologie* 3:1-39, 1904.

                                  C.A. 1 Sa 69m E F
                                  C.A. 1 Sa 69m E Microfilm

740. Recent contributions to the knowledge of Guatemala and West Salvador.
Manuscript: 27 leaves, typewritten; 28 cm.
English translation of: Neue Beitrage zur Kenntnis von Guatemala und Westsalvador. *Petermann's Mitteilungen* 47: 25-40, 1904.

                                  C.A. 1 Sa 69m E F
                                  C.A. 1 Sa 69m E Microfilm

741. The Verapaz and its inhabitants.
Manuscript: 28 leaves, typewritten; 28 cm.
English translation of: Die Verapaz und ihre Bewohner. *Das Ausland* 51:1011-1016, 52:1034-1036, 1891.

                                  C.A. 1 Sa 69m E F
                                  C.A. 1 Sa 69m E Microfilm

742. A visit among the eastern Lacandones.
Manuscript: 10 leaves, typewritten; 28 cm.
English translation of: Ein Besuch bei den östlichen Lacandonen. *Das Ausland* 45:892-895, 1891.

                                  C.A. 1 Sa 69m E F
                                  C.A. 1 Sa 69m E Microfilm

743. Schulz, Ramón P.C.

Contributions to the chronology and astronomy of ancient Central America.
Manuscript: 48 leaves, typewritten; 28 cm.
English translation of: Beiträge zur Chronologie und Astronomie des alten Zentralamerika. *Anthropos* 31:758-788, 1936.

                                  C.A. 9 Sch 84b E F

744. The so-called serpent numbers of the Maya Dresden Codex and the zero point of the Maya long count.
Manuscript: 22 leaves, typewritten; 28 cm.
English translation of: Los llamados números de serpiente del codice maya de Dresden y el punto cero de la cuenta larga maya. *El México Antiguo* 7:322-342, 1949. Includes a letter of transmittal from Schulz to Alfred M. Tozzer.

                                  C.A. 9 Sch 841 E F
                                  C.A. 9 Sch 841 E Microfilm

745. Schulz, Ramón P.C.

Some long count dates in the Dresden Codex.
Manuscript: 5 leaves, typewritten; 28 cm.
English translation of: Uber einige long-count Daten des Codex
Dresdensis. *Anthropos* 32:287-289, 1937.
C.A. 9 Sch 84u E F

746. Schwede, Rudolf

On the paper of the Maya codices and some ancient Mexican
picture writings.
Manuscript: 28 leaves, typewritten; 28 cm.
English translation of: *Uber das Papier der Maya-Codices und
einiger altmexikanischer Bilderhandschriften* ... Dresden :
Richard Bertling, 1912. Only a partial translation.
MEX 1 M 68 E F
MEX 1 M 68 E Microfilm

747. Seler, Eduard [1849-1922]

An alleged Aztec manuscript discovered in North America.
Manuscript: 3 leaves, typewritten; 28 cm.
English translation of: Eine angeblich in Nordamerika gefundene
Aztekenhandschrift. *Globus* 72:33, 1897.
MEX 1 Se 48m E F
MEX 1 Se 48m E Microfilm

748. American stone hatchets and their handles.
Manuscript: 2 leaves, typewritten; 28 cm.
English translation of: Uber amerikanische Steinbeile und
deren Schäftung. *Zeitschrift für Ethnologie* 27:357-358, 1895.
MEX 1 Se 48m E F
MEX 1 Se 48m E Microfilm

749. The ancient buildings of Hochob in the state of Campeche.
Manuscript: 2 leaves, typewritten; 28 cm.
English translation of: Die alten Bauten von Hochob in Staate
Campeche. *Zeitschrift für Ethnologie* 47:269-270, 1915.
MEX 3 Se 48al

750. Ancient Mexican attire and insignia of social and military
rank.
Manuscript: 121 leaves, typewritten; 28 cm.
English translation of: Altmexikanischer Schmuck und sociale
und militärische Rangabzeichen. *Zeitschrift für Ethnologie*
21:69-85, 1889, 23:114-144, 1891. Also in: *Gesammelte Abhand-
lungen* 2:509-519, 1904.
MEX 1 Se 48g E 2 F
MEX 1 Se 48g E 2 Microfilm
MEX 1 Se 48g E 3 F

751. Seler, Eduard [1849-1922]

Ancient Mexican bone rattles.
Manuscript: 23 leaves, typewritten; 28 cm.
English translation of: Altmexikanische Knochenrasseln.
Globus 74:85-93, 1898. Also in: *Gesammelte Abhandlungen*
2:672-694, 1904.

MEX 1 Se 48g E 2 F
MEX 1 Se 48g E 2 Microfilm
MEX 1 Se 48g E 3 F

752. Ancient Mexican shields.
Manuscript: 12 leaves, typewritten; 28 cm.
English translation of: Altmexikanische Schilde. *Internationales Archiv für Ethnographie* 5:168-172, 1892. Also in:
Gesammelte Abhandlungen 2:664-668, 1904.

MEX 1 Se 48g E 2 F
MEX 1 Se 48g E 2 Microfilm
MEX 1 Se 48g E 3 F
MEX 1 Se 48m E F
MEX 1 Se 48m E Microfilm

753. Ancient Mexican throwing sticks.
Manuscript: 30 leaves, typewritten; 28 cm.
English translation of: Altmexikanische Wurfbretter. *Internationales Archiv für Ethnographie* 3:137-148, 1890. Also in:
Gesammelte Abhandlungen 2:368-396, 1904.

MEX 1 Se 48g E 2 F
MEX 1 Se 48g E 2 Microfilm
MEX 1 Se 48g E 3 F

754. The ancient settlements in the district of the Huaxteca.
Manuscript: 20 leaves, typewritten; 28 cm.
English translation of: Die alten Ansiedlungen im Gebiete der
Huaxteca. *Zeitschrift für Ethnologie* 20:451-459, 1888. Also in:
Gesammelte Abhandlungen 2:168-183, 1904.

MEX 1 Se 48g E 2 F
MEX 1 Se 48g E 2 Microfilm
MEX 1 Se 48g E 3 F

755. The ancient settlements of Chaculá in the Nenton district of
the department of Huehuetenango in the Republic of Guatemala.
Manuscript: 242 leaves, typewritten; 28 cm.
English translation of: *Die alten Ansiedlungen von Chaculá in
Districkte Nenton des Departments Huehuetenango der Republik
Gautemala* ... Berlin : Dietrich Reimer, 1901.

C.A. 3 Se 4as E

756. Seler, Eduard [1849-1922]
      The ancient town of Chaculá.
      Manuscript: 11 leaves, typewritten; 28 cm.
      English translation of: Les anciennes villes de Chaculá.
      *Compte rendu XIIe Session du Congrès International des
      Américanistes*, Paris, pp. 263-270, 1900. Also in:
      Gesammelte Abhandlungen 2:247-256, 1904.
                    MEX 1 Se 48g E 2 F
                    MEX 1 Se 48g E 2 Microfilm
                    MEX 1 Se 48g E 3 F

757. The animal portrayals of the Mexican and Maya manuscripts.
      Manuscript: 191 leaves, typewritten; 28 cm.
      English translation of: Die Tierbilder der mexikanischen und
      Maya-Handschriften. *Zeitschrift für Ethnologie* 41:209-257,
      301-451, 784-846, 1909, 42:31-97, 242-287, 1910. Also in:
      Gesammelte Abhandlungen 4:453-758, 1923.
                    MEX 1 Se 48g E 2 F
                    MEX 1 Se 48g E 2 Microfilm
                    MEX 1 Se 48g E 3 F

758. Another ancient Mexican stone mask, the significance of which
      has been determined.
      Manuscript: 7 leaves, typewritten; 28 cm.
      English translation of: Eine andere mit Bestimmung versehene
      altmexikanische Steinmaske. *Globus* 84:173-176, 1903. Also in:
      Gesammelte Abhandlungen 2:953-958, 1904.
                    MEX 1 Se 48g E 2 F
                    MEX 1 Se 48g E 2 Microfilm
                    MEX 1 Se 48g E 3 F

759. Another quauhxicalli.
      Manuscript: 6 leaves, typewritten; 28 cm.
      English translation of: Ein anderes Quauhxicalli. *Ethno-
      logisches Notizblatt* 3:135-139, 1901. Also in: *Gesammelte
      Abhandlungen* 2:712-716, 1904.
                    MEX 1 Se 48g E 2 F
                    MEX 1 Se 48g E 2 Microfilm
                    MEX 1 Se 48g E 3 F

760. Antiquities from Guatemala (Chajcar).
      Manuscript: 7 leaves, typewritten; 28 cm.
      English translation of: Altertümer aus Guatemala (Chajcar).
      Veröffentlichungen aus dem Königlichen Museum für Völkerkunde
      4:21-53, 1895. Also in: *Gesammelte Abhandlungen* 3:578-640, 1908.
                    MEX 1 Se 48m E F
                    MEX 1 Se 48m E Microfilm

761. Seler, Eduard [1849-1922]

Antiquities from the Alta Verapaz.
Manuscript: 14 leaves, typewritten; 28 cm.
English translation of: Alterthümer aus der Alta Vera Paz,
Ethnologisches Notizblatt 1:20-26, 1895. Also in:
Gesammelte Abhandlungen 3:670-687, 1908.

MEX 1 Se 48g E 2 F
MEX 1 Se 48g E 2 Microfilm
MEX 1 Se 48g E 2 F

762. Antiquities of the Castillo de Teayo.
Manuscript: 36 leaves, typewritten; 28 cm.
English translation of: Die Alterthümer von Castillo de
Teayo. *Verhandlungen des XIV. Internationalen Amerikanisten-
Kongresses*, Stuttgart, pp. 263-304, 1904. Also in:
Gesammelte Abhandlungen 3:410-449, 1908.

MEX 1 Se 48g E 2 F
MEX 1 Se 48g E 2 Microfilm
MEX 1 Se 48g E 3 F

763. Archaeological expedition to Mexico.
Manuscript: 35 leaves, typewritten; 28 cm.
English translation of: Archäologische Reise in Mexiko.
Verhandlungen der Gesellschaft für Erdkunde zu Berlin,
February 2, 1889. Also in: *Gesammelte Abhandlungen* 2:107-
127, 1904.

MEX 1 Se 48g E 2 F
MEX 1 Se 48g E 2 Microfilm
MEX 1 Se 48g E 3 F

764. Archaeological expedition to South and Central America, 1910-1911.
Manuscript: 47 leaves, typewritten; 28 cm.
English translation of: Archäologische Reise in Sud- und
Mittelamerika, 1910-1911. *Zeitschrift für Ethnologie* 44:201-
242, 1912. Also in: *Gesammelte Abhandlungen* 5:115-151, 1915.

MEX 1 Se 48g E 2 F
MEX 1 Se 48g E 2 Microfilm
MEX 1 Se 48g E 3 F
MEX 1 Se 48m E F
MEX 1 Se 48m E Microfilm

765. Archaeological results of a trip to Mexico.
Manuscript: 42 leaves, typewritten; 28 cm.
English translation of: Die archäologischen Ergebnisse einer
ersten mexikanischen Reise. *Compte rendu VIIème Session du
Congrès International des Américanistes*, Berlin, pp. 111-145,
1888. Also in: *Gesammelte Abhandlungen* 2:290-367, 1904.

MEX 1 Se 48g E 2 F
MEX 1 Se 48g E 2 Microfilm
MEX 1 Se 48g E 3 F

766. Seler, Eduard [1849-1922]
The cedrela lintels of Tikal in the Basel Museum.
Manuscript: 37 leaves, typewritten; 28 cm.
English translation of: Die Cedrela-Holzplatten von Tikal
im Museum zu Basel. *Zeitschrift für Ethnologie* 32:101-126, 1900.
Also in: *Gesammelte Abhandlungen* 1:837-862, 1902.
MEX 1 Se 48g E 2 F
MEX 1 Se 48g E 2 Microfilm
MEX 1 Se 48g E 3 F

767. A chapter from the unpublished material written in the
Aztec language of the History by Sahagún (manuscript of
the Biblioteca del Palacio in Madrid).
Manuscript: 119 leaves, typewritten; 28 cm.
English translation of: Ein Kapitel aus den in aztekischer
Sprache geschrieben ingedruckten Materialen zu dem Geschichts-
werke des P. Sahagun (Ms. der Biblioteca del Paclacio zu Madrid).
Veröffentlichungen aus dem Königlichen Museum für Völkerkunde
1:117-174, 1890. Also in: *Gesammelte Abhandlungen* 2:420-508,
1904.
MEX 1 Se 48g E 2 F
MEX 1 Se 48g E 2 Microfilm
MEX 1 Se 48g E 3 F

768. Chichén Itzá: copies of the Temple of the Jaguars and the
Shields by Miss Adela Breton.
Manuscript: 2 leaves, typewritten; 28 cm.
English translation of: Chich'enitzá: Kopien aus dem Tempel
der Jaguare und der Schilde von Miss Adela Breton.
Verhandlungen des XIV. Internationalen Amerikanisten-Kongresses,
Stuttgart, pp. lxvii-lxix, 1904.
MEX 1 Se 48m E F
MEX 1 Se 48m E Microfilm

769. The conjugation system of the Maya language.
Manuscript: 100 leaves, typewritten; 28 cm.
English translation of: Das Konjugationssystem der Maya-Sprachen.
Inaugural-Dissertation, Leipzig ... Berlin : Druck von Gebr.
Unger (Th. Grimm), 1887.
C.A. 6 Se 48k E F

770. The corrections in the length of the year and in the length
of the Venus period in the Mexican picture writings.
Manuscript: 25 leaves, typewritten; 28 cm.
English translation of: Die Korrekturen der Jahreslänge und
der Länge der Venusperiode in den mexikanischen Bilderschriften.
Zeitschrift für Ethnologie 35:1-49, 1903. Also in: *Gesammelte
Abhandlungen* 3:199-220, 1908.
MEX 1 Se 48g E 2 F
MEX 1 Se 48g E 2 Microfilm
MEX 1 Se 48g E 3 F

771. Seler, Eduard [1849-1922]

Discussion of stone boxes, tepetlacalli, with representations of sacrifice and other similar remains.
Manuscript: 60 leaves, typewritten; 28 cm.
English translation of: Uber Steinkisten, Tepetlacalli, mit Opferdarstellungen und andere ähnliche Monumente. *Zeitschrift für Ethnologie* 36:244-290, 1904. Also in: *Gesammelte Abhandlungen* 2:717-766, 1904.

MEX 1 Se 48g E 2 F
MEX 1 Se 48g E 2 Microfilm
MEX 1 Se 48g E 3 F

772. The dog in ancient Mexico.
Manuscript: 4 leaves, typewritten; 28 cm.
English translation of: Der Hund bei den alten Mexikanern. *Compte rendu VIIème Session du Congrès International des Américanistes*, Berlin, pp. 321-334, 1888.

MEX 1 Se 48m E F
MEX 1 Se 48m E Microfilm

773. Eduard Seler sends a letter from Mexico [regarding the ruins at Palenque].
Manuscript: 9 leaves, typewritten; 28 cm.
English translation of: Hr. Eduard Seler sendet einen Brief aus Mexiko. *Zeitschrift für Ethnologie* 43:310-315, 1911.

MEX 1 Se 48m E F
MEX 1 Se 48m E Microfilm

774. The eighteen annual feasts of the Mexicans.
Manuscript: 245 leaves, typewritten; 28 cm.
English translation of: Die achtzehn Jahresfeste der Mexikaner. *Veröffentlichungen aus dem Königlichen Museum für Völkerkunde* 6:67-209, 1899.

MEX 3 Se 48am E F

775. Excavations at the site of the Templo Mayor in Mexico.
Manuscript: 52 leaves, typewritten; 28 cm.
English translation of: Die Ausgrabungen am Orte des Haupttempels in México. *Mitteilungen der Anthropologischen Gesellschaft in Wien* 31:113-137, 1901. Also in: *Gesammelte Abhandlungen* 2:767-904, 1904.

MEX 1 Se 48g E 2 F
MEX 1 Se 48g E 2 Microfilm
MEX 1 Se 48g E 3 F

776. Seler, Eduard [1849-1922]
The feast calendar of the Tzeltal and the Maya of Yucatán.
Manuscript: 10 leaves, typewritten; 28 cm.
English translation of: Der Festkalender der Tzeltal und der
Maya von Yucatan. *Zeitschrift für Ethnologie* 30:410-416, 1898.
Also in: *Gesammelte Abhandlungen* 1:706-711, 1902.
MEX 1 Se 48g E 2 F
MEX 1 Se 48g E 2 Microfilm
MEX 1 Se 48g E 3 F

777. Further contributions on Mexican chronology.
Manuscript: 3 leaves, typewritten; 28 cm.
English translation of: Neue Beiträge zur mexikanischen
Chronologie. *Zeitschrift für Ethnologie* 24:311-313, 1892.
MEX 1 Se 48m E F
MEX 1 Se 48m E Microfilm

778. The green stone idol from the Stuttgart Museum.
Manuscript: 17 leaves, typewritten; 28 cm.
English translation of: Das Grünsteinidol des Stuttgarter-
Museums. *Verhandlungen des XIV. Internationalen Amerikanisten-
Kongresses*, Stuttgart, pp. 241-261, 1904. Also in: *Gesammelte
Abhandlungen* 3:392-409, 1908.
MEX 1 Se 48g E 2 F
MEX 1 Se 48g E 2 Microfilm
MEX 1 Se 48g E 3 F

779. A hieroglyph vase from Nebaj in Guatemala.
Manuscript: 13 leaves, typewritten; 28 cm.
English translation of: Ein Hieroglyphengefäss aus Nebaj in
Guatemala. *Gesammelte Abhandlungen* 3:718-729, 1908.
MEX 1 Se 48g E 2 F
MEX 1 Se 48g E 2 Microfilm
MEX 1 Se 48g E 3 F

780. The Historical Exposition at Madrid.
Manuscript: 14 leaves, typewritten; 28 cm.
English translation of: Die historische Ausstellung in Madrid.
Internationales Archiv für Ethnographie 6:62-66, 1893.
MEX 1 Se 48m E F
MEX 1 Se 48m E Microfilm

781. The Huichol Indians of the State of Jalisco in Mexico.
Manuscript: 56 leaves, typewritten; 28 cm.
English translation of: Die Huichol-Indianer des Staates Jalisco
in México. *Mitteilungen der Anthropologischen Gesellschaft in
Wien* 31:138-163, 1901. Also in: *Gesammelte Abhandlungen* 3:355-
391, 1908.
MEX 1 Se 48g E 2 F
MEX 1 Se 48g E 2 Microfilm
MEX 1 Se 48g E 3 F

782. Seler, Eduard [1849-1922]

Idolatry among the modern Indians of Mexico.
Manuscript: 10 leaves, typewritten; 28 cm.
English translation of: Götzendienerei unter den heutigen
Indianern Méxicos. *Globus* 69:367-370, 1896. Also in: *Gesammelte
Abhandlungen* 2:87-93, 1904.

> MEX 1 Se 48g E 2 F
> MEX 1 Se 48g E 2 Microfilm
> MEX 1 Se 48g E 3 F

783. Jewelry of the ancient Mexicans and their art of working in
stone and the making of feather ornaments.
Manuscript: 58 leaves, typewritten; 28 cm.
English translation of: L'orfévrerie des anciens Mexicains et
leur art de travailler la pierre et de faire des ornements en
plumes. *Compte rendu de la VIIIème Session du Congrès International
des Américanistes*, Paris, pp. 401-452, 1890. Also in: *Gesammelte
Abhandlungen* 2:620-663, 1904.

> MEX 1 Se 48g E 2 F
> MEX 1 Se 48g E 2 Microfilm
> MEX 1 Se 48g E 3 F

784. The land register of Santiago Guevea.
Manuscript: 51 leaves, typewritten; 28 cm.
English translation of: Das Dorfbuch von Santiago Guevea.
Zeitschrift für Ethnologie 38:121-155, 1906. Also in:
Gesammelte Abhandlungen 3:121-155, 1908.

> MEX 1 Se 48g E 2 F
> MEX 1 Se 48g E 2 Microfilm
> MEX 1 Se 48g E 3 F

785. The legend of Quetzalcoatl and the Toltecs in records that
have become known in recent times.
Manuscript: 15 leaves, typewritten; 28 cm.
English translation of: Die Sage von Quetzalcouatl und den
Tolteken in der neuer Zeit bekannt gewordenen Quellen.
Verhandlungen des XVI. Internationalen Amerikanisten-Kongresses,
Wien, pp. 129-150, 1908. Also in: *Gesammelte Abhandlungen* 5:
178-196, 1915.

> MEX 1 Se 48g E 2 F
> MEX 1 Se 48g E 2 Microfilm
> MEX 1 Se 48g E 3 F
> MEX 1 Se 48m E F
> MEX 1 Se 48m E Microfilm

786. Seler, Eduard [1849-1922]
Leprosy in ancient Mexican documents.
Manuscript: 6 leaves, typewritten; 28 cm.
English translation of: Nachrichten über den Aussatz in alten
mexikanischen Quellen. *Zeitschrift für Ethnologie* 29:609-611,
1897. Also in: *Gesammelte Abhandlungen* 2:100-103, 1904.
MEX 1 Se 48g E 2 F
MEX 1 Se 48g E 2 Microfilm
MEX 1 Se 48g E 3 F

787. Magic and magicians in ancient Mexico.
Manuscript: 56 leaves, typewritten; 28 cm.
English translation of: Zaberei und Zauberer im alten Mexiko.
Veröffentlichungen aus dem Königlichen Museum für Völkerkunde
6:29-57, 1899.
MEX 3 Se 48am E F

788. Magic in ancient Mexico.
Manuscript: 10 leaves, typewritten; 28 cm.
English translation of: Zauberei im alten México. *Globus*
78:89-91, 1900. Also in: *Gesammelte Abhandlungen* 2:78-86, 1904.
MEX 1 Se 48g E 2 F
MEX 1 Se 48g E 2 Microfilm
MEX 1 Se 48g E 3 F

789. Mexican paintings [in the Lienzo de Tlaxcala].
Manuscript: 3 leaves, typewritten; 28 cm.
English translation of: Mexikanische Gemälde. *Zeitschrift für
Ethnologie* 25:178-179, 1893. Also in: *Gesammelte Abhandlungen*
2:669-671, 1904.
MEX 1 Se 48g E 2 F
MEX 1 Se 48g E 2 Microfilm
MEX 1 Se 48g E 3 F

790. Mexican sculptures from the Totonac region.
Manuscript: 3 leaves, typewritten; 28 cm.
English translation of: Mexikanische Skulpturen im Totonaken-
gebiete. *Gesammelte Abhandlungen* 3:543-544, 1908.
MEX 1 Se 48g E 2 F
MEX 1 Se 48g E 2 Microfilm
MEX 1 Se 48g E 3 F

791. Mixed forms of Mexican deities.
Manuscript: 6 leaves, typewritten; 28 cm.
English translation of: Mischformen mexikanischer Gottheiten.
Globus 87:110-112, 1905. Also in: *Gesammelte Abhandlungen* 3:
450-455, 1908.
MEX 1 Se 48g E 2 F
MEX 1 Se 48g E 2 Microfilm
MEX 1 Se 48g E 3 F

792. Seler, Eduard [1849-1922]

     The monuments of Huilocintla in Canton Tuxpan in the State of
     Veracruz.
     Manuscript: 8 leaves, typewritten; 28 cm.
     English translation of: Die Monumente von Huilocintla im Canton
     Tuxpan des Staates Vera Cruz. *Compte rendu de la XVème Session
     du Congrès International des Américanistes*, Quebec, vol. 2, pp.
     381-389, 1906. Also in: *Gesammelte Abhandlungen* 3:514-521, 1908.
                         MEX 1 Se 48g E 2 F
                         MEX 1 Se 48g E 2 Microfilm
                         MEX 1 Se 48g E 3 F

793. More concerning the vase from Chamá, Quetzalcoatl and Kukulcan.
     Manuscript: 15 leaves, typewritten; 28 cm.
     English translation of: Noch einmal das Gefäss von Chamá,
     Quetzalcouatl und Kukulcan. *Zeitschrift für Ethnologie* 28:
     222-231, 1896.
                         MEX 1 Se 48m E F
                         MEX 1 Se 48m E Microfilm

794. Musical instruments of Central America.
     Manuscript: 9 leaves, typewritten; 28 cm.
     English translation of: Mittelamerikanische Musikinstrumente.
     Globus 76:109-112, 1899. Also in: *Gesammelte Abhandlungen* 2:
     695-703, 1904.
                         MEX 1 Se 48g E 2 F
                         MEX 1 Se 48g E 2 Microfilm
                         MEX 1 Se 48g E 3 F

795. The nephrite slab in the Leiden Museum.
     Manuscript: 3 leaves, typewritten; 28 cm.
     English translation of: Leidener Nephritplatte. *Verhandlungen
     des XIV. Internationalen Amerikanisten-Kongresses*, Stuttgart,
     pp. lxv-lxvi, 1904.
                         MEX 1 Se 48m E F
                         MEX 1 Se 48m E Microfilm

796. Observations and studies on the ruins of Palenque.
     Manuscript: 118 leaves, typewritten; 28 cm.
     English translation of: *Beobachtungen und Studien in den Ruinen
     von Palenque.* Abhandlungen der Königlichen Preussischen Akademie
     der Wissenschaften, no. 5. Berlin, 1915.
                         C.A. 3 Se 4b E F

797. On the origin of ancient American civilization.
     Manuscript: 23 leaves, typewritten; 28 cm.
     English translation of: Über den Ursprung der altamerikanischen
     Kulturen. *Preussische Jahrbücher* 79:488-502, 1895. Also in:
     Gesammelte Abhandlungen 2:3-15, 1904.
                         MEX 1 Se 48g E 2 F
                         MEX 1 Se 48g E 2 Microfilm
                         MEX 1 Se 48g E 3 F

798. Seler, Eduard [1849-1922]
      On the origin of Central American civilizations.
      Manuscript: 24 leaves, typewritten; 28 cm.
      English translation of: Uber den Ursprung der mittelamerikanischen
      Kulturen. *Zeitschrift der Gesellschaft für Erdkunde zu Berlin*
      37:537-552, 1902. Also in: *Gesammelte Abhandlungen* 2:16-30,
      1904.
                          MEX 1 Se 48g E 2 F
                          MEX 1 Se 48g E 2 Microfilm
                          MEX 1 Se 48g E 3 F

799. On the origin of some forms of Quiché and Cakchiquel myths.
      Manuscript: 8 leaves, typewritten; 28 cm.
      English translation of: Uber die Herkunft einiger Gestalten
      der Quiché- und Cakchiquel-Mythen. *Archiv für Religionwissenschaft*
      1:91-97, 1898. Also in: *Gesammelte Abhandlungen* 3:573-577, 1908.
                          MEX 1 Se 48g E 2 F
                          MEX 1 Se 48g E 2 Microfilm
                          MEX 1 Se 48g E 3 F

800. On the words Anahuac and Náhuatl.
      Manuscript: 44 leaves, typewritten; 28 cm.
      English translation of: Uber die Worte Anauac und Nauatl.
      *Compte rendu de la Xème Session du Congrès International des
      Américanistes*, Stockholm, pp. 211-244, 1894. Also in: *Gesammelte
      Abhandlungen* 2:49-77, 1904.
                          MEX 1 Se 48g E 2 F
                          MEX 1 Se 48g E 2 Microfilm
                          MEX 1 Se 48g E 3 F

801. Overland from Mexico through Guatemala.
      Manuscript: 25 leaves, typewritten; 28 cm.
      English translation of: Von México über Land nach Guatemala.
      Verhandlungen der Gesellschaft für Erdkunde zu Berlin
      1897. Also in: *Gesammelte Abhandlungen* 2:215-229, 1904.
                          MEX 1 Se 48g E 2 F
                          MEX 1 Se 48g E 2 Microfilm
                          MEX 1 Se 48g E 3 F

802. Parallels in the Maya manuscripts.
      Manuscript: 11 leaves, typewritten; 28 cm.
      English translation of: Parallelen in den Maya-Handschriften.
      Globus 3:695-709, 1908.
                          MEX 1 Se 48g E 2 F
                          MEX 1 Se 48g E 2 Microfilm
                          MEX 1 Se 48g E 3 F

803. Seler, Eduard [1849-1922]
The pictorial representations of the annual feasts of the
Mexicans.
Manuscript: 17 leaves, typewritten; 28 cm.
English translation of: Die bildlichen Darstellungen der
mexikanischen Jahresfeste. *Veröffentlichungen aus dem
Königlichen Museum für Völkerkunde* 6:58-66, 1899.
MEX 3 Se 48am E F

804. Production of reliefs upon the monuments at Copán and Quiriguá
and the altar slabs at Palenque.
Manuscript: 93 leaves, typewritten; 28 cm.
English translation of: Die Monumente von Copan und Quiriguá
und die Altarplatten von Palenque. *Zeitschrift für Ethnologie*
31:670-738, 1899. Also in: *Gesammelte Abhandlungen* 1:712-
791, 1902.
MEX 1 Se 48g E 2 F
MEX 1 Se 48g E 2 Microfilm
MEX 1 Se 48g E 3 F

805. The pulque vessel of the Bilimec Collection in the Imperial
Museum of Natural History (Vienna).
Manuscript: 40 leaves, typewritten; 28 cm.
English translation of: Das Pulquegefäss der Bilimek'schen
Sammlung im k.k. naturhistorischen Hofmuseum. *Annalen des
K.K. Naturhistorischen Hofmuseums*, Bild 17, 1902. Also in:
Gesammelte Abhandlungen 2:913-952, 1904.
MEX 1 Se 48g E 2 F
MEX 1 Se 48g E 2 Microfilm
MEX 1 Se 48g E 3 F

806. Quauhxicalli. The Mexican vessel for sacrificial blood.
Manuscript: 8 leaves, typewritten; 28 cm.
English translation of: Quauhxicalli. Die Opferblutschale
der Mexikaner. *Ethnologisches Notizblatt* 2:14-21, 1899.
Also in: *Gesammelte Abhandlungen* 2:704-711, 1904.
MEX 1 Se 48g E 2 F
MEX 1 Se 48g E 2 Microfilm
MEX 1 Se 48g E 3 F

807. Quetzalcoatl facades of Yucatán structures.
Manuscript: 86 leaves, typewritten; 28 cm.
English translation of: *Die Quetzalcouatl-Fassaden yukatekischer
Bauten*. Abhandlungen der Königlichen Preussischen Akademie der
Wissenschaften, no. 2. Berlin, 1916.
C.A. 3 Se 4q E F

808. Seler, Eduard [1849-1922]
Quetzalcoatl-Kukulcan in Yucatán.
Manuscript: 52 leaves, typewritten; 28 cm.
English translation of: Quetzalcouatl-Kukulcan in Yucatán.
Zeitschrift für Ethnologie 30:377-410, 1898. Also in:
Gesammelte Abhandlungen 1:668-705, 1902.
MEX 1 Se 48g E 2 F
MEX 1 Se 48g E 2 Microfilm
MEX 1 Se 48g E 3 F

809. Religious songs of the ancient Mexicans.
Manuscript: 221 leaves, typewritten; 28 cm.
English translation of: Die religiösen Gesänge der alten
Mexikaner. *Gesammelte Abhandlungen* 2:959-1107, 1904.
MEX 1 Se 48g E 2 F
MEX 1 Se 48g E 2 Microfilm
MEX 1 Se 48g E 3 F

810. Remarks on a jade-like stone received from Prof. Buchner of
Munich.
Manuscript: 10 leaves, typewritten; 28 cm.
English translation of: Die Photographie eines hervorragenden
Stuckes aus dem mexikanischen Altertume. *Zeitschrift für
Ethnologie* 37:527-536, 1905. Also in: *Gesammelte Abhandlungen*
3:459-469, 1908.
MEX 1 Se 48g E 2 F
MEX 1 Se 48g E 2 Microfilm
MEX 1 Se 48g E 3 F

811. [Remarks on] Les Memoriales de Fray Toribio Motolinía, by
León Lejéal.
Manuscript: 2 leaves, typewritten; 28 cm.
English translation of: Memoriales des Fray Torobio Motolinía.
Verhandlungen des XIV. Internationalen Amerikanisten-Kongresses,
Stuttgart, pp. lix-lx, 1904.
MEX 1 Se 48m E F
MEX 1 Se 48m E F

812. Report on the chemical and physical examination of a Mexican
copper axe.
Manuscript: 4 leaves, typewritten; 28 cm.
English translation of: Bericht über die chemische und physikal-
ische Untersuchung einer mexikanischen Kupferaxt. *Compte rendu
de la XVème Session du Congrès International des Américanistes*,
Quebec, 2:405-411, 1906. Also in: *Gesammelte Abhandlungen* 3:
533-536, 1908.
MEX 1 Se 48g E 2 F
MEX 1 Se 48g E 2 Microfilm
MEX 1 Se 48g E 3 F

813. Seler, Eduard [1849-1922]
      Report on the Eighteenth International Congress of Americanists
      in London, May 27 to June 1, 1912.
      Manuscript: 31 leaves, typewritten; 28 cm.
      English translation of: Bericht über die achtzehnte Tagung des
      Internationalen Amerikanistenkongresses in London, 27 Mai bis
      1 Juni 1912. *Zeitschrift für Ethnologie* 44:525-548, 1912.
      Also in: *Gesammelte Abhandlungen* 5:152-167, 1915.
                              MEX 1 Se 48g E 2 F
                              MEX 1 Se 48g E 2 Microfilm
                              MEX 1 Se 48g E 3 F

814. Report on the examination of the ancient Mexican feather ornament
      in the Imperial Museum of Natural History (Vienna) by the
      commission appointed by the Congress.
      Manuscript: 5 leaves, typewritten; 28 cm.
      English translation of: Bericht über die Untersuchung des alt-
      mexikanischen Federschmucks im K.K. Naturhistorischen Hofmuseum
      (Wien) durch die von dem Kongresse gewählte Kommission.
      Verhandlungen des XVI. Internationalen Amerikanisten-Kongresses,
      Vienna, pp. 241-248, 1908. Also in: *Gesammelte Abhandlungen*
      5:171-176, 1915.
                              MEX 1 Se 48g E 2 F
                              MEX 1 Se 48g E 2 Microfilm
                              MEX 1 Se 48g E 3 F
                              MEX 1 Se 48m E F
                              MEX 1 Se 48m E Microfilm

815. [Review of] Brinton, Daniel G.: A Primer of Mayan Hieroglyphics.
      Manuscript: 4 leaves, typewritten; 28 cm.
      English translation of: Brinton, Daniel G.: *A Primer of Mayan
      Hieroglyphics*. University of Pennsylvania Series in Philology,
      Literature, and Archaeology, vol. 3, no. 2 ... Philadelphia, 1895.
      Deutsche Literaturzeitung 34:1326-1327, 1898.
                              MEX 1 Se 48m E F

816. [Review of] Chavero, A.: Pinturas jeroglíficas de la Colección
      Chavero.
      Manuscript: 3 leaves, typewritten; 28 cm.
      English translation of: Chavero, A.: *Pinturas Jeroglíficas de la
      Colección Chavero* ... México, 1901. *Zeitschrift für Ethnologie*
      33:266-267, 1901.
                              MEX 1 Se 48m E F
                              MEX 1 Se 48m E Microfilm

817. Seler, Eduard [1849-1922]
      [Review of] Hahn, Edward: Von der Hacke zum Pflug.
      Manuscript: 2 leaves, typewritten; 28 cm.
      English translation of: Hahn, Eduard: Von der Hack zum Pflug ...
      Leipzig : Quelle S. Meyer, 1914. *Zeitschrift für Ethnologie*
      47:379-380, 1915.
                                MEX 4 Se 48e E F

818. [Review of] Hamy, E. T.: Galerie Américaine du Musée d'Ethno-
      graphie du Trocadéro: choix de pieces archéologiques et ethno-
      graphiques, décrites et figurées.
      Manuscript: 5 leaves, typewritten; 28 cm.
      English translation of: Hamy, E.-T.: Galerie Américaine du Musée
      d'Ethnographie du Trocadéro: choix de pieces archéologiques et
      ethnographiques, décrites et figurées ... Paris, 1897. *Globus*
      74:181-182, 1898.
                                MEX 1 Se 48m E F
                                MEX 1 Se 48m E Microfilm

819. [Review of] Schellhas, Paul: Representations of Deities of the
      Maya Manuscripts.
      Manuscript: 4 leaves, typewritten; 28 cm.
      English translation of: Schellhas, Paul: *Representations of
      Deities of the Maya Manuscripts*. Papers of the Peabody Museum
      of American Archaeology and Ethnology, Harvard University, vol. 4,
      no. 1 ... Cambridge, Massachusetts. 1904. *Deutsche Literatur-
      zeitung* 21:1300-1301, 1904.
                                MEX 1 Se 48m E F
                                MEX 1 Se 48m E Microfilm

820. [Review of] Spence, Lewis: The Myths of Mexico and Peru.
      Manuscript: 2 leaves, typewritten; 28 cm.
      English translation of: Spence, Lewis: *The Myths of Mexico
      and Peru* ... London : G. Harrap, 1913.
                                MEX 4 Sp 32s E

821. The ruins of Chichén Itzá in Yucatán.
      Manuscript: 74 leaves, typewritten; 28 cm.
      English translation of: Die Ruinen von Chich'en Itza in Yukatan.
      Verhandlungen des XVI. Internationalen Amerikanisten-Kongresses,
      Vienna, pp. 151-239, 1908.
                                C.A. 3 Se 48r E F

822. Seler, Eduard [1849-1922]

The ruins of Chichén Itzá in Yucatán.
Manuscript: 204 leaves, typewritten; 28 cm.
English translation of: Die Ruinen von Chich'en Itza in
Yucatan. *Gesammelte Abhandlungen* 5:197-388, 1915. An expanded
version of Seler's Die Ruinen von Chich'en Itza in Yucatan
(1908).

    MEX 1 Se 48g E 2 F
    MEX 1 Se 48g E 2 Microfilm
    MEX 1 Se 48g E 3 F

823. The ruins of La Quemada in the State of Zacatecas.
Manuscript: 19 leaves, typewritten; 28 cm.
English translation of: Die Ruinen von La Quemada im Staate
Zacatecas. *Gesammelte Abhandlungen* 3:545-559, 1908.

    MEX 1 Se 48g E 2 F
    MEX 1 Se 48g E 2 Microfilm
    MEX 1 Se 48g E 3 F

824. The ruins of Uxmal.
Manuscript: 94 leaves, typewritten; 28 cm.
English translation of: *Die Ruinen von Uxmal*. Abhandlungen der
Königlichen Preussischen Akademie der Wissenschaften, no. 3,
Berlin, 1917.

    C.A. 3 Se 4ru E F

825. The ruins of Xochicalco.
Manuscript: 42 leaves, typewritten; 28 cm.
English translation of: Die Ruinen von Xochicalco. *Zeitschrift
für Ethnologie* 20:94-111, 1888. Also in: *Gesammelte Abhandlungen*
2:128-167, 1904.

    MEX 1 Se 48g E 2 F
    MEX 1 Se 48g E 2 Microfilm
    MEX 1 Se 48g E 3 F

826. The ruins on the Quie-ngola.
Manuscript: 14 leaves, typewritten; 28 cm.
English translation of: Die Ruinen auf dem Quie-ngola.
*Festschrift für Adolf Bastian zu seinem 70. Geburtstage am
26. Juni 1896.* pp. 419-433. Berlin : Dietrich Reimer, 1896.
Also in: *Gesammelte Abhandlungen* 2:184-199, 1904.

    MEX 1 Se 48g E 2 F
    MEX 1 Se 48g E 2 Microfilm
    MEX 1 Se 48g E 3 F

827. Seler, Eduard [1849-1922]
The so-called sacred vessels of the Zapotecs.
Manuscript: 11 leaves, typewritten; 28 cm.
English translation of: Die sog. sakralen Gefässe der Zapoteken.
Veröffentlichungen aus dem Königlichen Museum für Völkerkunde
1:182-185, 1890.
MEX 1 Se 48m E F
MEX 1 Se 48m E Microfilm

828. Some finely painted ancient pottery vessels from the Dr. Sologuren
Collection from Nochistlán and Cuicatlán in the State of Oaxaca.
Manuscript: 15 leaves, typewritten; 28 cm.
English translation of: Einige fein bemalte alte Thongefässe
der Dr. Sologuren'schen Sammlung aus Nochistlán und Cuicatlán
im Staate Oaxaca. *Compte Rendu du la XVème Session du Congrès
International des Américanistes*, Québec, 2:391-403, 1906. Also in:
Gesammelte Abhandlungen 3:522-532, 1908.
MEX 1 Se 48g E 2 F
MEX 1 Se 48g E 2 Microfilm
MEX 1 Se 48g E 3 F

829. Some more remarks on the monuments of Copán and Quiriguá.
Manuscript: 61 leaves, typewritten; 28 cm.
English translation of: Einiges mehr über die Monumente von
Copan und Quiriguá. *Zeitschrift für Ethnologie* 32:188-227, 1900.
Also in: *Gesammelte Abhandlungen* 1:792-836, 1902.
MEX 1 Se 48g E 2 F
MEX 1 Se 48g E 2 Microfilm
MEX 1 Se 48g E 3 F

830. Some older systems in the ruins of Uxmal.
Manuscript: 26 leaves, typewritten; 28 cm.
English translation of: Uber einige ältere Systeme in den
Ruinen von Uxmal. *Proceedings of the XVIII International Congress
of Americanists*, London, pp. 220-235, 1912.
MEX 1 M 68 E F

831. Some remarks on the natural bases of Mexican mythology.
Manuscript: 60 leaves, typewritten; 28 cm.
English translation of: Einiges über die natürlichen Grundlagen
mexikanischer Mythen. *Zeitschrift für Ethnologie* 39:1-41, 1907.
Also in: *Gesammelte Abhandlungen* 3:305-351, 1908.
MEX 1 Se 48g E 2 F
MEX 1 Se 48g E 2 Microfilm
MEX 1 Se 48g E 3 F

832. Seler, Eduard [1849-1922]
A stone figure from the Sierra of Zacatlan.
Manuscript: 9 leaves, typewritten; 28 cm.
English translation of: Eine Steinfigur aus der Sierra von
Zacatlan. *Boas Anniversary Volume*, pp. 299-305. New York, 1906.
Also in: *Gesammelte Abhandlungen* 3:537-542, 1908.
MEX 1 Se 48g E 2 F
MEX 1 Se 48g E 2 Microfilm
MEX 1 Se 48g E 3 F

833. The stucco facade of Acanceh in Yucatán.
Manuscript: 16 leaves, typewritten; 28 cm.
English translation of: Die Stuckfassade von Acanceh in Yukatan.
*Sitzungsberichte der Königlichen Preussischen Akademie der
Wissenschaften* 47:1011-1025, 1911. Also in: *Gesammelte Abhandlungen
lungen* 5:389-404, 1915.
MEX 1 Se 48g E 2 F
MEX 1 Se 48g E 2 Microfilm
MEX 1 Se 48g E 3 F

834. Studies in the ruins of Yucatán.
Manuscript: 10 leaves, typewritten; 28 cm.
English translation of: Studien in den Ruinen von Yukatan.
*Compte rendu de la XVème Session du Congrès International des
Américanistes*, Québec, 2:414-422, 1906. Also in: *Correspondenz-
blatt der Deutschen Gesellschaft für Anthropologie, Ethnologie
und Urgeschichte* 34:114-116, 1903. Also in: *Gesammelte
Abhandlungen* 3:710-717, 1908.
MEX 1 Se 48g E 2 F
MEX 1 Se 48g E 2 Microfilm
MEX 1 Se 48g E 3 F

835. The Teotihuacán culture of the Mexican plateau.
Manuscript: 216 leaves, typewritten; 28 cm.
English translation of: Die Teotihuacan-Kultur des Hochlandes
von Mexiko. *Gesammelte Abhandlungen* 5:405-585, 1915.
MEX 1 Se 48g E 2 F
MEX 1 Se 48g E 2 Microfilm
MEX 1 Se 48g E 3 F

836. The tonalamatl of the ancient Mexicans.
Manuscript: 21 leaves, typewritten; 28 cm.
English translation of: Das Tonalamatl der alten Mexikaner.
Zeitschrift für Ethnologie 30:165-177, 1898. Also in:
Gesammelte Abhandlungen 1:600-617, 1902.
MEX 1 Se 48g E 2 F
MEX 1 Se 48g E 2 Microfilm
MEX 1 Se 48g E 3 F

837.   Seler, Eduard [1849-1922]
       The tonalamatl of the Aubin Collection and related calendar
       books.
       Manuscript: 252 leaves, typewritten; 28 cm.
       English translation of: Das Tonalamatl der Aubin'schen Sammlung
       und die verwandten Kalender bucher. *Compte rendu de la VIIème
       Session du Congrès International des Américanistes*, Berlin,
       pp. 521-735, 1888.
                                    MEX 7 Se 48to E F

838.   Three objects from Mexico.
       Manuscript: 4 leaves, typewritten; 28 cm.
       English translation of: Drei Gegenstände aus Mexico. *Zeitschrift
       für Ethnologie* 37:441-444, 1905. Also in: *Gesammelte Abhand-
       lungen* 3:456-458, 1908.
                                    MEX 1 Se 48g E 2 F
                                    MEX 1 Se 48g E 2 Microfilm
                                    MEX 1 Se 48g E 3 F

839.   Three travel letters from Pueblo Viejo Quen Santo and Chaculá.
       Manuscript: 29 leaves, typewritten; 28 cm.
       English translation of: Drei Reisebriefe aus Pueblo Viejo Quen
       Santo und Chaculá. *Gesammelte Abhandlungen* 2:230-246, 1904.
                                    MEX 1 Se 48g E 2 F
                                    MEX 1 Se 48g E 2 Microfilm
                                    MEX 1 Se 48g E 3 F

840.   The true length of the katun of the Maya chronicles and the
       beginning of the year in the Dresden manuscript and on the
       stela of Copán.
       Manuscript: 18 leaves, typewritten; 28 cm.
       English translation of: Die Wirkliche Länge des Katun's der
       Maya-Chroniken und der Jahresanfang in der Dresdener Handschrift
       und auf den Copan-Stelen. *Zeitschrift für Ethnologie* 27:441-449,
       1895. Also in: *Gesammelte Abhandlungen* 1:577-587, 1902.
                                    MEX 1 Se 48g E 2 F
                                    MEX 1 Se 48g E 2 Microfilm
                                    MEX 1 Se 48g E 3 F

841.   Two notable specimens from ancient Mexico in the Christy
       Collection in London.
       Manuscript: 8 leaves, typewritten; 28 cm.
       English translation of: Zwei hervorragende Stücke der altmexikan-
       ischen Sammlung der Christy Collection in London. *Globus* 80:
       223-226, 1901. Also in: *Gesammelte Abhandlungen* 2:905-912, 1904.
                                    MEX 1 Se 48g E 2 F
                                    MEX 1 Se 48g E 2 Microfilm
                                    MEX 1 Se 48g E 3 F

842. Seler, Eduard [1849-1922]
    Two spring months in Yucatán.
    Manuscript: 17 leaves, typewritten; 28 cm.
    English translation of: Zwei Frühlingsmonate in Yucatán.
    Festschrift zu P. Ascherson's 70. Geburtstage. pp. 371-382.
    Berlin, 1904. Also in: *Gesammelte Abhandlungen* 3:563-572,
    1908.

    MEX 1 Se 48g E 2 F
    MEX 1 Se 48g E 2 Microfilm
    MEX 1 Se 48g E 3 F

843. Wall sculptures in the Temple of the Pulque God at Tepoztlán.
    Manuscript: 28 leaves, typewritten; 28 cm.
    English translation of: Die Wandskulpturen im Tempel des
    Pulquegottes von Tepoztlan. *Compte Rendu de la XVème Session
    du Congrès International des Américanistes*, Québec, 2:351-370,
    1906. Also in: *Gesammelte Abhandlungen* 3:487-513, 1908.

    MEX 1 Se 48g E 2 F
    MEX 1 Se 48g E 2 Microfilm
    MEX 1 Se 48g E 3 F

844. Where was Aztlán, the home of the Aztecs?
    Manuscript: 21 leaves, typewritten; 28 cm.
    English translation of: Wo lag Aztlan, die Heimath der Azteken?
    Globus 65:317-324, 1894. Also in: *Gesammelte Abhandlungen* 2:31-
    48, 1904.

    MEX 1 Se 48g E 2 F
    MEX 1 Se 48g E 2 Microfilm
    MEX 1 Se 48g E 3 F

845. A winter-term in Mexico and Yucatán.
    Manuscript: 41 leaves, typewritten; 28 cm.
    English translation of: Ein Wintersemester in Mexico und
    Yucatan. *Zeitschrift für Gesellschaft für Erdkunde zu Berlin*
    38:477-502, 1903. Also in: *Gesammelte Abhandlungen* 2:257-286,
    1904.

    MEX 1 Se 48g E 2 F
    MEX 1 Se 48g E 2 Microfilm
    MEX 1 Se 48g E 3 F

846. The wooden drum of Malinalco and the atl-tlachinolli sign.
    Manuscript: 96 leaves, typewritten; 28 cm.
    English translation of: Die holzgeschnitzte Pauke von Malinalco
    und das Zeichen atl-tlachinolli. *Mitteilungen der Anthropologischen
    Gesellschaft in Wien* 34:222-274, 1904. Also in: *Gesammelte
    Abhandlungen* 3:221-304, 1908.

    MEX 1 Se 48g E 2 F
    MEX 1 Se 48g E 2 Microfilm
    MEX 1 Se 48g E 3 F

847. Seler-Sachs, Caecilie [1855-1935]

   The Huaxteca Collection of the Royal Museum of Ethnology at
   Berlin collected by Eduard and Caecilie Seler in 1888.
   Manuscript: 55 leaves, typewritten; 28 cm.
   English translation of: Die Huaxteca-Sammlung des Kgl. Museums
   für Völkerkunde zu Berlin gesammelt von Eduard und Caecilie
   Seler im Jahre 1888. *Baessler Archiv* 5:98-135, 1913.
                                                MEX 3 Se 4 E F

848. A short account of an archaeological journey through Mexico
   and Central America.
   Manuscript: 13 leaves, typewritten; 28 cm.
   English translation of: Kürzer Bericht über archäologische
   Reise durch Mexiko und Mittelamerika. *Globus* 72:85-88, 1897.
                                                MEX 1 M 68 E F
                                                MEX 1 M 68 E Microfilm

849. Small pottery objects from Lake Chapala, Mexico.

   Manuscript: 3 leaves, typewritten; 28 cm.
   English translation of: Irdene Kleingeräte aus dem Chapalasee,
   Mexiko. *Globus* 72:240-241, 1897.
                                                MEX 1 M 68 E F
                                                MEX 1 M 68 E Microfilm

850. Stempell, W.

   Representations of animals in the Maya manuscripts.
   Manuscript: 47 leaves, typewritten; 28 cm.
   English translation of: Die Tierbilder der Mayahandschriften.
   Zeitschrift für Ethnologie 5:704-743, 1908.
                                                C.A. 7 St 4r

851. Strebel, Hermann [b. 1849]

   Animal ornaments on pottery vessels from ancient Mexico.
   Manuscript: 76 leaves, typewritten; 28 cm.
   English translation of: Uber Tierornamente auf Thongefässen
   aus Alt-Mexiko. *Veröffentlichungen der Königlichen Museum für
   Völkerkunde* 6:1-28, 1899.
                                                MEX 3 St 8an E F
                                                MEX 3 St 8an E Microfilm

852. On the interpretation of an ancient Mexican ornament motif.
   Manuscript: 12 leaves, typewritten; 28 cm.
   English translation of: Zur Deutung eines altmexikanischen
   Ornamentmotivs. *Globus* 71:197-201, 1897.
                                                MEX 1 M 68 E F
                                                MEX 1 M 68 E Microfilm

853. Strebel, Hermann [b. 1849]

Ornaments on earthen vessels from ancient Mexico.
Manuscript: 3 leaves, typewritten; 28 cm.
English translation of: Ornamente auf Thongefässen aus Alt-
Mexiko. *Verhandlungen des XIV. Internationalen Amerikanisten-
Kongresses*, Stuttgart, pp. 305-307, 1904.
PAM S

854. Termer, Franz [1894-1968]

The archaeology of Guatemala.
Manuscript: 41 leaves, typewritten; 28 cm.
English translation of: Zur Archäologie von Guatemala.
Baessler Archiv 14:167-191, 1930.
C.A. 3 T 273z E F

855. The significance of the Pipiles in the cultural configuration of
Guatemala: a contribution to the historical ethnography of
northern Central America.
Manuscript: 14 leaves, typewritten; 28 cm.
English translation of: Die Bedeutung der Pipiles für die
Kulturgestaltung in Guatemala. *Baessler Archiv* 19:108-113,
1936.
PAM T

856. Uhle, Max [1856-1944]

Specimens of American archaeology selected from the Royal
Museum of Ethnography.
Manuscript: 89 leaves, typewritten; 28 cm.
English translation of: Ausgewählte Stücke des K. Museums
für Völkerkunde zur Archäologie Amerikas. *Veröffentlichungen
aus dem Königlichen Museum für Völkerkunde* 1: 1-44,
1899.
C.A. 3 Uh 6

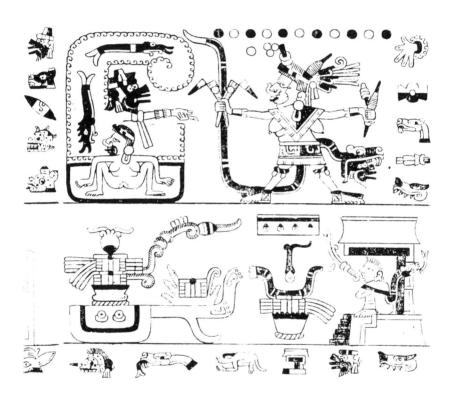

Copy of *Codex Laud* by Annie G. Hunter (no. 376)

INDEX OF PERSONAL NAMES

INDEX OF PLACE NAMES

Jalisco
  see Mexico-Jalisco
Jalpan
  765
Java
  361
Jilitla
  765
Jocotenango
  350-353
Jocotitlán
  195
Jolomax
  736
Juquilá
  358
Kabáh
  517, 553
Kalamté
  736
Kaua
  68, 69
Kichmoo
  553
Kochilá
  114
Labna
  549, 553
Lagos Miramar
  417
Laguna de Términos
  187, 240
Lake Atitlán
  319
Lake Nicaragua
  614
Lake Petén
  589
La Muñeca
  515
Lanquín
  see San Agustín Lanquín
Las Mercedes
  736
Las Pacayas
  736
Las Quebradas
  736
Lemoa
  see San Sebastian Lemoa

Loltún
  549
London, England
  366
Los Dolores
  119
Los Llanos
  9
Madrid
  366
Malinalco
  846
Mama
  501
Manché
  see San Miguel Manché
Maní
  306, 381, 458, 462
Marihuana
  516
Matagalpa
  197
Maxcanú
  355
Mayapán
  513, 592
Menché Tinamit
  see Yaxchilán
Mérida
  59, 72, 79, 102, 211, 250,
  317, 355, 362, 478, 501, 546-
  548, 553, 845
Mexico-Campeche
  355, 357, 433-437, 484, 485,
  505, 515, 516, 522, 732, 736,
  749
Mexico-Central
  25, 55, 91, 153, 157, 176,
  204, 209, 236-239, 248, 311,
  312, 333, 361, 368, 372-375,
  378, 379, 382, 388, 397, 403,
  406, 410, 440, 455, 481, 518,
  519, 521, 531, 546, 547, 548,
  561, 571, 580, 585, 593, 600,
  630, 632, 666, 667, 679, 714,
  723, 763-765, 775, 789, 800,
  805, 810, 814, 835, 841, 843,
  845, 849
Mexico-Chiapas
  12, 21-23, 35, 36, 43, 81, 94,

Mexico-Chiapas (continued)
100, 154, 162, 184, 200, 201,
202, 208, 261, 327, 331, 409,
413, 493, 495, 499, 505, 540,
564, 567, 587, 637, 638, 669,
684-686, 736, 773, 776, 796,
801, 848
Mexico-Colima
438
Mexico-Hidalgo
410, 543, 845
Mexico-Jalisco
609, 698, 713, 715, 717, 781
Mexico-Michoacán
37-40, 48, 54, 55, 83, 84, 106,
139-143, 156, 177, 255, 293,
669, 670, 751
Mexico-Morelos
397
Mexico-Oaxaca
15, 33, 49, 92, 122, 123, 128-
130, 144, 150, 159, 160, 174,
205, 227, 266, 270, 273, 327,
358, 370, 376, 380, 409, 410,
413, 420, 440, 441, 494, 499,
630, 723, 764, 782, 784, 801,
826-828, 848
Mexico-Puebla
160, 176, 421, 422, 456, 481
Mexico-Quintana Roo
357, 472, 505, 515, 516, 604,
732, 736
Mexico-Tlaxcala
765, 789, 845
Mexico-Veracruz
174, 356, 413, 536, 537, 668,
792, 845
Mexico-Yucatán
2, 13, 31, 42, 57, 59, 64-
74, 79, 85-87, 89, 90, 95,
101, 102, 105, 111, 114, 115,
124, 131, 136, 145, 147, 163-
166, 178, 182, 185, 193, 199,
211, 213, 215, 232-234, 248,
250, 251, 256, 302, 306, 313,
316, 317, 327, 328, 345, 346,
355, 357, 359, 362-365, 381,
387, 426, 430-432, 443, 444,
452-454, 458, 459, 462, 472,
476, 478-480, 486-488, 496,
501-505, 507, 511, 513, 514

517, 520, 523. 524, 545, 549-
555, 562, 564, 571, 581, 582,
592, 598, 604, 608, 630, 662,
692-695, 720, 721, 723, 736,
762, 768, 776, 807, 808, 821,
822, 824, 830, 833, 834, 845,
856
Mexico-Zacatecas
823
Michoacán
see Mexico-Michoacán
Milpa Alta
593
Mitla
327
Mixteca Alta Region
828
Mocochá
2, 501
Momostenango
see Santiago Momostenango
Monte Alban
630
Morelos
see Mexico-Morelos
Moskito Coast
149
Motul
501
Moxopipe
501
Muna
501
Naachtun
515
Nah
70
Namotivá
169
Naranjo
612, 682, 686, 688
Nebaj
107
Nexitza
173
Nicaragua
120, 149, 193, 230, 330, 408,
525, 614, 674, 675
Nicoya
675

-213-

Zapotitlán
193
Zinanché
501
Zumpango
247

-218-

INDEX OF SUBJECTS

Cacchi
  see Kekchí
Cacchiquel
  see Cakchiquel
Caché-Linguistics
  Vocabulary
  16
Cahabón Manuscript
  348, 349
Cakchiquel-Ethnohistory
  Calendar
  51
Cakchiquel-Linguistics
  660
  Christian Doctrine
  11, 30, 170-172, 180, 245,
  283, 497
  Grammar
  18, 30, 148, 267, 291, 304,
  305, 450, 451
  Texts
  11, 51, 170-172, 180, 245,
  276, 283, 497
  Vocabulary
  19, 50, 88, 148, 152, 247,
  257, 258, 290, 291, 294-296,
  301
Calendar-Aztec
  55, 153, 360, 368, 378, 379,
  455, 458, 477, 561, 619, 623,
  624, 636, 646, 658, 663, 770,
  777, 786, 837
Calendar-Cakchiquel
  51
Calendar-Chiapanec
  43
Calendar-Kekchí
  53, 112, 597
Calendar-Maya
  51-53, 67-74, 371, 377, 381,
  386, 395, 396, 458, 520, 597,
  634-658, 664, 681-690, 745,
  776, 840
Calendar-Mixtec
  370, 376
Calendar-Quiché
  52
Calendar-Tarascan
  54, 55
Calendar-Tzeltal
  776

Calendar-Yucatec Maya
  67-74, 520
Calendario de Paris
  see Codex Borbonicus
Calendario o Rueda del Año
  see Colección Chavero no. 3
Carib-Ethnography
  731
Carib-Linguistics
  660
Carnegie Institution of Washington
  317, 332, 365, 434, 448, 472,
  514-516, 555
Carrillo Ancona Collection
  72, 250
Census-Central Mexico
  167, 176
Census-Yucatán
  213, 316, 486, 487, 523, 524
Central American Exposition, 1897
  724
Chaneabal
  see Tojolabal
Chiapanec-Ethnography
  Calendar
  43
  Cofradía
  162
  Traditional History
  43
Chiapanec-Linguistics
  413, 660
  Christian Doctrine
  36, 125, 200, 201
  Grammar
  12, 43
  Texts
  36, 125, 162, 200, 201
Chicomuceltec-Linguistics
  413
Chilam Balam
  511
  Calkini
  64, 65
  Chumayel
  66, 335, 345, 362-364, 458
  Ixil
  67
  Kaua
  68, 69, 603

Jinca
  see Xinca
John Carter Brown Library,
  Providence
  101, 122, 123, 148, 174, 223,
  494
John S. Guggenheim Foundation
  347
Katun
  602, 603, 840
Kekchí-Ethnography
  725, 727, 741, 794
  Calendar
  53, 112, 597
  Cosmology
  597
  Dance Dramas
  307-309, 323-326
  Dwellings
  727, 741
  Land Documents
  109, 262, 390, 391, 558-560,
  735
  Subsistence
  597, 727
  Wills
  109, 418
Kekchí-Linguistics
  449, 660
  Christian Doctrine
  58, 217, 228, 235, 490, 508,
  597
  Grammar
  58
  Texts
  53, 58, 109, 217, 228, 235,
  262, 323-326, 348, 349, 418,
  490, 508, 558-560, 595, 597
  Vocabulary
  596, 597
Königlichen Bibliothek, Berlin
  427
Königlichen Museum für Völkerkunde, Berlin
  680, 714, 760, 814, 841, 847,
  856
Königlichen Naturhistorischen
  Hofmuseums, Vienna
  805, 814
Labrets
  856

Lacandón-Ethnography
  63, 119, 155, 158, 417, 567,
  725, 742
  Dwellings
  417, 742
  Subsistence
  417
La Gaceta de Guatemala
  340-342
Land Documents
  Cacalchen
  164
  Chicxulub
  89, 90
  Chimolab
  262
  Ebtún
  166
  Kochila
  114
  Maní
  306, 462, 603
  San Cristóbal Totonicapán
  110, 216
  San Francisco El Alto
  216
  San Juan Bautista Tabi
  496
  San Juan Chamelco
  109, 558-560
  San Miguel Tucurú
  390, 391, 559
  San Pedro Carchá
  390, 391, 558, 560, 725
  Santiago Guevea
  784
  Santiago Momostenango
  110
  Teabo
  215
  Ticul
  111
  Xochimilco
  388
La Prensa, Mérida
  453
Latin American (Miscellaneous)
  Collection, Library of Congress,
  Washington, D.C.
  2, 6-8, 11-15, 19, 20, 22-24,
  26, 27, 30, 34, 36, 39-42, 48,

Latin American (Miscellaneous)
Collection, Library of Congress,
Washington, D.C. (continued)
49, 51-54, 56, 58-61, 64-73,
75-78, 80, 81, 83, 85-89, 91,
92, 95, 100-102, 105-111, 114-
117, 121-127, 131, 133-135,
143, 146-148, 151-154, 156,
159, 162-167, 169-176, 178,
181, 183-185, 187-191, 194,
198, 201, 206, 209, 211, 212,
215-221, 224, 227, 228, 231,
233, 236, 237, 239, 242-245,
247, 249, 250, 252-256, 258,
260-264, 267, 269-271, 273,
276, 277, 280, 281, 286-288,
290-291, 294, 297, 299, 301,
304-309
Latin American Collection,
University of Texas, Austin
186
Latin American Library, Tulane
University, New Orleans
6, 8, 12-14, 18, 20, 23, 25,
25, 35, 39-41, 48, 54, 58,
60, 61, 68, 70-73, 77, 83,
89, 91, 92, 104, 106-109,
111, 125, 134, 147, 151,
156, 159, 160, 163, 164, 167,
170, 173, 175, 181, 183, 187,
191, 197, 198, 201, 204, 217,
221, 224, 228, 243, 245, 247,
262, 267, 270, 271, 273, 277,
296, 297, 300, 462, 464-466,
496
Leiden Plaque
645
Lenca-Ethnography
674, 725
Lenca-Linguistics
660
León Collection
106, 125
Leprosy-Aztec
786
Libro de Judio
478, 479
Libro de los Cocomes de Cacalchen
164, 345
Libro della China
see Codex Cospi

Lienzo de Amoltepec
see Lienzo de Santa María
Yolotepec
Lienzo de Astata
see Lienzo de Tecciztlán y
Tequatepec
Lienzo de San Pedro Ixcatlán
441
Lienzo de San Pedro Yolox
420
Lienzo de Santa María Yolotepec
358
Lienzo de Tecciztlán y Tequatepec
481
Lienzo de Tlaxcala
789
Lienzo de Tuxtepec
see Lienzo de San Pedro Ixcatlán
Lienzo de Zacatepec
757
Linguistics-Historical
413, 544
Loque
see Zoque
Macuilxochitl
714
Magic-Aztec
787, 788
Maler Collection
64, 68, 74
Mam-Ethnography
839
Mam-Linguistics
Christian Doctrine
126
Grammar
424
Texts
126
Vocabulary
117, 424
Manché
see Chol
Mangue-Linguistics
Texts
169, 230
Manuscrit de Veletri
33
Mapa de Cuauhtlantzinco
456

Vocabulary (continued)
Quiché
34, 41, 50, 56, 116, 152,
289, 301, 383, 424, 590,
591
Sumo
149
Talamanca
45
Tarascan
139, 140, 255, 293
Tepehua
543
Tojolabal
44
Totonac
300
Twaka
149
Tzeltal
23, 331
Tzotzil
100
Vizeita
16
Xinca
303
Yucatec Maya
101, 102, 114, 302, 507, 592
Zapotec
84, 123, 130, 173, 266, 494
Zoque
130, 146, 223
Wall Paintings-Central Mexican
835
Wall Paintings-Maya
346, 768, 821
Weapons-Kekchí
725
Wills-Kekchí
109, 418
Wills-Quiché
110, 113
Wills-Yucatec Maya
111
Writing Systems-Aztec
708
Writing Systems-Maya
336, 412, 430-432, 436, 535,
607, 618, 621, 622, 631, 655-
658

Writing Systems-Mixtec
440
Writing Systems-Pipil
400
Writing Systems-Tarascan
670
Writing Systems-Zapotec
440
Xinca-Linguistics
660
Grammar
450, 451
Vocabulary
303
Xiu Chronicles
306, 345, 600-603
Yucatec Maya-Ethnography
553, 567, 581, 739
Apiculture
553
Calendar
67-74, 520
Cosmology
13, 66-69, 554
Herbals
68-74, 163, 165, 178, 199,
211, 476, 478, 479
Fisheries
328
Land Documents
89, 90, 111, 114, 164, 166,
215, 306, 462, 496, 603
Music
553
Tribute Schedules
182, 545
Wills
111
Yucatec Maya-Linguistics
660
Christian Doctrine
2, 42, 59, 86, 87, 95, 105,
115, 124, 131, 147, 185, 206,
215, 232-234, 248, 250, 251,
256, 365, 459
Grammar
85, 387, 506, 573, 767
Texts
2, 42, 57, 59, 86, 87, 89, 90,
95, 105, 111, 114, 115, 124,
131, 136, 147, 163-166, 178,

REFERENCES

Anders, Ferdinand
1967   Wort- und Sachregister zu Eduard Seler Gesammelte Abhandlungen
        zur Amerikanischen Sprach- und Altertumskunde. Graz : Akademische
        Druck- u. Verlagsanstalt.

Arjona, Mireya Priego de
1937   Notas acerca de bibliografía yucateca. Museo Arqueológico e
        Historico de Yucatán, Publicación Especial no. 4. Mérida :
        Talleres Graficos del Sudeste.

Bandelier, Adolphe F.
1881   Notes on the bibliography of Yucatan and Central America,
        comprising Yucatan, Chiapas, Guatemala (the ruins of Palenque,
        Ocosingo, and Copan), and Oaxaca; a list of some of the writers
        on this subject from the sixteenth century to the present time.
        Worcester, Massachusetts : Charles Hamilton.

Beristain y Martin de Sousa, Jose M.
1816-   Bibliotheca Hispano-Americana Septentrional ó catálogo y
1821   noticia de los literatos que ó nacidos, ó educados, ó florecientos
        en la America Septentrional española han dado á luz algun
        escrito, ó lo han dexado preparado para la prensa. México.

Bowditch, Charles P.
1912   Letter to William E. Gates, October 17, 1912. Charles P.
        Bowditch Papers, Peabody Museum of Archaeology and Ethnology,
        Harvard University, Cambridge, Massachusetts.

Brasseur de Bourbourg, Charles Etienne
1871   Bibliothèque Mexico-Guatémalienne, précédée d'un coup d'oeil
        sur les études américaines dans leurs rapports avec les études
        classiques et suivie du tableau par ordre alphabétique des
        ouvrages de linguistique américaine contenus dans le même
        volume, rédigée et mise en ordre d'après les documents de sa
        collection américaine. Paris : Maisonneuve.

Breton, Adela C.
1921   Charles Pickering Bowditch. Man 21:123.

-240-

Bright, William
1967   Inventory of descriptive materials. In Linguistics, edited by
        Norman A. McQuown. pp. 9-62. Handbook of Middle American
        Indians, vol. 5. Austin : University of Texas Press.

Brinton, Daniel G.
1869   A notice of some manuscripts in Central American languages.
        American Journal of Science and Arts 47:222-230.

1897   The missing authorities on Maya antiquities. American
        Anthropologist 10:183-191.

1900   Catalogue of the Berendt Linguistic Collection. Philadelphia :
        Department of Archaeology and Paleontology, University of
        Pennsylvania.

Brunhouse, Robert L.
1975   William E. Gates. In Pursuit of the ancient Maya: some
        archaeologists of yesterday. pp. 129-167. Albuquerque :
        University of New Mexico Press.

Butler, Ruth Lapham
1937   A Check-list of manuscripts in the Edward E. Ayer Collection,
        The Newberry Library. Chicago : The Newberry Library.

1941   A Bibliographical check-list of North and Middle American
        Indian linguistics in the Edward E. Ayer Collection. Chicago :
        The Newberry Library.

Campbell, Lyle R.
1977   Quichean linguistic prehistory. University of California
        Publications in Linguistics, vol. 81. Berkeley : University
        of California Press.

Carmack, Robert M.
1973   Quichean civilization: the ethnohistoric, ethnographic, and
        archaeological sources. Berkeley and Los Angeles : University
        of California Press.

Catalogue of the John Carter Brown Library in Brown University, Providence,
1919-   Rhode Island. 3 vols. Providence : John Carter Brown Library,
1931   Brown University.

Chavero, Alfredo
1903   Apuntes viejos de bibliografía mexicana. México : tipografía
        J. I. Guerrero.

Cline, Howard F.
1961   A provisional listing of Middle American Indian materials
        in the Division of Manuscripts, Library of Congress, from the
        Indian Language Collection, and related materials in the Latin
        American (Miscellaneous) Collection. Handbook of Middle
        American Indians Project Working Papers, no. 6. Washington, D.C.

1962   The Gates Collection. III. A listing of Gates photocopies in
        the McComas inventory of 1940, and photocopies represented in
        the collections at Brigham Young University, Provo, Utah. The
        linguistic documents, the pictorial documents. Handbook of
        Middle American Indians Project Working Papers, no. 16.
        Washington, D.C.

Freeman, John F.
1966   A Guide to manuscripts relating to the American Indian in the
        Library of the American Philosophical Society. Memoirs of
        the American Philosophical Society, vol. 65. Philadelphia :
        American Philosophical Society.

Gates, William E.
1918   Letter to Charles P. Bowditch, October 31, 1918. Charles P.
        Bowditch Papers, Peabody Museum of Archaeology and Ethnology,
        Harvard University, Cambridge, Massachusetts.

1924   The William E. Gates Collection; manuscripts, documents,
        printed literature relating to Mexico and Central America, with
        special significance to linguistics, history, politics and
        economics, covering five centuries of Mexican civilization
        from the Aztec period to the present time. New York : American
        Art Association.

1937   The Maya Society and its work. Baltimore : The Maya Society.

[1940] The Gates Collection of Middle American literature. Section A.

Gibson, Charles and John B. Glass
1975   A census of Middle American prose manuscripts in the
        native historical tradition. In Guide to ethnohistorical
        sources, part 4, edited by Howard F. Cline. pp. 322-400.
        Handbook of Middle American Indians, vol. 15. Austin :
        University of Texas Press.

Glass, John B.
1975a   A catalog of falsified Middle American pictorial manuscripts.
        In Guide to ethnohistorical sources, part 3, edited by Howard
        F. Cline. pp. 297-310. Handbook of Middle American Indians,
        vol. 14. Austin : University of Texas Press.

Glass, John B.
1975b A census of Middle American Testerian manuscripts. In Guide
       to ethnohistorical sources, part 3, edited by Howard F. Cline.
       pp. 281-296. Handbook of Middle American Indians, vol. 14.
       Austin : University of Texas Press.

Glass, John B. and Donald Robertson
1975   A census of native Middle American pictorial manuscripts.
       In Guide to ethnohistorical sources, part 3, edited by
       Howard F. Cline. pp. 81-252. Handbook of Middle American
       Indians, vol. 14. Austin : University of Texas Press.

Gropp, Arthur E.
1934   Manuscripts in the Department of Middle American Research.
       rev. ed. Middle American Pamphlets, no. 5. New Orleans :
       Department of Middle American Research, The Tulane University
       of Louisiana.

Hammond, George P.
1972   A Guide to the manuscript collection of the Bancroft Library.
       2 vols. Berkeley and Los Angeles : University of California
       Press.

Leclerc, Charles
1878   Bibliotheca Americana; historie, géographie, voyages,
       archéologie et linguistique des deux Amériques et des Iles
       Philippines. Paris : Maisonneuve.

Lejeal, Léon
1902   Bibliothèque de bibliographies critiques publiée par la
       Société des Etudes Historiques: les antiquités Mexicaines
       (Mexique, Yucatan, Amérique-Centrale). Paris : Alphonse
       Picard.

Lowe, Gareth W., Lillie B. Bargaehr, and Hollis Scott
1973   William E. Gates: bibliography and preliminary inventory
       to his papers in the Brigham Young University Library. University
       Archives, Manuscript Division, Manuscript no. 279. Provo, Utah :
       Brigham Young University Library.

Marcou, P.
1921   Charles Pickering Bowditch. Journal de la Société des
       Américanistes de Paris 13:323-324.

Moore, Charles
1921   Manuscripts in public and private collections in the United
       States. Washington : Library of Congress.

Omont, Henri
1925   Catalogue des manuscrits américains de la Bibliothèque
        Nationale. Paris : Edouard Champion.

Orozco, Federico Gómez de
1925   Catálogo de la colección de manuscritos relativos a la
        historía de América formada por Joaquin García Icazbalceta.
        México : Monografías Bibliografías Mexicanas.

Pilling, James C.
1885   Proofsheets of a bibliography of the languages of the North
        American Indians. Smithsonian Institution-Bureau of Ethnology,
        Miscellaneous Publication, no. 2. Washington, D.C. :
        Government Printing Office.

Pinart, Alphonse L.
1883   Catalogue de livres rares et precieux manuscrits et imprimés
        principalement sur l'Amérique et sur les langues du monde
        entier composant la bibliothèque de M. Alph.-L. Pinart et
        comprenant en totalité la bibliothèque Mexico-Guatémalienne
        de M. l'abbe Brasseur de Bourbourg. Paris : Labitte.

Sanchez G., Daniel
1920   Catálogo de los escritos franciscanos de la provincia
        serafica del santismo nombre de Jésus de Guatemala. Guatemala :
        Tipografía San Antonio.

Seler, Eduard
1902-   Gesammelte Abhandlungen zur amerikanischen Sprach- und Alter-
1915   thumskunde von Eduard Seler. 5 vols. Berlin : A. Asher.

Stephens, John L.
1843   Incidents of travel in Yucatan. 2 vols. New York : Harper.

Streit, Robert
1916-   Bibliotheca missionum. 3 vols. Münster i. W. : Aschendorffschen
1927   Buchhandlungen.

Teixidor, Felipé
1937   Bibliografía yucateca. Mérida : Talleres Graficos del Sudeste.

Tozzer, Alfred M.
1921   Charles Pickering Bowditch. American Anthropologist 23:353-359.

1922   Charles Pickering Bowditch. Proceedings of the American
        Academy of Arts and Sciences 57:476-478.

Tristan, José M.
1949   Bibliografía maya yucateca. Rochester, New York.

Valle, Rafael H.
1937-   Bibliografía maya. México : Instituto Panamericano de
1940   Geografía e Historia.

Vela, David
1956   Bibliografía cakchiquel. In Método para aprender a hablar,
        leer y escribir la lengua cakchiquel, by Alfredo Herbruger
        and Eduardo Díaz Barrios. pp. 371-399. Guatemala :
        Tipografía Nacional.

Verneau, R.
1922   Charles Pickering Bowditch. L'Anthropologie 31:612-613.

Weeks, John M.
1984   Spanish administrative documents relating to Middle
        American Indians at Tozzer Library, Harvard University.
        Vanderbilt University Publications in Anthropology monograph
        series, Nashville, Tennessee. in press.

William E. Gates [obituary]
1940a   American Historical Review 46:254.

1940b   Baltimore Sun, April 25.

1940c   New York Times, April 25.